ADAM STYLE

Steven Parissien

ADAM STYLE

The Preservation Press
National Trust for Historic Preservation

Contents

	Preface	7
Introduction	The Age of Adam	9
Chapter One	Adam Style	30
Chapter Two	The Architectural Shell	58
Chapter Three	Fixtures and Fittings	91
Chapter Four	Services	127
Chapter Five	Colours and Coverings	152
Chapter Six	Furniture	183
Chapter Seven	Revivals	212
	Directory of Designers	224
	Glossary	227
	Contacts and Sources	230
	Further Reading	234
	Index	238

FOR VAL

The Preservation Press
National Trust for Historic Preservation
1785 Massachusetts Avenue, N.W.
Washington, D.C. 20036

The National Trust for Historic Preservation in the United States is the only national
private nonprofit organization chartered by Congress to encourage public participation in the
preservation of sites, buildings and objects significant in American history and culture. Support is
provided by membership dues, endowment funds, contributions and grants from federal
agencies, including the U.S. Department of the Interior, under provisions of the National Historic
Preservation Act of 1966. The opinions expressed in this publication
do not necessarily reflect the views or policies of the Interior Department.
For information about membership, write to the Trust at the above address.

Library of Congress Cataloging-in-Publication Data

Parissien, Steven.
    Adam style/Steven Parissien.
        P.   cm.
    Includes bibliographical references and index.
    ISBN 0-89133-197-2
    1. Architecture, Domestic – Great Britain. 2. Neoclassicism
    (Architecture) – Great Britain. 3. Architecture, Modern –
    17th-18th centuries – Great Britain. 4. Decoration and
    ornament – Great Britain – Neoclassicism. 5. Adam, Robert,
    1728-1792 – Criticism and interpretation. I. Title.
NA7328.P23 1992   92-7346
720'.92 – dc20   CIP

Originally published in Great Britain by Phaidon Press Limited
Copyright © 1992 Phaidon Press Limited
Text © 1992 Steven Parissien

Printed and bound in Singapore 1992

Designed by Pocknell and Green

ACKNOWLEDGMENTS

I am indebted to the following for their help and advice:
Patrick Baty, Tony Herbert, Timothy Mowl, Chris Salmond
Annabel Westman and Adam White

Especial thanks go to Kit Wedd
for her dedicated proofreading, inspirational advice and continual support

20, St James's Square was a sumptuous townhouse, built by Robert Adam and his
brothers for Sir Watkin Williams Wynne between 1771 and 1774. The pictures on pages one and
three *(frontispiece)* show views of the recently restored interior, featuring some of the most
characteristic elements of the Neo-Classical period: bright colours, delicate ironwork, anthemia
and swags. The picture on page five shows a ceiling detail from the house; even in his
grandest houses, Adam's use of gilding was rare

The endpapers show fragile motifs and delicate colouring in a wallpaper design of 1775

Soon after Robert Adam died, on 3 March 1792, the highly respected and widely read *Gentleman's Magazine* published a hagiographical portrait of the architect and designer which concluded that Adam 'had produced a total change in the architecture of the country'. For once, the obituarist's eulogies were wholly justified. Robert Adam, the outstanding artistic figure of the day, had transformed the architectural and decorative worlds of Britain and America, bringing a new grace, lightness and humour to exteriors and interiors alike. So successful was he that to many observers of the nineteenth and twentieth centuries the style of Robert Adam and his contemporaries - the thirty or so years after 1755 - is synonymous with the whole of the 120-year-long Georgian period. For many of us, still, 'Adam Style' represents all that is most attractive and typical of Georgian decoration.

What we now know as 'Adam Style' is not, of course, simply the creation of one man, unusually gifted though Robert Adam undoubtedly was. Other great architects and craftsmen helped to define this radically new style - among them two figures whose genius for design and for marketing were fully equal to Adam's own: Thomas Chippendale and Josiah Wedgwood. Thus in examining the origins and development of what can be termed 'Adam Style', other individuals and other influences, as well as the direct inspiration provided by the Adam family, must be identified and explored. As a result, this is by no means a biography of Robert Adam (much as we need a good, full, modern study of the great man himself), but a general overview of the architectural and decorative style which so often takes his name.

Adam Style has been written specifically to fill the wide gap between the ubiquitous, glossy yet terribly thin home decoration picture-books and the more inaccessible, scholarly works of historians and architects. It tells the story of the average English house from the mid-1750s to the mid-1780s, the period which corresponds to the highly productive career of Robert Adam.

Like its companion volume, *Regency Style,* it does not deal with familiar themes such as the great houses and great architects of the time. There are countless studies of the marvellous mansions and castles erected by Adam and his contemporaries, but precious few which look at how the vast mass of the population built and disposed their homes. *Adam Style* seeks to correct this dramatic imbalance, providing a colourful picture of how the house of the Adam period was designed, how it was built, how it was decorated and furnished, and how it was used. The result is, I hope, an informative and accessible guide, as relevant to the refurbisher or redecorator as to those who are simply interested in this most fascinating and lively of periods. It can be dipped into or read right through, as you wish. And in case it has encouraged you to learn more about the subject, included at the end of the book are sections detailing Further Reading as well as expert bodies whom you can consult.

Adam Style does not seek to persuade you to turn the clock back to 1760. Nor does it provide instant remedies to historical problems which are actually far more complex than most populist 'style' guides would dare to admit. Instead, it outlines the way in which the British and colonial middle classes of the period built and disposed their homes, and provides the design parameters within which any would-be decorators or restorers can make their own, personal choices. For those who are captivated by the buildings and the society of Adam's day, I hope that this book will open doors to further exploration of the Georgian era.

Steven Parissien

'Blest age, when all men may procure
The title of a connoisseur;
When noble and ignoble herd
Are governed by a single word'   *(Robert Lloyd, 1759)*

Opposite: *Robert Adam, by George Willison, c.1773. Dressed as a conservative gentleman and holding the portfolio of his drawings of the ruins of the Emperor's Palace at Spalatro, Adam in this portrait hardly looks like the man who declared himself to have brought about a revolution in taste.*

Elevation of Lansdowne House in London's Berkeley Square, from Robert and James Adam's Works in Architecture, *which appeared after 1773.*

The house was begun c.1762 for the Adams' great patron and George III's great friend, the Third Earl of Bute. Much of it was rebuilt after 1929; the original drawing room, however, still survives intact in the Museum of Arts in Philadelphia.

The 'Age of Adam', as James Lees-Milne aptly termed it in 1947, is the colourful and eventful era which approximately corresponds to the career of the great architect and designer Robert Adam - roughly, the period from 1755 to 1785. (By 1770 Robert Adam was possibly the most celebrated architect in the world; by 1785, though, he was being eclipsed by younger and more versatile rivals, and had retreated to his native Scotland.) These thirty years witnessed the flowering of what is often regarded as the quintessential 'Georgian' decorative style. They were also, though, years of immense political and social change.

This fascinating period's borders are neatly defined by two great wars. The Seven Years War of 1756-63 was a worldwide struggle which effectively created the British Empire: the British won notable gains in the East and West Indies, while managing to consolidate and extend their North American possessions. (In Voltaire's opinion, however, Britain and France were merely 'fighting over a few acres of snow on the borders of Canada', spending 'more money on this glorious war than the whole of Canada is worth'.) The American Revolution of 1775-83, however, seemed to many observers to represent the death-knell of Britain's nascent imperial ambitions, as the youthful and audacious American colonies successfully shook themselves free from increasingly suffocating imperial ties. 'Well!' exclaimed Horace Walpole presciently at the War's start in 1775, 'we had better have gone on robbing the Indies; it was a more lucrative trade.'

The era of Robert Adam was also a time of revolution in other areas of human endeavour. The Industrial Revolution was, if not born, then at least christened in 1779, when Pritchard and Darby erected their stunningly novel and graceful iron bridge over the river at Coalbrookdale in Shropshire. The political world, too, was greatly shaken by the accession in 1760 of the young George III - a monarch determined to break the comfortable oligarchy of the Whig grandees once and for all. The new king sought to achieve this by dispensing with the traditional Whig politicians (now ably headed by William Pitt, Earl of Chatham) and instead using his (highly inexperienced) former tutor, the 3rd Earl of Bute, to create a government independent of any party loyalty. The young monarch's new dogma - which, worryingly enough for parliament, appeared to be aiming at absolutist, monarchical rule - was made crystal clear in a letter he wrote to Bute in November 1760, soon after his accession:

'I am happy to think that I have at present the real love of my subjects, and lay it down for certain that if I do not show them that I will not permit ministers to trample on me, that my subjects will in time come to esteem me unworthy of the Crown I wear.'

Bute's government was, in the event, a dismal failure. The Scottish earl - both 'insolent and cowardly' and 'rash and timid', according to the Earl of Shelburne - was clearly incapable of running an administration; by January 1763 he was in constant fear of assassination by the mob, wailing that 'The angel Gabriel could not at present govern this country.' However, excepting figures such as Bute, the Age of Adam was a indeed an era of great men. Not only did William Pitt the Elder grace the parliamentary stage, but also his talented and precocious son - Prime Minister in 1784 at the tender age of twenty-four. It was a time of military heroes: of General James Wolfe, posthumous victor

The world's first cast-iron bridge and the wonder of the age: Abraham Darby's famous bridge at Coalbrookdale, Shropshire, of 1779, as depicted in a print published by Boydell in 1788.

Opposite: *George III in suitably kingly pose, in an official portrait by Mather Brown. In private, the king preferred to adopt the role of the simple country squire - a predilection which won him the nickname 'Farmer George'.*

Below: *a plate from Hogarth's satirical series The Times, of 1762 - expressly designed by the conservative artist to prop up the unpopular government of the Earl of Bute in the face of the attacks of William Pitt the Elder. A fireman from the Union Office (the Union of England and Scotland) is trying to put out the fire in Britain's part of the globe (the Seven Years War), opposed by rival firemen from the Temple Coffee House (signifying Pitt's brother-in-law Earl Temple). Pitt himself is represented as the notorious and overbearing figure of Henry VIII, fanning the fire with bellows.*

John Stuart, Third Earl of Bute, in an engraving by W. T. Mote. Brought into government by a devoted George III in 1761, he was out of office by 1763. At the end of the decade, however, he was still widely (though erroneously) regarded by the Whigs as the eminence grise *behind the King's anti-party policies.*

of Quebec; of George Washington, the Father of the new United States; of dashing naval figures from Admiral Rodney, scourge of the French, to John Paul Jones, the swashbuckling antagonist of the complacent British. It was a time, too, of great inventors and entrepreneurs: of the amazing polymath Benjamin Franklin in America, and the energetic manufacturer Matthew Boulton in Britain. The arts prospered in the hands of skilled practitioners such as the mercurial playwright-politician Richard Brinsley Sheridan, the composer Thomas Arne (the author of 'Rule Britannia'), internationally-renowned artists Joseph Reynolds and Thomas Gainsborough, and legendary actors such as David Garrick.

       Three men in particular dominated their respective professions during this time: the architect Robert Adam, the ceramicist Josiah Wedgwood and the cabinet-maker Thomas Chippendale - all three of whom are now popularly regarded as the most famous past exponents of their crafts. It was a time of great women, too: Angelica Kaufmann, Eleanor Coade and Hester Bateman excelled in the visual arts; Sarah Siddons and Mrs Jordan triumphed on the stage; while radical writer Catherine Macaulay and radical aristocrat Georgiana, Duchess of Devonshire, shocked the male establishment with their unconventional behaviour - Macaulay marrying a man half her age, the Duchess buying votes for the radical Whig Charles James Fox with publicly proffered kisses.

       The politics of the period were nothing if not colourful. The expiring Earl of Chatham was melodramatically carried in a litter into Parliament in order to denounce Britain's conduct of the American War. Lord George Sackville was court-

martialled for cowardice after the Battle of Minden in 1759 - being declared 'unfit to serve His Majesty in any capacity whatsoever' - only to re-emerge (now in the guise of Lord George Germain) as Secretary for the Colonies in 1775, in which capacity he was directly responsible for the ill-fated operations in America. (Sackville's elder brother, meanwhile, had cut down all the trees at his vast, ancestral estate of Knole in Kent, and had been declared mentally incompetent by his family.) Even after his removal from government the unappealing and pathetic Earl of Bute was persistently - and unaccountably - regarded by the Whig leaders as the real ruler of Britain, the 'Minister Behind the Curtain' who was, they alleged, in truth the *eminence grise* behind George III's ambition of ridding himself of parliamentary democracy.

Opposite: *James Stuart's adaptation of the legendary Athenian 'Tower of the Winds', built in the grounds of Shugborough, Staffordshire in 1764.*

A chastely Neo-Classical sugar temple, re-created for Fairfax House in York. Delightful culinary conceits of this type were all the rage on the fashionable tables of mid-Georgian Britain.

*The anti-Catholic Gordon
Riots of 1780 in full flow, as
depicted in a graphic,
contemporary cartoon
showing the burning of the
notorious Newgate Prison.*

When King George did finally find to his liking a Prime Minister who could fill Bute's place in his affections, his choice was an astonishingly inept one. Lord North, Prime Minister between 1770 and 1782, was not only disastrously indecisive, and increasingly blind, but retained such a low opinion of his own (admittedly meagre) abilities that he was for twelve long years continually attempting to resign. In January 1782, faced with the imminent loss of America, he wrote in typical vein to the king:

'I am ensensible how unfit I have always been, and how much more unfit I am now to decide in matters of nicety and difficulty, and if I had not repeatedly laid before Your Majesty my incapacity, and humbly advised Your Majesty more than once a year during the past ten years to place your affairs in other hands.'

Having been sharply attacked by Fox in the Commons in 1778, North could only moan that 'My mind, always weak, is now ten times weaker than it was' and ask 'Let me die disgraced, for that I can not now avoid.' This was the man who - aided by a disgraced army officer (Lord Germain) and a notorious rake (the Earl of Sandwich) - was charged with saving the American colonies for Britain.

The Age of Elegance was also a period of increasing social repression. An act of 1753, brought in on behalf of the 'Merchants, Traders and Insurers of the City of London', prescribed hanging for the crime of stealing shipwrecked goods; 'The existing laws', as Douglas Hay notes, 'were declared to be too gentle.' In 1764 the death penalty was, at the request of the English Linen Company, additionally applied to those who stole linen; in 1769 it was extended to food rioters, too. In Dr Hay's words, 'As the decades passed, the maturing trade, commerce and industry of England spawned more laws to protect particular kinds of property'. Two-thirds of those who, between 1760 and 1788, were found guilty of forgery - the greatest insult to private property and to unfettered capitalism - were executed.

Although there is evidence to suggest that, as the number of capital crimes mounted, so local judges were increasingly reluctant to sentence transgressors to death, the severity of the judicial system helped maintain Georgian society's natural inclination towards violence and brutality. To take just one example, on 5 March 1762 James Woodforde recorded in his diary that:

'... Judge Willmott condemned one Shadrach Smith, a gypsy, for robbing a girl of 2 shillings and beating her, in a very cruel manner; this man's son was the most principal Witness against his Father, and he was that had him hanged, or condemned to be hanged, he insisted upon his son's witnessing against, though the Judge was much against it.'

It was a time of politically-inspired violence, too. The national 'Wilkes and Liberty' riots of the 1760s, sparked by the highly controversial figure of radical MP John Wilkes, not only rocked the political establishment, but founded a strong radical tradition in Britain which in turn provided a useful incidence of extra-parliamentary pressure for the frustrated colonists. Across the Atlantic, the comedy of the Boston Tea Party of 1773 led inexorably to the bloody tragedy of the American Revolution of 1775. And at the height of the ensuing war, in 1780, London was paralysed by the 'No Popery' mobs rampaging through the streets at the behest of the fanatic anti-Catholic and 'class traitor' Lord George Gordon - although social historian Dorothy George has concluded that 'the excesses of the Gordon Riots'

The American Revolution in full spate, and seen in engravings of the time. Above: General Howe's Redcoats riding triumphantly through Manhattan in 1776. Below: a taste of things to come - British forces facing defeat at the Battle of Bunker Hill of 1775.

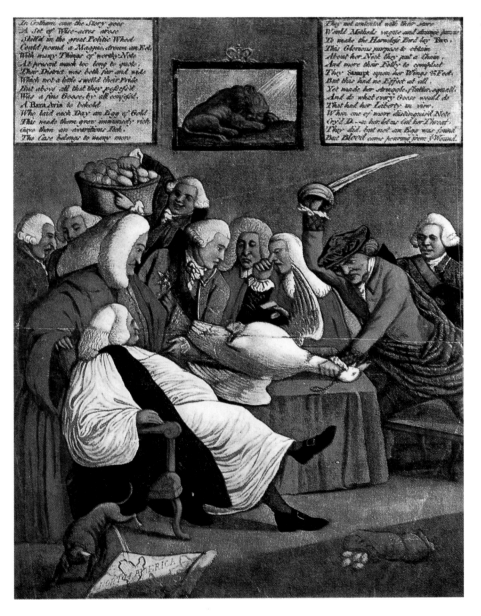

A cartoon from The Broadside of 1770, berating the British government's brusque and unyielding policy towards the American colonies (represented by the sacrifical bird) at the time of the so-called 'Boston Massacre'.

were to be explained more by 'the effects of drink and a swamping of the forces of order by the inhabitants of the dangerous districts in London who were always ready for pillage' rather than pure anti-Catholic passion.

Violence was endemic in mid-Georgian society. In 1769 Benjmain Franklin reported from England that 'I have seen, within a year, riots in the country, about corn; riots about elections; riots about workhouses; riots of colliers, riots of weavers, riots of coal-heavers; riots of sawyres; riots of Wilkesites; riots of government chairmen' and even 'riots of smugglers'. Drury Lane Theatre, the West End home of Garrick's and Sheridan's greatest triumphs, was repeatedly wrecked by rioting theatre-goers in 1755, 1763, 1770 and 1776. In 1770 even the august halls of Winchester School echoed to the cries of a violent insurrection by the pupils, which caused the local militia to read the Riot Act to the rebellious schoolchildren.

The thirty years which followed 1755 were also, however, a time of noble deeds - and famous deaths. General James Wolfe's dramatic expiry on the Heights of Abraham was seen as a fittingly romantic climax to the 'annus mirabilis' of 1759, during which Britain's armies and navies crushed the forces of France at Fort Niagara, Ticonderoga, Guadeloupe, Lagos, Madras and, of course, Quebec. ('No nation', exclaimed the Sussex shopkeeper Thomas Turner in 1759, 'had ever greater occasion to adore the Almighty Disposer of all events than Albion, whose forces meet with success in all quarters of the world.') The execution of Admiral Byng in 1757, for failing to hold the island of Minorca, was especially celebrated. The threat of popular violence had, it seemed, helped to bring a noted admiral to the scaffold. (Horace Walpole told his friend Horace Mann that 'papers were fixed on the Exchange, with these words, "Shoot Byng, or take care of your King".') The French satirist Voltaire, though, pretended to see the execution as a distinctly beneficial act - famously quipping in his *Candide* of 1759 that 'it pays to shoot an Admiral from time to time, to encourage the others.'

Defenders of the British Constitution were quick to use Byng's death to advertise the impartiality of British law. Equally helpful for the legal establishment (though, in reality, equally unrepresentative) was the case of Lord Ferrers, executed at Tyburn in 1760 for killing his steward. However, Ferrers's execution was, in the event, no ordinary death: the homicidal peer was hanged 'in his silver brocade wedding suit, on a scaffold equipped with black silk cushions for the mourners', while his hanging was attended by thousands of excited day-trippers. Horace Walpole was one of these. Confiding to George Montagu that Ferrers 'was soon out of pain, and quite dead in four

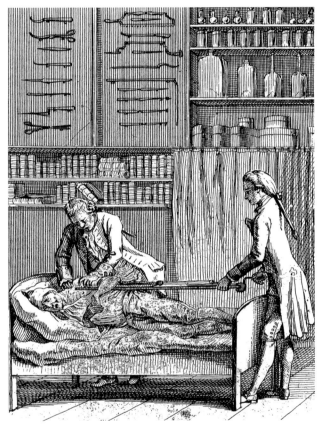

minutes', he observed the mob tearing off his clothes for relics, and the body being - as was the custom for murderers - 'conveyed back with the said pomp to Surgeons' hall, to be dissected'.

Lord Ferrers's death notwithstanding, the peerage of Britain stood a far better chance of living to a ripe old age than the vast majority of the population. The average death rate in London at the beginning of our period was one in twenty - a statistic that had actually worsened since 1700, when the figure for the capital stood at one in twenty-five. Life was cheap, and the cure for social ills or for rampant disease was often worse than the original problem. Of 2,379 children sent to London workhouses between 1750 and 1755, only 168 were alive at the start of 1756. Modern medicine was still in its infancy: frogs were still tied around the neck to cure nose bleeds - which were also, in the case of males, to be cured by 'soaking or washing the Testicles in the sharpest vinegar' - while tooth decay was invariably dealt with by quixotic folk remedies such as smearing the rotting area with honey (!), introducing a magnet into the mouth or, most

Opposite: another scene, of 1762 or 63, from Hogarth's pro-government series The Times. *Here Hogarth depicts the 'garden of good government' being watered by 'the pump of royal patronage', operated by Bute (at bottom left). Parliament is shown to the left: the Lords are slumbering and indifferent whilst in the Commons Pitt and his followers fire at the Dove of Peace (representing the negotiations to end the Seven Years War). On the right two notorious figures - the political radical John Wilkes, and the hoaxer Mrs Fanny - are in the pillory.*

Above left: *Earl Ferrers's celebrated execution of 1760 inevitably attracted much attention from the cartoonists of the day, some of whom attempted to portray the event as a shining example of the impartiality of British justice. However, whilst Ferrers was sent to the scaffold, most miscreant peers of the time were never even prosecuted for equally heinous crimes.*

Above: *Penzel's gruesome engraving* Setting a Limb, 1784, *epitomizes the medical standards of the day.*

bizarrely, placing roast turnip parings behind the ear. During the 1770s the Manchester Infirmary discovered that the traditional fishermen's remedy for rickets or rheumatism, cod liver oil (with its large amounts of what we now call vitamin D), actually had considerable medical worth; at the same time, however, Cornishmen were still passing their children through holes in the middle of prehistoric stones in order to cure rickets.

While Georgian medicines could kill, equally eccentric and harmful concoctions were prescribed as beauty aids. A 1784 recipe, designed to banish the freckles that betokened a common, outdoor existence, and requiring a solution of ashes boiled in water, was actually quite benign by the standards of the day. In practice, the pursuit of beauty necessitated considerable sacrifices of health and longevity. Sometimes these sacrifices were terminal: in 1760 Maria Gunning, the Countess of Coventry and the most famous beauty of the day - who attracted cartloads of onlookers wherever she travelled - died, aged only twenty-seven, as a result of excessive use of white lead as a cosmetic to whiten her precious skin. Lead poisoning also accounted for another celebrated victim seven years later when Kitty Fisher, the hugely successful courtesan and latterly the 'companion' of the 3rd Earl of Bristol, died from the effects of lead-based cosmetics.

Such tragedies did not, however, prompt any dramatic re-assessment of the requirements of fashion or the accepted ideals of beauty. Indeed, vanity remained endemic among the upper and middle classes of Adam's day. Since high foreheads and high hairstyles were fashionable, for example, numerous practices were recommended in order to prevent hair growing on the forehead; these ranged from the odd - rubbing walnut oil into the skin - to the decidedly unenticing, such as the application of bandages 'dipped in vinegar in which cat's dung has been steeped'. Meanwhile, during the 1770s the fashion for women was to wear their wigs higher and higher. From the mid-1760s onwards, daring men - the widely-satirized 'macaronis' - began to wear their own hair, dressed in the fashion of a wig; by 1775 Fag, in Sheridan's play *The Rivals*, was exclaiming that 'None of the London whips of any degree of *ton* wear *wigs* now.' Women, however, persisted in ever-more ludicrous sculptural compositions, based on foundations of wire or cotton and topped with enormous feathers and, on occasion, wooden or glass ornaments. Inevitably, the increasing amounts of rice-based wig powder needed to lend these bizarre creations the correct degree of whiteness - in order to properly emphasize the eyes - attracted numerous vermin to the heads of the fashion-conscious. Fortunately and unsurprisingly, by the very end of the period a reaction had set in. In 1785 Betsy Sheridan (the playwright's sister) was noting that 'all who have fine hair go without [powder], and if you have not quite enough 'tis but buying a few curls'.

Not all fashions were as impractical as the towering hairstyles of the 1770s. The ever-enterprising Josiah Wedgwood began to manufacture porcelain false teeth at his Stoke-on-Trent works - a technological breakthrough sorely needed by those whose natural beauty was not enhanced by two rows of blackened stumps. As was often said at the time, now it was possible not only to eat *off* Wedgwood china, but *with* it, too. And another felicitous invention was helping to offset the

The Macaroni Bricklayer
and the Macaroni Dressing
Room: *cartoons of 1772
depicting the lengths to
which the young arbiters of
fashion would go. The word
'macaroni' was used to
denote anything fashionably
- if not eccentrically - new.*

rancid odours emanating from the barely-washed of Europe and America. One of the most helpful by-products of the Seven Years War was the invention and manufacture of 'Aqua Admirabilis', a scent originally devised by the Farina brothers of Köln, in the German Rhineland, to enable soldiers to mask the whiff of battle. By 1780 this perfume, now popularly known as 'Eau de Cologne' after its originators, was being extensively used by both men and women in fashionable society.

The generous application of Eau de Cologne and the proliferation of ludicrous hairstyles were two of the many fashions whose cue was - in contrast to much of the architecture of the period - taken by Britain and her American colonies from recent developments in France. Sadly, though, while the opulent Versailles courts of Louis XV and the ill-fated Louis XVI provided glittering models for culture and fashion the world over, London's Court of St James's languished far behind in terms of cultural inspiration. George III - in dramatic contrast to his eldest son (later Prince Regent and subsequently George IV) - was no arbiter of taste. He loathed Shakespeare (although, amusingly enough, he managed to read *King Lear* when he himself went 'mad'), was singularly uninterested in music (unless it was of the jingoistic and martial 'Rule Britannia' variety), and collected almost nothing. He preferred instead to be regarded by the nation as a frugal squire, 'Farmer George', who differed little in his tastes and requirements from most of his subjects. Under his influence, the dress of the British court remained far behind not only that of Versailles, but also that of the fashionable society of London, Bath or Philadelphia. Artistic and architectural innovation, too, tended to spring not

from royal patronage or encouragement, but from the individual geniuses of men such as Robert Adam and Thomas Chippendale.

Outside George III's ascetic court, however, conspicuous excess was by no means unknown. Dr Johnson was not alone in regularly downing three whole bottles of port after dinner; even the rural Somerset clergyman James Woodforde - whose diaries reveal much about the unabashed gluttony of the period - was a hearty and enthusiastic trencherman. Woodforde's record of a 'very genteel Dinner' for nine people for 10th June 1784, for example, listed the following dishes:

'Soals and Lobster Sauce, Spring Chicken boiled and a Tongue, a Piece of rost Beef, Soup, a Fillet of Veal rosted with Morells and Trufles, and Pigeon Pye for the first course - sweetbreads, a green Goose and Peas, Apricot Pye, Cheesecakes, Stewed Mushrooms and Trifle.'

Such culinary extravagance also often proved remarkably unhealthy (see Chapter Five,

The suitably dramatic Parliamentary collapse of William Pitt, Earl of Chatham - a result of his deathbed denunciation of the North government's conduct of the American War - provided a marvellous subject for contemporary artists. This romanticized representation is by the American artist J. S. Copley and dates from 1779.

below), and must, inevitably, have accounted for a good proportion of the untimely deaths of the Georgian upper and middle classes.

Extravagance was also displayed to an increasing degree in the middle-class home, as the newly prosperous 'middling sorts' found themselves able - through a combination of increased personal wealth and the introduction of labour-saving industrial processes - to own items which had previously been regarded as luxuries only destined for the rich. The very latest furniture, carpets and wallpapers were snapped up as soon as they appeared; whereas, for example, in 1713 only 197,000 yards of taxed wallpaper were sold in Britain, by 1785 2.1 million yards were being purchased annually. And while there was considerable interest in the recently discovered remains of the Ancient world, no-one wanted antiques. Far more popular were the new, Neo-Classical designs of men such as Adam and Wedgwood, both of whom excelled at manipulating public taste and, additionally, at marketing their own considerable talents.

The American War - and in particular the intervention of France, Spain and the United Provinces on the colonists' side in 1778 - prompted a temporary halt to much of this ostentatious display of wealth. Wise heads had already counselled against the folly of Britain's originally coercive yet latterly half-hearted campaigns. As early as 1774 Horace Walpole daringly suggested that 'we could even afford to lose America.' 'You cannot, I venture to say it, you CANNOT conquer America,' Chatham had thundered after the dismal news of the surrender at Saratoga reached the mother country in November 1777. A few weeks later the ailing Chatham, now close to death, rose in the House of Lords to declare that England had engaged in a 'ruinous' war 'through the means of false hope, false pride and promised advantages of the most romantic and improbable nature'. 'Oh God, it is all over!' cried Lord North presciently when news of Cornwallis's surrender at Yorktown - when the revolutionaries' band allegedly played 'The World Turned Upside Town' - reached him on 25th November 1781.

As historian Paul Kennedy has recently said of the American War: 'It had hardly been a glorious conflict for the British, who had lost their largest colony and seen their national debt rise to about 220 million.' However, in dramatic contrast to the economic chaos experienced by the French - who were actually on the winning side - sound financial measures quickly restored a large measure of health to the British economy. In general, the American War did surprisingly little, at least until the early 1780s, to hamper the economic growth of Britain during this period; in particular, it caused only a temporary abatement of the phenomenal growth of building work being undertaken in the country.

The massive development of London during the Age of Adam caused much contemporary comment. In 1779 Dr Richard Price noted that 'The increase of buildings in London has for several years been the subject of general observation' and that 'It deserves particular notice that it is derived from the increase of luxury' - 'an evil', he continued, 'which, while it flatters, never fails to destroy.' In 1756 work began on the New Road linking Paddington in the west to Islington in the north; as the road progressed, so the speculator-builders erected large, new housing estates about its path. By 1780 the foreign visitor von Archenholtz was contrasting the

Sir Lawrence Dundas and his Grandson, *Johan Zoffany, 1769-70. Set in the library of his town house, 19 Arlington Street, Mayfair, which had been newly decorated by Robert Adam, this portrait provides one of the most accurate contemporary depictions of a mid-eighteenth century interior. It features a 'Turkey' carpet (with typical red and blue decoration); fashionable blue wallpaper with a golden fillet above the dado; simple horsechair-covered chairs and tables arranged against the walls; chocolate-coloured skirting; a typical crowded picture hang; and blue damask curtains hung in the new 'French' (side-drawn) style.*

dilapidated East End of London ('the streets there are narrow, dark and ill-paved') with the impressive new West End that was being erected to the south of the New Road:

'The houses here are mostly new and elegant; the squares are superb, the streets straight and open ... If all London were as well built, there would be nothing in the world to compare with it.' Not all of this new building work, however, was being expertly executed. In 1764 the *London Chronicle* warned 'those who are to inhabit the many piles of new buildings that are daily rising in this metropolis' of the dangers of cheap brick construction, resulting from the practice of making bricks (which were fired in temporary kilns on site) from any local materials that came to hand:

'When we consider the practice among some of the bricklayers about this time ... we must shudder at the evil ... The demand for bricks had raised the price of brick earth so greatly that the makers are tempted to mix the slop of the street, ashes, scavengers' dirt and everything that will make the brick earth or clay go as far as possible.'

The long-awaited and much-needed repaving of the nation's streets began in 1762 with the Westminster Paving Act. Before this measure the maintenance of the street and pavement in Westminster - as in other towns and cities in Britain and America - had rested with the individual householder, responsible for the immediate area outside his or her front door. The 1762 Act introduced paving commissioners, provided for gutters at the side of roads (instead of the insanitary central channels) and the regular scavenging of streets for rubbish, authorized the removal of illegal traders and illegally-projecting balconies and

bow windows, and announced the immediate replacement of cobbles with stout, durable Purbeck stone. The effect of the Act on the West End streets was considerable: in 1787 the paving in Westminster was described by one admiring observer as 'an undertaking which has introduced a degree of elegance and symmetry into the streets of the metropolis, that is the admiration of all Europe'.

Other cities rapidly followed Westminster's lead. Manchester (whose population, like Liverpool's, was to treble between 1760 and 1800) passed a similar Cleaning and Lighting Act in 1765. Such legislation helped to make the quality of the environment better in a very tangible way. As one schoolteacher remarked in 1781:

'The streets are ... better and more regularly cleansed; and by the addition of several new works, water is become much more plentiful than it was heretofore; and this has been a great means of contribution ... to greater cleanliness in our houses.'

The provision of better street-lighting - at least in the centres of London and the other great cities of both Britain and America - was an improvement which met with especially widespread applause. The tourist von Archenholtz, who was Prussian, was particularly impressed with London's street lamps when he visited the country in 1780, declaring that 'nothing can be more superb':

'The lamps, which have two or four branches, are enclosed in crystal globes and fixed on posts at a little distance from each other. They are lighted at sunset in winter as well as in summer whether the moon shines or not. In Oxford Road [now Oxford Street] alone there are more lamps than in all the city of Paris.'

The countryside also witnessed considerable

change during this period. Industrial advances help substantially improve crop yields; thus during the forty years after 1760 corn production in Britain increased by a massive fifty per cent. At the same time the pressure for development meant that many fields or areas of common land were being enclosed for new housing. As the historian T. S. Ashton wrote in 1948:

'Areas that for centuries had been cultivated as open fields, or had lain untended as common pasture, were hedged or fenced; hamlets grew into populous towns; and chimneystacks rose to dwarf the ancient spires.'

The implementation of enclosures was at its height during the 1770s, not only laying the way for ambitious new building development, but also throwing a mass of dispossessed rural poor onto the riot-torn streets of nearby towns or cities. And with new houses came new communications. Whereas in 1750 some 143 turnpike trusts governed 3,400 miles of British road, by 1170 there were 500 such trusts, administering more than 15,000 miles of road. And in 1759 the first industrial canal, linking Manchester with the Worsley coalpits, was built by James Brindley for the Duke of Bridgwater, inaugurating the great age of canals.

Such industrial progress was not to everyone's taste. Doctor Johnson - angered, in this instance, by the abolition of public executions at Tyburn Hill - moaned with some justification in 1783 that 'The age is running mad after innovation.' However, despite the qualms of conservatives such as the admirable Dr Johnson, the Age of Adam was also the age of the great industrial inventions - and the great industrial entrepreneurs. As early as 1757

Josiah Tucker was remarking of Birmingham that 'almost every Master and Manufacturer hath a new invention of his own, and is daily improving on those of others'.

Innovation was particularly marked in the area of textile production and other mill-related manufactures. John Kay's flying shuttle had been invented in 1733; it was not until the 1760s, however, that it came into widespread use, after which it was augmented by a breathtakingly ingenious series of industrial improvements. Hargreaves's spinning jenny of 1766 allowed a number of threads to be spun at once, and by 1785 there were 20,000 such machines at work. Arkwright's water-frame of 1769 allowed the use, for the first time, of a strong warp thread as well as a tough weft, while his carding patent of 1775 brought mechanized efficiency closer to hand in textile production. Watt's steam-engine patent, also of 1775, was of paramount importance in providing the power needed for Industrial Britain. Already in 1781 the great Birmingham entrepreneur Matthew Boulton was enthusiastically commenting that 'The people in London, Manchester and Birmingham are all steam mill mad.'

The effects of the Industrial Revolution were not only to be seen in the mills of Adam's day. Houses, too - even the most modest terrace development or rural cottage - reflected the pace of technological change in the materials with which they were constructed and the methods with which they were built. How this was expressed, and how, in turn, industrial advances changed the way architects approached the aesthetics of design, will be seen in the following chapters.

An idyllic, Arcadian landscape by Claude of 1650. Such Utopian views did much to inspire the Neo-Classicists of the 1750s and 60s.

'God damn my blood, my Lord, is this your Grecian arch? What villainy! What absurdity? If this be Grecian, give me Chinese, give me Gothick! Anything is better than this! For shame, my Lord, pull it down and burn it'

(Lord de la Warr on James Stuart's Greek arch at Nuneham Park, Oxon, built for Earl Harcourt in 1764)

Right: *the frontispiece of Stuart and Revett's enormously influential* Antiquities of Athens *of 1762.*

Opposite: *Edinburgh's sedate and elegant Charlotte Square, designed by Robert Adam late in his career and begun in 1791.*

The choice of 1755 as a starting date for this book, while it is not meant to signify that that particular year had any immense architectural or social significance, is not a wholly random one. In that year James Stuart, the son of a Scots sailor, and his companion Nicholas Revett, the scion of proud Suffolk gentry, returned from many years' study of the ancient ruins of Italy and Greece. Their experiences had not been solely academic ones: having eschewed a predecessor's example of hiring a troop of Turkish cavalry to guard them (Greece had long been a dangerous outpost of the Ottoman Empire), Revett was subsequently attacked by pirates, and both students had to flee Athens following yet another palace coup.

Stuart and Revett were a strangely-assorted couple. Revett was a calm, studious dilettante whose private means allowed him the luxury of never having to run an architectural practice. Stuart, on the other hand, was an extrovert and notoriously slothful genius, who took as his second wife the sixteen-year-old Greek daughter of his *first* wife. (Following his second marriage his child-bride was immediately dispatched to school to become literate.) Stuart, according to Professor Crook, 'ended his days playing skittles in the afternoon, and drinking in public houses in the evening.' Yet the fruit of Revett and Stuart's long sojourn abroad was to effect a fundamental change in architecture and design, the drama of which was being re-enacted anew in Britain and America a century later.

For seven years after their return Stuart and Revett worked on the magisterial record of their labours, *The Antiquities of Athens*. This volume was so widely anticipated by professionals and public alike that, even before its publication in 1762, the project was satirized in a public print *(The Five Orders of PERRIWIGS)* by the aging William Hogarth. Stuart and Revett's avowed aim was to provide an invaluable reference work for scholars and architects, which described for the English-speaking world the as yet largely undiscovered architectural treasures of ancient Greece ('Greece', they avowed, 'appears principally to merit our Attention') in meticulous and accurate detail. They aimed to correct the imprecision of past works, whose 'Descriptions are so confused, and their Measures so inaccurate' that they had proved of little use to architects or builders. In the Preface the authors declared that:

'if accurate Representations of these Originals were published, the World would be enabled to form, not only more extensive, but juster Ideas than have hitherto been obtained, concerning Architecture, and the state in which it existed during the best ages of antiquity.'

Even renowned interpretations of antiquity such as those penned by Palladio and Desgodetz, it was alleged, 'cannot be said to afford a sufficient variety of Examples for restoring even the three Orders of Columns'. What was wanted, believed Stuart and Revett, was a finely-crafted record of some of the most astonishing monuments of Ancient Greece - 'the Place where the most beautiful Edifices were erected, and where the purest and most elegant Examples of ancient Architecture are to be disovered'.

However, although their record did exercise enormous influence on the literary and architectural worlds of Britain and the colonies, in practice it proved too esoteric for the average builder to use. More determinedly populist works, such as Stephen

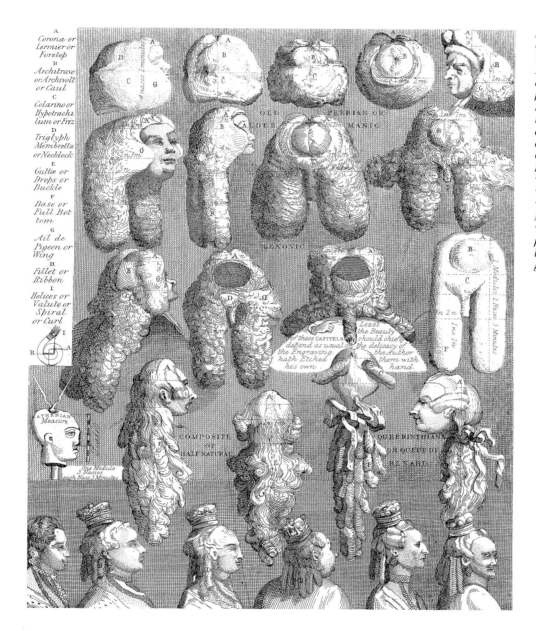

Hogarth's The Five Orders of Perriwigs *of November 1761 was a satire on* The Antiquities of Athens *which appeared even before the publication of Stuart and Revett's much-anticipated work. In place of the customary five classical orders (Doric, Tuscan, Ionic, Corinthian and Composite) Hogarth has suggested 'Episcopal', 'Old Peerian' or 'Aldermanic', 'Lexonic', 'Queerinthian' and 'Half Natural' wigs. The head of 'Athenian' Stuart himself is pictured on the left, his nose broken off to give him a genuinely antique look.*

Opposite: *one of the coloured engravings published by Stuart and Revett in their* Antiquities of Athens *1762. This one shows Hadrian's Arch.*

Above and left: *two engaging classical fantasies.* Above: *Piranesi's view of two Roman roads flanked by colossal funerary monuments, in an etching of c.1756, and,* below, *the frontispiece for Joshua Kirby's* The Perspective of Architecture *of 1761, engraved by William Woollet after Hogarth.*

At the same time, the books hurried out by Wood's imitators - notably Le Roy's *Ruines des Plus Beaux Monuments de la Gréce* of 1758 and Robert Sayer's *Ruins of Athens* of 1759 - were rushed, scrappy and inaccurate. Far more important to the history of Neo-Classicism than either of these works was Winckelmann's *Reflections on the Imitation of Greek Works in Painting and Sculpture* of 1755. 'The only way for us to become great', Winckelmann had portentously announced, 'lies in the imitation of the Greeks.' Yet Winckelmann's book was not translated into English until 1765 - three years after *The Antiquities of Athens* had taken the English-speaking world by storm - and the rancorous German scholar remained a lifelong enemy of the archaelogical precision of Stuart and Revett.

The *Antiquities of Athens* enthralled and inspired a generation of architects, designers and collectors. Its appearance, for example, encouraged the great diplomat-collector Sir William Hamilton (now, unfortunately, better known as the cuckolded spouse of Nelson's celebrated mistress) to launch the so-called 'Etruscan' style with the publication of his *Collection of Etruscan, Greek and Roman Antiques* in 1766-7. (Sir William's own collection was bought by the British Museum, which in 1772 became the first public gallery in the world to exhibit Greek ceramics.) The distinct black and red-coloured Etruscan scenes and motifs which featured prominently in Hamilton's book were in turn made popular by Robert Adam, who used them copiously at Osterley Park and other large-scale commissions of the 1770s.

The earliest truly Neo-Classical building, however, was erected some time before Adam's Osterley. James Stuart, no longer in partnership

Riou's *The Grecian Orders* of 1768, were subsequently needed to re-interpret the new, Neo-Classical message in simpler terms for the building and decorating trades.

Stuart and Revett were by no means the first who sought to depict the architectural wonders of ancient civilizations. Robert Wood's *Ruins of Palmyra* of 1753 - lauded by Horace Walpole as 'a noble book' - and its companion volume on Baalbec of 1757 caused a great stir in Britain (and, incidentally, encouraged Robert Adam to publish his similarly-organized study of *Spalatro* in 1764). However, the scope of Wood's volumes was limited.

The Etruscan Room at Home House, Portman Square, London. Etruscan decoration, concentrating on the use of the terracotta and black colours which adorned ancient Etruscan pottery, was all the rage in the grander homes by the mid-1760s.

with Revett, built a Greek temple at Hagley Park in Worcestershire, of 1758-9, that was the first building in the world to use the Greek order since the days of Ancient Greece. The fact that such obviously Mediterranean-inspired edifices were not wholly suitable for the English climate had already been widely remarked upon. Two years before the Hagley temple was begun, the poet James Cawthorn bemoaned the irrelevance of much contemporary design:

'Is there a portal, colonnade, or dome
The pride of Naples, or the boast of Rome?
We raise it here in storms of wind and hail,
On the bleak bosom of a sunless vale;
Careless alike of climate, soil and place,
The cast of Nature and the smiles of Grace.
Hence all our stucco'd walls, Mosaic floors,
Palladian windows and Venetian doors.'

James Stuart's sumptuous interiors of 1759-65 at Spencer House in London's St James's, however, saw the new Neo-Classical ideology being adapted for a more practical and domestic context. The end result was splendid, and shocking. Too shocking for some: even Robert Adam observed of Stuart's ceilings that they were 'Greek to the teeth ... but by God they are not handsome.'

Stuart's former partner, Revett, built a few exquisite monuments in the new Grecian style that were perhaps rather less offensive to conservative contemporaries than Stuart's early efforts. His lakeside temple at West Wycombe Park, Buckinghamshire, of 1778-80, neatly combined the taste for Greek with the well-established English landscape tradition, creating a sublime Arcadian vision which not only recalled the paintings of Poussin and Lorrain but also echoed the more

recent work of celebrated English landscape artists such as Richard Wilson.

Even Stuart and Revett, however, baulked at utilizing some of the more dramatically primitive forms being discovered in Greece; as a result buildings executed in the true, austere 'Greek Revival' style did not begin to appear until the mid-1780s. In the meantime, the two preceding decades were dominated by one man's personal interpretation of the startling new finds of the antique world, an interpretation which - being somewhat more palatable to contemporary tastes than the undiluted Grecian forms of the more academic practitioners - inspired generations of designers, craftsmen and house-owners.

Robert Adam was born in Kirkcaldy, Fife, on 3 July 1728. The second of four brothers, and the son of the well-established Scots architect William

Revett's austere yet poetically Neo-Classical Island Temple, built in the late 1770s by the lake at West Wycombe Park, Buckinghamshire, and appearing in an evocative archive photo.

Above and left: *the first true crescent: John Wood the Younger's Royal Crescent in Bath, begun in 1767. As historian Stefan Muthesius has observed, 'one not only has a full view of the lawn in front and the valley beyond; the terrace itself can be seen in its full curve and grandeur from many angles and many distances.' Wood's use of the giant order of columns to link first and second floors, in a manner which suggests a massive and continuous colonnade, was particularly striking and novel.*

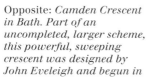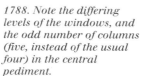

Opposite: *Camden Crescent in Bath. Part of an uncompleted, larger scheme, this powerful, sweeping crescent was designed by John Eveleigh and begun in* 1788. *Note the differing levels of the windows, and the odd number of columns (five, instead of the usual four) in the central pediment.*

Adam, he went to school with the future economist Adam Smith. In 1754 Robert and his brother James travelled to Italy and beyond, meeting, architectural luminaries such as Piranesi and measuring the Roman palace of Split in Dalmatia (now Croatia). The results of their labours were lavishly published in the form of the book Ruins of the Emperor Diocletian at Spalatro in 1764. Unlike Stuart and Revett, however, the Adam brothers never actually got to Greece. In 1756 Robert suggested to James that they journey there merely in order to rush out a book which would knock The Antiquities of Athens off its lofty and academically-precise pedestal. 'We would furnish a very tolerable Work to Rival Stuart and Rivets in three months time and return home laden with Laurel', Robert optimistically declared. Yet in the event they never went. Instead, they returned in 1758 to England where, if they did not immediately eclipse Stuart and Revett, they were soon being widely acclaimed.

The principal reason for this rapid success lay partly in astute marketing. The Adams - not only Robert and James, but also their eldest brother, John - often collaborated on architectural projects. Yet it was generally Robert's name that was pushed to the fore, a practice which branded what may have actually been a group effort in a personal, easily-recognizable form. At the same time the Adams were assiduous in cultivating valuable patrons. Thus in 1761 their fellow-Scot the Earl of Bute, by now effectively in charge of government patronage, persuaded his former pupil George III to appoint Robert Adam as one of the two new Architects of the King's Works. And when Robert was, thanks to invaluable political influence, elected MP for Bute's Scottish pocket borough of Kinross in 1769, his

brother James succeeded him in this Works post. The success of the Adams' gold-digging is testified to by the fact that, at his funeral in 1792, Robert Adam's coffin was borne by pall-bearers who were almost to a man former clients, and who were all members of the aristocracy.

Occasionally, however, the Adam brothers' overweening ambition came seriously unstuck. In 1768 the family took a 99-year lease on a portion of land on the north side of the River Thames in the heart of the City of Westminster. Their avowed aim was to reclaim this marshy terrain in order 'to raise palaces upon an inoffensive heap of mud', as a contemporary put it. More precisely, they sought to build twenty-four First Rate houses, all of which were to be treated in daringly novel fashion as a single, unified architectural composition: the 'Adelphi'.

The result was certainly a visual success; as the Adams boasted later, the houses were indeed

Opposite and this page: *the Circus in Bath, begun by John Wood the Elder in 1754. The frieze motifs are a jumble of masonic, Druidic and Judaic symbols. Wood was a highly eccentric character who based the proportions of his Circus on Stonehenge and legendary Druid temples.*

A contemporary engraving of the grand, Thames-side elevation of Adelphi Terrace, the centrepiece of the Adam brothers' ill-fated Adelphi scheme. The heroic scale and palatial proportions of their ambitious composition - the first to be actually termed a 'terrace' - are very evident in this view.

'remarkably strong and substantial, and finished in the most elegant and complete measure, much beyond the common style of London houses'. However, the financing soon proved decidedly shaky. The Adams had anticipated that the government would hire the enormous vaults they had constructed underneath the terrace; but their stock with the government - no longer managed by the pliable Bute - was not as high as they presumed. The Treasury failed to take the carrot, and the development crashed ignominiously. 3,000 workmen were summarily dismissed, while critics, long envious of the Adams' seemingly unstoppable rise, queued to gloat over the ruins. Even closer acquaintances shook their heads. The Scots philosopher David Hume wrote to the Adams' former schoolmate, Adam Smith, that 'To me the scheme of the Adelphi always appeared so imprudent, that my wonder is how they could have gone on so long.'

Feverish attempts were made to salvage something from the wreck. Celebrated friends of the Adam family were persuaded to support the scheme in a very public fashion; thus David Garrick took a house in the Adelphi, as did Robert Adam himself, while Josiah Wedgwood even installed a showroom for his vastly popular ceramics in the terrace. Finally, a public lottery was devised in 1774 as the only way in which the Adams could save their personal fortunes. The lottery did indeed avert bankruptcy, but the project remained a financial disaster.

The Adams did not dwell on the setback of the Adelphi for long. In 1773 Robert and James published their *Works in Architecture* - in fact a blatant self-advertisement whose text was very

much in the vein of Stuart and Revett's masterpiece (Greece and Rome, the brothers averred, should 'serve as models which we should imitate, and as standards by which we ought to judge'), but whose illustrations were startlingly novel. Their boastful claim that 'We have not trod in the paths of others, nor derived aid from their labours' was, for once, quite justified.

The importance of the *Works in Architecture* for the design of the average house of the time lies not so much in the actual buildings featured - which largely comprised the grandest of the Adams' recent commissions - as in its definition of the essence of 'Adam Style'. Pausing to note that 'Architecture has already become more elegant and more interesting,' the text outlined what was to become one of Robert Adam's guiding principles in design: the concept of 'movement'. To the Adams, and to Robert in particular, 'movement' was 'an agreeable and diversified contour, that groups and contrasts like a picture, and creates a variety of light and shade, which gives great spirit, beauty and affect to the composition'. In the wrong hands, they were careful to warn, it could cause havoc. As James Adam had written in 1762:

'At the same time as I mention this movement as absolutely necessary for attaining to great elegance in the Elevation, yet I must not omit a caution not to give into excess of this kind, not to torment the eye with too frequent decorations which, like the abuse or too great profusion of all beauty, will undoubtedly tire the spectator'.

Robert Adam's great achievement was to provide a synthesis of fashions, new and old, which could be applied to all manner of buildings and everyday objects. His decorative style, as outlined in

Adam's Eating Room at Osterley Park, Middlesex, and (left) an Adam design for an urn. The design of the marvellous plaster ceiling of the Eating Room - based on Bacchic emblems - has been attributed to Adam's great rival William Chambers. The pink and green colour scheme is Adam's own, of 1762; the inset medallions are painted by Antonio Zucchi.

Opposite: *Zoffany's painting of Charles Towneley and colleagues, of c.1781, shows connoisseurs admiring a jumbled collection of recently-imported classical statuary at his home of 14 Queen Anne's Gate, London. Note the splendid carpet.*

A perspective of 1775 by Thomas Malton, showing how proportion governed the standard Georgian interior. All the elements of the house are, in terms of size, directly related to each other and to the scale of the human figure seen ascending the stairs.

Above: *The grand entrance hall at Somerset House, on London's Strand. Erected to the design of William Chambers after 1776, Somerset House has been hailed as Chambers's masterpiece. Now the home of the Courtauld Institute's galleries, it is, ironically, almost adjacent to the site of the Adam brothers' largely-demolished Adelphi.*

Opposite: *the drawing room from the Moffatt Ladd House, Portsmouth, New Hampshire. Note the Chippendale-style chairs, the re-created wallpaper, with its Neo-Classical swags and medallions, and the delicate proportions (and tiled inset) of the chimneypiece.*

the Works and seen in his vast output of buildings and artefacts, was undeniably daring and revolutionary. He made great use of the recent, well-publicized Greek and Roman archaeological discoveries, not in a slavish, academic way, as many of his successors were to do, but in a highly personal and at times distinctly light-hearted fashion, in order to effect a sea-change in decorative taste. Everything he touched he remoulded in his own image. The heavy Palladian motifs of the previous forty years were tamed, reduced in scale and given movement and vivacity. At the same time, the recent fripperies of the Rococo style - a fashion borrowed from France which had appealed to many of the most fashionable patrons of the 1740s and 50s - were banished from the interior, their place taken by simpler and more overtly architectural forms.

Other French innovations, such as a liking for sequences of differently shaped rooms (a device first exploited by Sir Robert Taylor), were adapted by Adam to fit even the most cramped and modest townhouse. Archaeological themes, whether from the pages of Winckelmann or Stuart and Revett, or direct from the ruins of Rome or Herculaneum, were applied in the most light and delicate manner possible, in sites often far removed in spirit and function from their original contexts. To this stimulating and intriguing cocktail Adam added Renaissance details, borrowed from the Italian master-architects of the sixteenth and seventeenth centuries. The result was, in Sir John Summerson's words, 'a personal revision and reconstruction of the antique into which many threads from a variety of sources were drawn and interwoven'. Equally importantly, it was a particularly British style, which followed decades of Italian-derived, Dutch-influenced and French-inspired architectural fashion.

The effect that this exciting new combination of themes and cultures had on the decorative taste of Europe and especially America cannot be overstated. For once, the immodest prose of an architect's self-promoting pattern-book actually does justice to the drama and significance of his work. As Adam wrote in Works in Architecture:

'The massive entablature, the ponderous compartment ceiling, the tabernacle frame almost the only species of ornament formerly known in the country are now universally exploded and in their place we have adopted a beautiful variety of light mouldings, gracefully formed, delicately enriched and arranged with propriety and skill.'

Robert Adam was the first to devise an overall, integrated 'look' for interiors, anticipating by thirty years the Regency decorating manuals which preached this doctrine. As the eminent architectural historian Howard Colvin has written:

'... ingenious and imaginative planning

Buildings in the typically reticent and well-proportioned mid-Georgian streetscape of Bath. Adam Fergusson noted of the city in the 1950s that 'it had a harmony of style and grace unmatched on such a scale anywhere else.' Despite the depredations of the 1960s and 70s, Bath remains a uniquely Georgian city, built almost entirely out of the local, honey-coloured limestone. Its special status has recently been officially recognized in the declaration of Bath as a World Heritage Site.

ensured a progression of varied and interesting shapes in place of the simple rectangular rooms of earlier Georgian architecture, and walls, ceilings, chimneypieces, carpets and furniture - down even to details like doorknobs and candlesticks - were designed as part of an elegant, varied and highly sophisticated decorative scheme.'

In Adam's interiors, as well as those directly or indirectly inspired by Adam, major architectural features were less pronounced than formerly, and were subordinated to the overall scheme. Gone was the intrusive, heavy and at times overly academic style of the Palladians; in its stead appeared decorative schemes of low relief in which the chimneypiece was often the only element which truly projected into the room. Even large pieces of furniture were included in this overall treatment, becoming as much a part of the architecture of the wall as did the doors and windows.

The Adam brothers were not, of course, the only major architects working in Britain during the 1760s and 70s. Robert Adam did, however, remain by far the most influential and popular architect of the day, a fact bitterly resented by his rivals. No-one had more reason to envy Robert Adam's success than his great rival William Chambers. The dour son of a Scottish merchant, Chambers developed into an architect who, in the words of James Lees-Milne, 'stood for officialdom and those comfortable prejudices enshrined in the bosom of his royal master', George III. To the conservative Chambers, Robert Adam's daring innovations were little more than 'filigrane toy work'. He staunchly believed that his own style of orthodox Palladianism with a veneer of dull, academic Neo-Classicism was in reality closer to 'the true style ... of the Ancients'.

Chambers's career ran exactly parallel to that of Robert Adam. Like Adam a Scot (although one who was actually born in Sweden), he returned from study in Italy in 1758, quickly built up a large practice, was created Surveyor-General of the reformed Office of Works in 1782, and died in 1796, only four years after Adam. Despite his undoubted success, however, he was never truly able to cope with the easy popularity of Adam's new designs. 'Was there ever such a brace of self-puffing Scotch coxcombs?', he blustered after the appearance of the *The Works in Architecture* of Robert and James Adam in 1773. His own *Treatise on Civil Architecture*, published fourteen years before, had been a far more restrained and philosophical work, which rejected excessive ornament and undue movement and stood by the tried and trusted Palladian principles of the past three decades. 'Variety in ornaments must not be carried to excess', warned Chambers sternly, since 'In architecture they are only acessories, and therefore they should not be too striking, not capable of long detaining the attention from the main object.'

Robert Adam's other principal rival was the young, mercurial and prodigiously talented yet notoriously lazy and careless architect James Wyatt. Wyatt, too, was overshadowed by the Adams, at least until the 1780s; unlike the haughty Chambers, however, he was content at first to borrow from the Adam Style when it suited him. Joseph Farington's Diary records that in 1804, long after Adam's death, Wyatt - typically economical with the truth - told George III 'that when he came from Italy he found the public taste corrupted by the Adams and he was obliged to comply with it'. Wyatt could build in Greek, Roman or Gothic. His Pantheon, opened to

Vol:II.

Girandoles in the first Drawing room
Girandoles dans la première Salle d'Assemblée

Curtain Cornice of the Bed Chamber
Corniche aux Rideaux de la Chambre à coucher

N.º I.

Curtain Cornice of the Etruscan room
Corniche aux Rideaux de la Chambre Etrusque

Plate VIII.

Girandole in the Nich of the Etruscan room
Girandole dans la Niche de la Chambre Etrusque

Girandoles in the Etruscan room
Girandoles dans la Chambre Etrusque

Folding Doors of the third Drawing room
Portes à deux Battans pour la troisième Salle d'Assemblée

Folding Doors for the Etruscan room
Portes à deux Battans pour la Chambre Etrusque

Top of a Commode in the Countess of Derby's Dressing room
Dessus d'une Commode dans la Chambre à Toilette de Mad.me la Comtesse de Derby

Front of a Commode in the Countess of Derby's Dressing room
Façade d'une Commode dans la Chambre à Toilette de Mad.me la Comtesse de Derby

Opposite and this page: *designs for the decoration of interiors from the Adams' Works in Architecture of 1773-78 with* (left) *'Designs of coloured ornaments for Pannels'. The delicacy of line, tempered by an adherence to strongly architectural forms and combined with the frequent use of Neo-Classical motifs such as the urn, the vase and the drop, epitomizes the Adam Style.*

This page and opposite: *the Harrison Gray Otis House in Boston, built after 1795 by Charles Bulfinch - the outstanding American architect of the early Federal period, and the leading exponent of the Adam Style in the United States. Whilst the exterior is conservatively Palladian (aside from the large fanlight over the front door), the interior betrays elements characteristic of the delicate style of Adam and his contemporaries. The bold colouring is evocatively Neo-Classical.*

great acclaim in London's Oxford Street in 1772 (but sadly burnt down in 1792), caused an immediate sensation, temporarily eclipsing the Adams' fame. Many people began to discover that they preferred the cooler, more obviously showy 'Grecian' style of Wyatt and his contemporaries. The Pantheon prompted Lady Mary Coke to declare that '[Wyatt's] designs I prefer to those of Mr Adams', while in 1782 Horace Walpole wrote admiringly of James Stuart's grand house for Elizabeth Montagu in Portman Square that 'It is grand, not tawdry, or larded and embroidered and pomponned with shreds and remnants, and clinquant like all the harlequinades of Adam, which never let the eye repose a moment.'

Whatever invective Walpole may have used, however, it did not detract from the profound influence Robert Adam's style exercised on the designs of his own time, and indeed on those of the two centuries which have elapsed since his death in 1792. His immediate influence in America, for example, was pronounced. Before the termination of the War of Independence in 1783 America was almost wholly reliant on English designs. As textile historian Florence Montgomery has observed:

'Being for the most part Englishmen, the colonists had a natural preference for English fashions which they saw in the rich furniture, curtains, and bed hangings brought to the colonies by royal governors and imported by wealthy merchants.'

The Antiquities of Athens and the third edition of Chippendale's *Director* proved very popular in America; soon after its publication in 1773 the Adam brothers' *Works in Architecture* had become an important element of any self-respecting colonial arts library. Already in 1775 George Washington was incorporating Adamesque elements into the new dining room at his home of Mount Vernon in Virginia.

By 1790 the 'Adam Style' - or, as it was known in the United States, the 'Federal Style' - was all the rage along the east coast of America. One of the first wholly Adam-influenced American houses was The Woodlands in Philadelphia, built in 1787-9 to the design of its owner, William Hamilton. The most celebrated exponent in America of the Adam Style, however, was the architect Charles Bulfinch. Having undertaken the Grand Tour in accustomed fashion between 1875 and 1787, during the 1790s Bulfinch brought Adam Style to a large number of New England homes - perhaps the most famous survivor of which is Boston's Harrison Gray Otis House of 1795. It is indeed ironic that what was in origin a very English stylistic synthesis remained popular in America long after the States had won their political independence. Even twenty years after Adam's death - when the Adam Style was deemed to be entirely out of fashion in Britain - homes were still being built in America in this most lively and gracious of styles.

This page and opposite: Robert Adam's Kenwood, built in the 1760s on a ridge high on Hampstead Heath,

north of London, for the First Earl of Mansfield. Its stuccoed principal elevation was daringly revolutionary.

'My son, observe . . . those mouldering walls, and humid floor'

(Oliver Goldsmith, The Vicar of Wakefield, *1766)*

The entrance to 20 St James's Square, London (built in 1771-4 for Sir Watkin Williams Wynn), as envisaged by Adam (right) *and as it is today* (opposite). *The vast, intricate fanlight and the sinuously Neo-Classical ironwork are typical of Robert Adam's personal style.*

As Britain and her colonies prospered, so there was a corresponding rush to translate sudden wealth into bricks and mortar. After 1755, for example, many of the *nouveaux riches* began to commission architects such as Sir Robert Taylor to build small, highly compact villas in the country; these comparatively modest, medium-sized buildings were soon all the rage for successful businessmen or professionals. Taylor - who, Hardwick famously recorded, 'nearly divided the practice of the profession' between himself and James Paine 'till Mr Robert Adam entered the lists' - provided, in the shape of his Harleyford Manor in Buckinghamshire, the ideal social centre for the aspiring middle classes. The exterior appeared reasonably plain: every elevation was faced in humble brickwork, rather than expensive stone, and the external walls were designed to be wholly astylar, without columns or pilasters of any kind. Harleyford was, nevertheless, grand enough to impress visitors, while remaining small enough to be run cheaply, yet compact enough to allow entertainments to be conducted on a suitably lavish scale.

Taylor's Harleyford revolutionized the concept of the villa, and brought this hitherto prohibitively expensive luxury within reach of the aspiring middle classes. Its principal rooms were on the ground floor, not the first floor, and the whole room plan was built around the central staircase. Each room was accordingly reached without having to trespass through another, an arrangement which perfectly suited the typical Georgian ball or rout, with its wide variety of entertainments. To emphasize the varying functions of the rooms, as well as to help accommodate them within the tight room plan, Taylor also employed a number of differing room shapes, a novelty later seized upon by Robert Adam for his great houses. Not surprisingly, Harleyford was an immediate success, and Taylor's villa practice rapidly took off. Similar villas were soon built at Coptfold in Essex (1755-6, now demolished), Barlaston in Staffordshire (1755-6, for the Leek lawyer Thomas Mills) and, perfecting the style of the compact country villa, Danson in Kent (1762-7) and Asgill House in Richmond (1761-4), built for the banker Sir Charles Asgill. However, Taylor remained a Palladian at heart: by the time it was finished, in 1767, buildings such as Danson had begun to look very conservative when compared to the new designs of Robert Adam. Taylor's use of traditional English Palladian devices, such as large areas of blank wallspace punctuated by small windows, now appeared distinctly old-fashioned when set beside the latest Neo-Classical compositions. Even the modest *Kentish Traveller's Companion* complained that the fenestration at Danson was mean - a feature which, it declared, suggested that 'the architect did not imagine that sleeping in airy chambers might contribute to the health of the family.'

The imposing side elevation of the Nathaniel Russell House, Charleston, South Carolina. Note the exaggerated keystones and lengthened windows.

Opposite: *an aquatint of the completed Adelphi Terrace from the River Thames, by Thomas Malton.*

For those whose new-found wealth did not quite amount to the riches of a Mills or an Asgill, there were a variety of grandly-appointed terraced housing developments springing up all over Britain and the east coast of America. After the Treaty of Paris had ended the Seven Years War in 1763 there was a great building boom that did not abate until the intensification of the American War in the late 1770s. The Adam brothers' Adelphi scheme of 1768-74 set a high standard for these new terrace developments. Although, as we have seen, the scheme proved a financial flop, the Adelphi was the first development in which the houses had been conceived as an architectural composition, on the scale of an Italian palace, rather than merely as a succession of identical houses. It was also the first time the Thames had been bordered with architecture specially devised to exploit the scenic properties of the waterfront - which until then had been covered with ramshackle warehousing and nondescript docks.

Surpassing the Adelphi in scale, however, was a vast new development in the Scottish capital: Edinburgh New Town, a complex of grand, stone-built streets laid out from *c.*1762 to a design by James Craig. The fashionable watering-hole of Bath was not to be outshone by Edinburgh, though. Bath's vision proved even more ambitious: John Wood junior, son of the architect of Queen Square, was commissioned not only to complete his father's monumental Circus (begun in 1754), but also to add a large development of his own - what became the magnificent Royal Crescent of 1767-75. This marvellous sweeping terrace, given added emphasis by the verticality and monumentality of the grand Ionic order, was unrivalled anywhere in the world, and became the model for grandiose housing projects for the next sixty years.

Rivalling the new, stone-clad terraces of Edinburgh and Bath was London's brick-and-stucco Bedford Square. As in Edinburgh's George Street or Bath's Royal Crescent, the basic proportions of the Palladian era were retained in Bedford Square, all of the elevations being built so that each façade approximated to a square-and-a-half, even though it was created by a number of hands. It was also the first London square to realize the old Palladian dream of a palace front applied to a domestically-scaled building. James Ralph's *Critical Review* of 1783 called the completed composition 'proof of the improvement of our taste'; in his view 'the regularity and symmetry of the pavements, and the neatness of the iron rails' made it far superior 'to any square in Europe'.

Of course, not all mid-Georgian terraces were constructed to the high standard of Bedford Square. Yet however sloppy the work, the basic principles of design remained the same in every elevation: the Palladian proportions, the importance

of the fenestration, the use of the latest materials, the pursuit of grandeur in even the most modest façade, and inclusion of the orders where it was felt necessary to give a particular emphasis. The end result was peculiarly British. As Sir John Summerson wrote in 1945:

'The insistent verticality of the [Georgian] London house is idiomatic. The French learnt at an early date to live horizontally and most, if not all, continental capitals followed the French lead.'

The designer of mid-Georgian urban-development squares and terraces was rarely an architect of the calibre of Robert Adam, William Chambers or John Wood. Most terrace developments were erected by speculator-builders,

who took on the ground rents, built the carcass, and then sold on the leasehold or (less usually) the freehold, leaving the new owner to decide on the finishing of the interiors. The social commentator Pierre-Jean Grosley remarked in 1765 that 'All the houses in London excepting a few in the heart of the city belong to undertakers, who build upon ground of which a lease is taken for 40, 60 or 99 years'.

By 1785, a wealth of pattern books was available to help the more untutored builder or craftsman to execute the latest fashions. The Neo-Classical gospel preached by Stuart and Revett and the Adam brothers was repeated in a more everyday idiom in more basic publications by authors such as William Pain, whose *Practical Builder* of 1774 was

Panorama (left) *and detail* (opposite) *of John Wood the Younger's Royal Crescent in Bath of 1767-75. Justly termed by Charles Robertson 'one of the great set pieces of European architecture', it has not always been so* *extravagantly praised: a critic of 1773 complained that 'The wretched attempt to make a centre to the Crescent where none was necessary is absurd and preposterous, in a high degree.'*

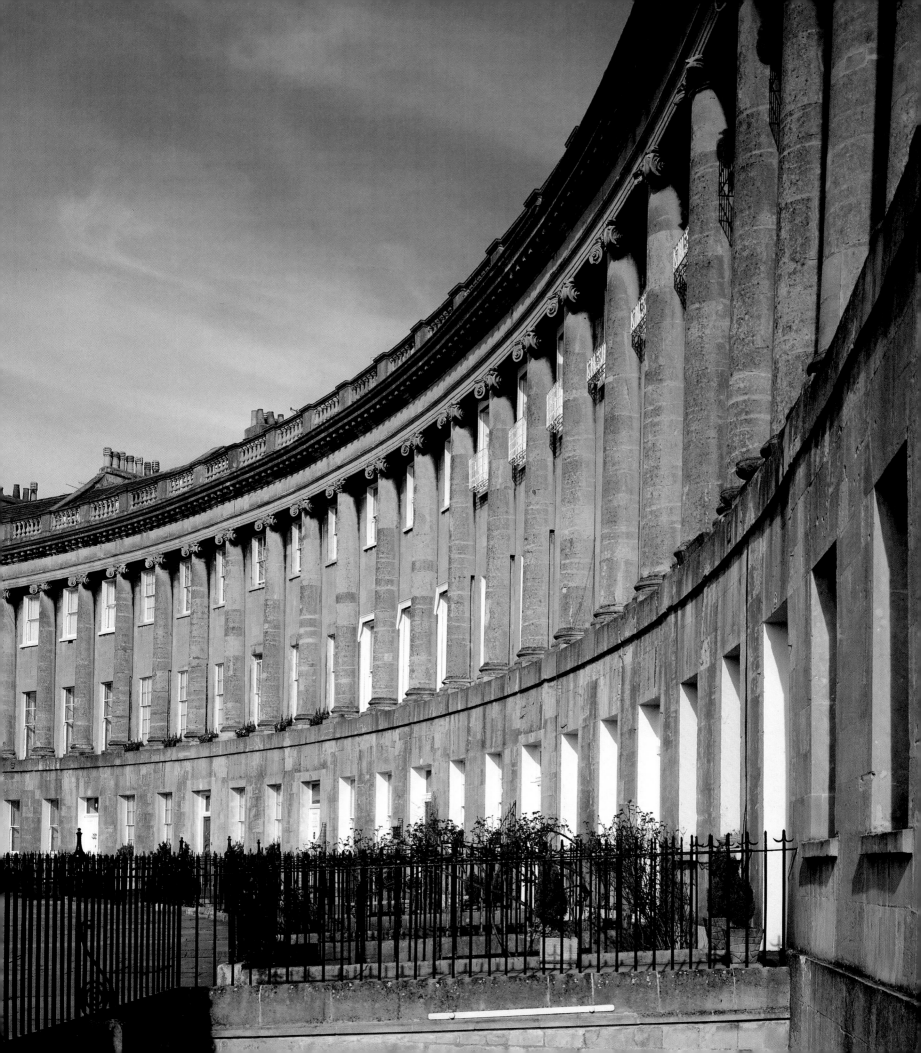

quick to pay tribute to the Adams in observing the 'very great revolution' which had recently occurred in 'the ornamental Department'.

Despite the existence of tough building regulations which dated from the years following the Great Fire of London of 1666, there was still a significant need to regulate unscrupulous speculators and dishonest builders. In 1766 Gwynn's *London and Westminster Improv'd* bemoaned the fact that, while 'the rage of building has been carried to so great a height for several years past, as to have increased this metropolis in an atonishing manner', there was yet a 'want of ... publick direction' of the building work - the reason 'why so wretched an use has been made of so valuable and desirable an opportunity of displaying taste and elegance' in Westminster. This 'public direction' was finally supplied in the form of the 1774 Building Act. Drafted by architects Robert Taylor and George

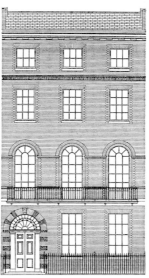

'First Rate', 'Second Rate' and 'Fourth Rate' house types, as classified by the 1774 Building Act (taken from a builders' manual of 1825).

Dance, it was aimed at solving the very problems enunciated by Gwynn and others. In an attempt to end jerry-building it laid down four types or 'rates' of house which could be built in future. Each rate had its own, well-defined limits. The First Rate house was worth over £850 a year in ground rent, occupying more than 900 square feet of space. At the other end of the scale, the Fourth Rate was a house worth less than £150 a year, which occupied less than 350 square feet. Within each category was a list of building requirements.

The 1774 Act certainly helped to raise building standards, although it by no means eradicated the poor-quality building of the period. Yet it also led, inevitably, to a degree of design standardization which, as expressed in some of the terraces of London or Dublin, could prove increasingly dull. In less than gifted hands building regulations could, in Summerson's memorable words, promote the 'inexpressible monotony of the typical London street', more graphically condemned as 'one damn Georgian building after another'.

The basic plan of the Georgian home was much the same for First Rate as for Fourth Rate houses. In 1772 Grosley observed that 'a subterraneous storey, occupied by kitchen and offices', was a common feature in most terrace houses. This basement did not need to function as a store for coal: since the 1720s coal had - at least in the larger towns and cities - been stored in specially-built vaults which ran under the street itself. In 1756 Isaac Ware noted that 'the basement is naturally the kitchen', although it could additionally serve as accommodation for the servants if the garrets proved too small, in which case 'a bed for a man or 2 maid servants is contrived to be let down in the

London's Bedford Square. Built between 1775 and 1783, this was the first real example of a uniform London square. The centrepiece of each of the sides was pedimented and stuccoed to give the composition added emphasis and symmetry.

Details of individual Bedford Square elevations, showing the elegant proportions of the scheme. The square's centrepieces were originally faced in Liardet's ill-fated stucco, and included the classical solecism of a five-pilaster portico.

kitchen.' Ware was not very happy about the practice of installing basements below ground level. However, he accepted its inevitability in tightly knit urban communities such as the capital: 'The lower story in these common houses in *London* is sunk entirely under ground, for which reason it is damp, unwholesome, and uncomfortable; but the excuse has weight: ground-rent is so dear in *London* that every method is to be used to make the most of the ground plan.'

Up on the ground floor, Ware's *Complete Body of Architecture* of 1756 observed that 'In common houses the fore parlour is the best room.' Old-fashioned Palladian rules dictated that most rooms of importance should, in true Italian practice, be sited on the first floor; however, even Ware acknowledged that there were 'sound functional reasons for making the ground floor the major floor'. Many of the smaller Georgian homes simply could not afford the luxury of having the principal rooms on the first floor; there simply was not sufficient space. Thus drawing rooms (or more humble parlours) were often placed on the ground floor, in order to be near the main entrance, while dining rooms were removed down a floor, to be nearer the kitchen and to create an easy progression for guests who were being entertained in the drawing room prior to eating. Ware, however, remained suspicious of this un-Palladian trend: 'A fore parlour is a room of very little use or value in a small house,' he stoutly declared; 'it is too near the street, and too much in the way of disturbance from the entry.'

At the rear of the ground floor even the most urban of developments often had a small garden. From the little evidence we have concerning

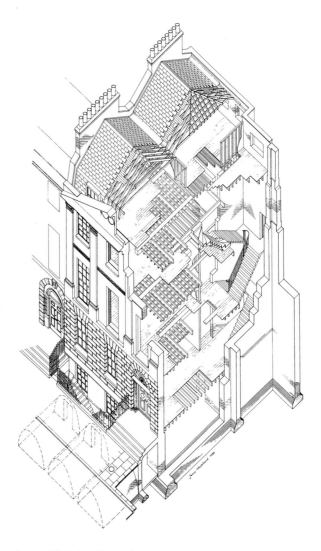

James Whitehead's modern axonometric drawing of 32 Bedford Square shows exactly how a house of this type was constructed. Note the M-shaped roof with its vulnerable central gutter, the ascent of the stair, and the patterns of the floor joists.

The gardens of homes belonging to officers at Chatham Dockyard, Kent, as depicted in an extremely rare model of the 1770s. The gardens (which still survive today in some form) are placed on a higher level than the houses themselves. The importance accorded to the broad, gravel walks is immediately obvious; as historian Neil Burton has pointed out: 'Grass played a very small part in such gardens'.

gardens of this time, they appear to have been largely symmetrical, with formal flower beds and small grassed areas arranged about wide gravel paths. The flowers planted there were often perfumed, their scents permeating the rearward rooms of the house during spring and summer. Honeysuckle was a particular favourite, as were roses, sweet peas and stocks. These could be blended with traditional, unperfumed varieties such as asters, marigolds, lupins, carnations and pansies. The flower beds and gravel walks in turn led to a somewhat less fragrant feature: the 'bog-house', to which the drains led, generally sited at the far end of the garden.

The first floor of many grander homes still contained the drawing and dining rooms; in more modest dwellings, it housed the principal bedrooms, too. Ware and, later, La Rochfoucauld testified to the inclusion of bedrooms at this level, the Frenchman noting that, in sharp contrast to modern practice, they were generally placed at the front, not the rear, of the house. Other, less important bedrooms - the children's, perhaps, or the lodger's - would be

placed on the plainer and meaner second floor, while the attic was reserved for servants, whose beds were often let down from the attic walls.

The problem of where to put the servants was a perennial one. Nearly every mid-Georgian household of any pretension employed them. Ware stated that a family of two or three would have three or four servants, yet many homes possessed far more - perhaps as many as fifteen for a large townhouse. If outbuildings existed, these would have been used to house the servants; otherwise, they would sleep in the attic, or under a table in the basement kitchen.

'Adam Style' depended as much on the materials available to the architect and builder as on pure Neo-Classical theory. Indeed, the change in the aspect of the average home - whether part of a grand terrace in Bath or a humble stone or brick cottage in the provinces - was due largely to the effect of the Industrial Revolution, which introduced new, more efficient materials and methods, while consigning many traditional, vernacular materials (among them clay, clunch and cob) to obsolescence.

The effect of the Industrial Revolution was especially apparent in the production of one of the most basic of building materials, brick. Increasingly, brick kilns were fired not with traditional fuels such as wood, charcoal or bracken, but with coal. This allowed kilns to attain higher temperatures than before, enabling a greater range of brick colours to be produced, the colour being determined not only by the colour of the clay but also by the temperature of the firing. In 1756 Isaac Ware was to make the observation that 'The degree of burning makes a considerable difference in the condition of the bricks, but their principal distinction is from the

Contrasting examples of late eighteenth-century brick terraces from different parts of London.

A new brick kiln from Isaac Ware's A Complete Body of Architecture *of 1756; and, far right, a carefully rendered exercise in the construction of brick and stone arches from T. Carter's* The Builders Magazine *of 1774.*

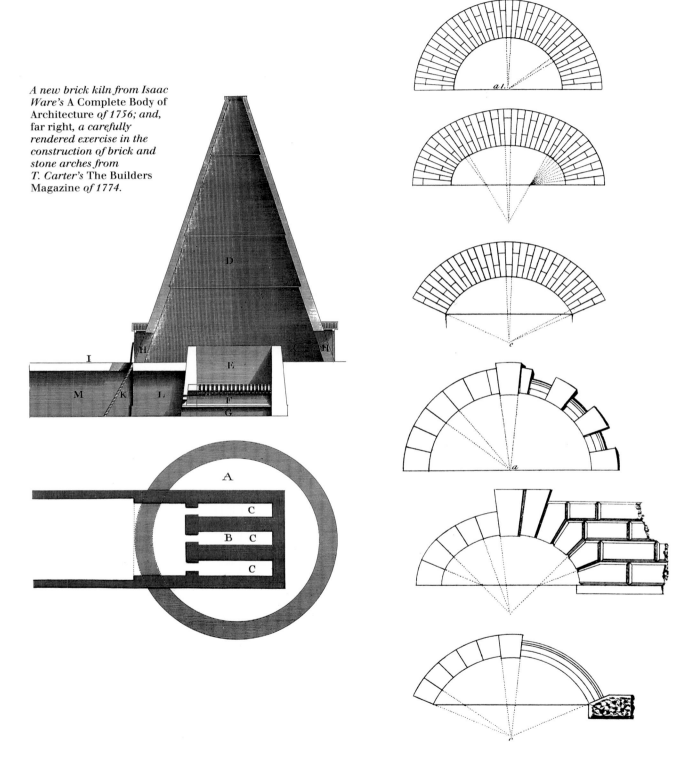

nature of the materials with which they are made'.

No longer had architects and builders to rely wholly on the ubiquitous 'hot' red brick which characterized the brick buildings of the late seventeenth-century and the first half of the eighteenth century. Bricks could now be made that were brown, yellow, grey or (particularly in the eastern counties) white or cream in colour. It was also easier to produce the blue-grey 'vitrified' bricks. These were produced by placing unburnt bricks close to the fire-holes in the clamp or kiln, the intense heat reacting with the clay during firing to produce a silvery, glazed effect. Not only were vitrified headers (the end faces of the brick) often used in combination with red stretchers (the long, side faces) to produce the delightful chequered wall pattern so common in southern England; now whole walls could be cheaply constructed from vitrified headers and stretchers, with red brickwork being used only as a dressing.

Such technological advances married well with changing aesthetic tastes. The middle classes who sought to buy a house in town wanted a reflection of their recent wealth which was as opulent and up-to-date as possible. To them, red brickwork was far too redolent of old-fashioned values and of the humble dwellings of past decades. Since the grandest homes were built in - or at least faced with - stone, they wanted the next-best thing: brick, coloured or finished to resemble expensive stone. As with so many Georgian building 'shams', the idea was not to deceive or to mimic, but merely to suggest the superior material. Hence the sudden popularity of cream, yellow or grey bricks - all of which could, at a distance, be imagined to be stone, and none of which carried the stigma of being

associated with last year's fashion. The cream brick came of age when Henry Holland used this material, and not stone, to face the imposing front elevation of Brooks's Club, built in 1776-8 in the heart of London's fashionable St James's district.

The bricks that Holland used to face Brooks's were by this time usually known as 'stocks'. The 'stock board' was in origin the wooden base on which hand-made bricks had been moulded, but by Adam's time a 'stock' had come to denote any well-shaped, good-quality facing brick. The 1776 contract for erecting Bedford Square, for example, called for the use of 'hard place bricks with good grey stocks in uniform colour' - 'place' bricks being the inferior products used behind the more impressive outer skin of good brick or stucco. By the mid-eighteenth century stocks were twice as expensive as place bricks. Even more costly - four times more expensive - were what were called 'cutting bricks'. This category comprised softer, finely crafted products, which could be shaped as required and used to create brick arches and surrounds. Also known as 'rubbed' or 'gauged' bricks, they were so well-made that it only required a very thin line of white mortar to point their joints. Such work was costly, however. By the mid-eighteenth century a practice had become common by which such fine brickwork was deliberately mimicked using poorer-quality bricks: 'tuck-pointing'. This involved surrounding badly cut or worn bricks with a base mortar the same colour as the bricks themselves, then inserting a white 'tucking' mortar in a straight line between the bricks to simulate the visual effect of neat joints. Tuck pointing can still be found today, particularly in larger housing developments, and is certainly worth reproducing if it exists; if properly

Terrace details from Bath's Paragon, begun in 1768. The warm limestone contributes much to the city's enduring architectural character, proving far more durable than brick construction elsewhere. As Adam Fergusson has written, 'Eighteenth-century Bath had virtually no decay in it;' even 'the terraced cottages of the grooms, the ostlers, the stonemasons, the buhlcutters, the roadmakers and the Sedan chair carriers - and of the pimps, the pickpockets and the whores - were of brand new Bath stone.' Sadly, many of these terraces, having survived two centuries of atmospheric assault, were demolished by Bath City Council after 1945; however, most of those that remain today appear to be safe from future development.

executed, the wall should look from the street as if it is simply made of high-quality, well-pointed bricks. Some builders, however, have in their enthusiasm resorted to an ugly pastiche of this technique, in which white mortar lines are ruled directly across the faces of the actual bricks. This is not a very happy solution: it not only looks ridiculous, but the white mortar rapidly falls off if improperly bedded.

Another Georgian alternative to purchasing expensive facing bricks was to employ mathematical tiles: ceramic tiles, laid in courses on top of wooden laths, which when laid resembled bricks. These tiles were particularly popular by the mid-eighteenth century. When the new stucco began to crumble away from the external walls of David Garrick's houses in Hampton and Chevening, his widow immediately replaced the render with mathematical tiles, exclaiming that 'the new tiling now made use of to cover houses would be the only durable material that my house will or would admit.' In fact, mathematical tiles were not as new as Mrs Garrick believed. They were a late seventeenth century invention, but it took the industrial improvements of the mid-eighteenth century to encourage their production - in as many colours as the clay and the firing temperature would permit - on a large scale, especially in the southeastern counties of Kent and Sussex. The production of both mathematical tiles and bricks was undoubtedly affected by the brick tax of 1784, a measure designed to help pay for the recent, costly American War only finally concluded the previous year. However, the tax - two shillings and sixpence per 1000 bricks and three shillings per 1000 mathematical tiles - did little to reduce the popularity of these ever-popular ceramics.

As already noted, products such as mathematical tiles and practices such as tuck-pointing were devised as honest shams, whose real character could be discerned on any close inspection of the front wall. Behind the immediate façade, however, many builders perpetrated the most blatant acts of professional dishonesty, which often threatened the structural integrity of the whole house. Much speculative housing was designed to endure only as long as the first lease, so there was often little behind the outer four-inch skin of facing bricks and badly sited, ill-seasoned timbers. Even on the ground floor, the outer skin of bricks was all-too-frequently poorly anchored to the inner skin of inferior place bricks. The common result was that front façades simply fell off. This was not helped by the fact that in the larger towns even facing bricks could be of very disappointing quality. Grosley remarked of one such typical terrace in 1765:

'It is true the outside appears to be of brick, but the wall consists only of a single row of bricks, these being made of the first earth that comes to hand, and only just warmed at the fire ... In the near quarters of London, brick is often made upon the spot where the buildings themselves are erected and the workmen make use of the earth which they find in digging the foundations. With this earth they mix the ashes gathered in London by the dustmen.'

Within the walls, Grosley observed, 'small pieces of deal supply the place of beams' in many speculative developments, while inside the rooms 'all the wainscoting is of deal and the thinnest that can be found.' It is thus quite astonishing that so many of these Georgian houses have survived into the late twentieth century - an accident which perhaps says more about the generally high level of craft skills available to Georgian building

Right: *a doorway from the Circus in Bath, the top two panels of the door having been substituted by an intriguing oval pane. Opposite: ovals punctuate the parapet above, which is topped by Wood's bizarre, oversized acorn finials. As Mowl and Earnshaw's splendid biography of the architect notes, Wood's obsessions 'seem to have trapped him in a pattern of provincial intellectualism which drew him further and further apart from standard thinking on classical architecture and world history ... That self-confidence which drove him to reshape Bath in a short lifetime made him an outrageously bad historian. He was spiteful, ungenerous and adapted all information to suit previously fixed notions.'*

contractors than about the quality of the materials they were using.

Stone construction was generally more reliable than brick, but it was also, even in areas of plentiful local stone, a good deal more expensive. High-class developments such as Edinburgh New Town were able to display work by the very best stonemasons; in the New Town itself the sandstone façades were treated in a variety of ways in the same elevation: arranged in random rubble courses, as rock-faced ashlar, as rusticated ashlar or as smooth ashlar. However, not all stone houses were necessarily built to these exacting standards. Even in exclusive Bath, the stunning new terraces of golden limestone were not always as solid as they appeared to be. In 1771 the novelist Tobias Smollett wrote of the city's recently built streets:

'The rage of building has laid hold on such a number of adventurers, that one sees new houses staring up in every out-let and every corner of Bath; contrived without judgement, executed without solidity, built so slight, with the soft crumbling stone found in this neighbourhood, that I should never sleep quietly in one of them.'

If stone proved too expensive, or was unavailable locally, a new alternative presented itself in the 1770s: stucco, a cheap substitute which could be incised and painted so as to suggest courses of fine ashlar. 'Stucco' was originally an Italian term to denote a mix of lime and marble, but by 1770 it was widely used in Britain to mean any internal or external lime-based or gypsum-based plasterwork. It was only later in the nineteenth century that 'stucco' came to specifically signify the external lime render applied in three, four or five thin coats to the exterior of the house. It is, however, probably less confusing to stick with this modern definition.

The composition of stucco as we now know it was largely unknown in Britain and America before Adam's day. In 1765 the Reverend David Wark patented the first true modern stucco. Within a few years the Adam brothers, displaying once again their abundance of marketing acumen, quickly seized on this new opportunity, acquiring Wark's patent in 1768. Six years later they replaced Wark's stucco with an allegedly more reliable product in the form of Liardet's stucco, patented in 1773. Both Wark's and Liardet's stuccoes were oil-based, not water-based, as is commonly the practice today. The use of boiled linseed oil in the recipe would, it was widely believed, help protect the brickwork beneath. Unfortunately for Liardet - and

Details of Coade Stone work in London: a doorway keystone and a vermiculated quoin from Bedford Square (top), *and* (bottom) *an anthemion capital from Chandos House, and a Neo-Classical frieze and pediment medallion from Portland Place.*

for the enthusiastic Adams - this was not the case; in reality, the oil-based render effectively served to trap moisture in the brickwork behind, which not only helped to cause decay within the bricks but quickly forced the stucco off the wall.

In the early 1770s, however, these disadvantages were not yet apparent, and stucco was soon all the rage. By 1779 Sheridan's *Critic* was being asked to concoct a pamphlet posing as 'a Detester of Visible Brickwork, in favour of the new invented Stucco ... in the style of Junius'. Liardet's product was first used by the Adams at 11 St James's Square, and subsequently on all manner of Adam façades. The relationship between Liardet and the Adams was always a dificult one. Liardet - 'a troublesome, jealous body' wrote William Adam in 1781 - was lent large sums of money by the Adam family after 1774, in the anticipation that he would make his fortune from his stucco; this did not prevent him from attempting to sue the Adams in 1782, in a protracted case that ran on for five whole years.

Nor was Liardet the only obstacle to the Adams' monopoly on the use of this exciting new invention. In 1778 Lord Chief Justice Mansfield, presiding over a case of stucco patent rights being contested by the Adams and their former clerk of works, John Johnson, found in favour of the Adams. This was not, it must be admitted, an entirely impartial judgement: Mansfield was currently employing the Adams to build him a house at Kenwood on Hampstead Heath, a vast mansion which was then being comprehensively, and most expensively, covered in stucco. Mansfield - who did originally demur at the cost of the stucco, suggesting that parian marble (the durable, pale ceramic much

used by Victorian designers) would have proved cheaper - thus had a rather pressing vested interest in the Adams' use of stucco, and in their continued control of stucco production.

In the longer term this legal victory did the Adams little good. By the 1780s, as the architectural historian and stucco expert Frank Kelsall has noted, the outlook for Liardet's stucco suddenly looked rather grim:

'Oil-based stuccoes began to fall off buildings with increasing regularity, to the great financial embarrassment of the Adam brothers who, for instance, had £1,500 damages awarded them... for the failed stucco at Chevening.'

Oil-based stucco had proved a failure, and the Adams had, as at the Adelphi, been made to look fools. (Indeed, it may have been this professional and financial disaster which prompted Robert Adam to retire to Scotland in the early 1780s.) The disillusioned Adams accordingly paid no attention to Bryan Higgins's new water-based stucco, patented in 1779. This, although an inferior and unreliable product, was the direct ancestor of modern stuccoes; yet it was not until four years after Robert Adam's death, in 1796, that the first commercially-successful water-based stucco appeared. This product, 'Parker's Cement', was patented by yet another bored and stuccophile cleric, the Reverend David Parker. (This close link between the late Georgian clergy and external plasters is something still to be fully investigated.)

The stuccoes of Liardet and his rivals could, it was claimed, be cast from moulds. However, a far more reliable product existed for those who sought to adorn their homes with fashionable cast ornaments. 'Coade Stone' was a very hard and

Left: *delicate Neo-Classical ironwork of the 1770s and 80s in London and Bath - including an anthemion boot-scraper.*

Opposite: *the brick-and-stucco facade of 7 Adam Street, virtually the last survivor of the Adams' Adelphi scheme. The Neo-Classically-patterned stucco pilasters represented a radical new approach to the external decoration of middle-class housing.*

highly durable ceramic marketed after 1769 from her factory in Lambeth, south London, by the remarkable Eleanor Coade. Coade's personal ambition was undoubted; she hired the celebrated sculptor John Bacon to design the grander pieces and, unlike Josiah Wedgwood and his unsuccessful ceramic plaques, won commissions from every leading architect of the day. By 1774 most external cast ornamentation being applied to houses in London's new West End was being made not in stone or in stucco but in Coade Stone.

While Coade Stone was occasionally used for structural work - with rather unfortunate long-term effects on the stability of the masonry - its use was generally limited to cast statuary or applied decoration. Cast iron, on the other hand, could actually alter the shape of structures in which it was used. Improved casting techniques allowed iron railings and balusters, often provided with additional ornamentation made from cast lead, to be manufactured in an increasing variety of delicate and suitably Neo-Classical patterns as demanded by the leading designers of the day. Robert Adam's own 'Heart and Honeysuckle' anthemion-based design, first used at 7 Adam Street in the Adelphi in 1774, profoundly influenced the design of iron balconies over the next sixty years. And iron railings with prominent Greek motifs such as urn finials and anthemia were increasingly found in the more fashionable streets of Britain and America.

While Robert Adam was responsible for some of the latest cast-iron designs, much new ironwork owed its manufacture to another of the Adam brothers. Robert's brother John Adam was actually a partner in the most famous of the new iron foundries, Carron and Company of Falkirk, in the Adams' native Scotland. Carron's, together with their great rivals the Coalbrookdale Company, based in the new industrial heartland of Shropshire, dominated the domestic cast-iron market during the second half of the eighteenth century.

Iron was not used only for decorating the outside of new homes. Architects also began to used it for expressly structural purposes, an innovation, dating from Adam's day, which was later fully exploited by Regency and Victorian designers. The up-to-the-minute homes erected in London's Bedford Square, for example, were equipped with 'Hartley's fire-plates': overlapping sheets of iron, nailed to joists. This invention, patented in 1773, was designed to limit the spread of fire. To prove his point Hartley, ever the showman, invited George III, Queen Caroline and the Prince of Wales to the 'fireproof house' in Putney to which he had had fitted his fireplates. While the royal family were being sumptuously entertained on the first floor, Hartley lit a fire on the ground floor which was soon blazing merrily, without at all inconveniencing the royal party upstairs. Hartley was clearly not without

A splendid ironwork baluster ending in a flourish, from Adam's 20 St James's Square.

This portrait of the artist Paul Sandby by Francis Cotes tells us much about the manner in which the window area was treated, as well as what the fashionable artist of the period was wearing. Clearly evident is a brass shutter handle and grained (not white) window joinery. Above is a detail of the shutter box of a rather grander window - one of those lighting the Long Gallery at Adam's Syon House, London. The gilded, Neo-Classical detailing (of c.1763) is exquisite.

a considerable talent in the field of public relations, even if his iron plates had the unfortunate habit of corroding and warping with age.

Cast iron and stucco were not the only new materials being applied to the homes of this period. The provision of roofing slates also had a sizable effect on both the design and the appearance of the mid-Georgian house. In 1765 Lord Penrhyn began to develop the export of slate from his Welsh quarries to London, with the consequence that slate for roofs became suddenly much cheaper.

Until the 1760s the principal roofing material in urban and rural areas had been the clay tile, either in the form of a 'plain', rectangular tile or an S-shaped 'pantile'. Plain tiles were punctured by two nail holes, used for fixing the tile to the wooden roof battens. Others were provided with 'nibs', right-angled projections from which the tile hung on the batten, which were originally formed by pushing the clay forward with the thumb. (Most eighteenth-century roofing tiles carried no maker's name, being produced locally, and anonymously, by individuals or by small workshops; thus thumb and finger prints are often the only clue to the identity of the maker.) The pantile was an early eighteenth-century development, very common by the 1750s: an S-shaped, nibbed product which could be interlinked with its fellows without the aid of wooden pegs or iron nails.

By the 1780s, however, Welsh blue slates were replacing clay tiles on roofs not only in London but in other large towns and cities too. As early as 1756 Isaac Ware had declared a preference for slates as opposed to clay tiles. 'The great value of slate', he advised in his *Complete Body of Architecture*, 'consists in its foundness in thin peices, and in its fine texture, by which it resists the endurance of wet.' By 1785 British slates - fixed by nailing into battens - could be had in four basic varieties: blue-grey slates from the Lake District; grey slates from mid-Wales; blue or rarer plum red slates from northwest Wales; and grey-green 'Delabole' slates from Cornwall. In certain rural areas such as the Lake District, slates were laid in diminishing courses, the size of the slates in each row decreasing as the tiling approached the apex of the roof. This visually appealing arrangement transferred much of the weight of the roof covering to the strong outer walls, rather than to the fragile roof apex, and also provided a greater uninterrupted surface area at the eaves, from which the rainwater could run off into the gutter or onto the ground. This technique was also used when laying stone 'slates', found in areas with good local stone and little or no slate or clay tile manufacture. The Welsh slates which, after 1765, were appearing so regularly on the roofs of London were, on the other hand, nearly always of uniform size.

Roofs and walls were by no means the only beneficiaries of improved technology in the house of Adam's day. Windows became larger as the manufacture of 'Crown glass' (largely concentrated in Newcastle) became more sophisticated. Crown glass, the most superior type of Georgian glass, was made by spinning out a globe of molten glass to form a large circle, which was then cut up into panes; inferior 'cylinder', 'broad' or 'muff' glass was made by swinging the molten glass over a pit to lengthen it, then opening out the resulting cylinder. With larger, stronger panes, there was now less need for bulky glazing bars to give hefty structural support to the glass in the multi-pane sash windows

Left: *Crown glass manufacture, as explained in Diderot and D'Alembert's wonderfully comprehensive* Encyclopaedia *of 1751-7.*

Above: *detail of Georgian windows seen through a modern glass which seeks to replicate the effect of genuine Georgian examples. Encouragingly, Crown glass is now being made in Britain again, for the first time since the 1930s.*

The most typical of mid-Georgian sash configurations was the six-panes-over-six arrangement. In some instances the dimensions of each pane were supposed to derive from the proportions of the golden section. However, in practice there were no set rules for pane sizes; in smaller towns some sash panes were constructed to be broader than they were tall.

that still remained by far the most common form of fenestration in Britain and America. Thus glazing-bar profiles on the outer surface of the windows grew increasingly thin and shapely, matching the trend towards refined elegance *inside* the home.

Windows could also be larger, since the larger panes of glass were now strong enough to be introduced into the sash window format without any need for a complex grid of wooden supports. By the 1770s, it was the height of fashion to lower the cills of first-floor windows and to fit larger sashes in the enlarged spaces. The 1776 building contract for Bedford Square, for example, included the provision that 'liberty [was] to be given to cut down any of the windows so low as the floors of the rooms.'

Window panes were never of one, standard size during the Georgian era. Sometimes they were even broader than they were tall. Nor was the common six-over-six pane pattern always adhered to. In 1759 William Chambers alleged that the most frequently found arrangement of panes was 'three in the breadth and four in the height, whatever the dimensions of the window', although modern observation does not appear to bear this claim out. (Chambers's *Treatise* also observed that 'The Sashes of the Windows are generally made of Oak,' a claim which testifies more to the fact that Chambers's practice was confined to the great and good than it does to the widespread use of oak, and not pine or fir, for window joinery.)

Unfortunately, the size of the window was still limited by constraints other than the necessity of making stronger glass. The hated window tax was actually extended in 1766, to cover all houses with seven windows or more. This unhelpful measure - not finally repealed until 1851 - had the effect of reducing the circulation of air and the admission of light in the house, since many windows were now bricked up. The long-term result was an inevitable increase in gloom, damp and disease.

A more constructive piece of legislation was the already-mentioned 1774 Building Act, whose measures, designed to regulate the size and configuration of windows aimed to reduce the risk of fire entering the house via the external woodwork. Window joinery had already, in accordance with the Building Act of 1709, to be recessed four inches from the wall's outer face; now it was to be largely concealed behind the brick, stone or stuccoed face, with only a small amount visible to the street. The act also wisely limited the extent of the newly fashionable bow-fronted shop windows, preventing them from protruding more than ten inches into the street. This saved many pedestrians - now able to walk on the narrow pavement, and not forced out into the road - from a grisly death under the wheels of a passing carriage.

By the time of the 1774 Act, traditional wooden sash pulleys were being replaced by more durable iron or brass examples. Even the colours of the windows were changing. Window joinery, particularly when set into light-coloured brick, stone or stucco, was now often painted not the 'broken' off-white so common earlier in the century, but darker greys, browns or even greens. Sometimes, too, the windows were grained, inside and out, to mimic seasoned oak or Jamaican mahogany - finishes specifically designed to set off the light colour of the surrounding masonry. The ubiquitous white-painted sash was more an innovation, or perhaps a revival, of the late nineteenth century. And the bright, bleached whites so often

Left: *typical doorways of the period,* (from top left) *Dublin, Bath, Boston, Massachusetts and London's Bedford Square.*

Opposite: *the doorway at the Adams' 7 Adam Street: delicate, assured, well-proportioned and enticing.*

inappropriately used for old windows today are more a postwar enthusiasm, having no historical foundation whatsoever.

Mid-Georgian front doors were generally found painted in a variety of dark colours, especially browns and greens. Despite what is often believed (and, alas, practised) today, Georgian front or internal doors were *never* stripped. Unless the wood was of a particularly expensive and handsome kind, the Georgians had far more sense than to seek to expose the knotty, irregular surfaces of inferior pine or fir. The six-panelled door was the most common arrangement for front entrances; however, like the six-over-six pane sash, this configuration was by no means the only form used during this time. Eight-, five- or three-panel doors were commonly found in the 1760s, 70s and 80s, the bottom two panels often fused and raised to stile level in order to prevent feet from inadvertently kicking through the wood.

By the end of our period the numbering of front doors had begun, at least in the capital. Reminiscing about the mid-1760s some forty years later, James Malcolm recalled that in London 'the nobility introduced brass plates or doorplates with their names engraved on them', and that 'the numbering of the houses' was becoming fashionable. However, for most households of Adam's time the only furniture that was applied to the front door was a simple, black-painted and centrally-placed iron doorknob. Doors of this period were rarely over-filled with iron or brass ornament; if any door furniture was added, it would always have been - in contrast to the elaborate fanlight above - deliberately modest.

By 1755 the doorcase was still generally arranged in the typically Palladian 'temple front' or 'aedicular' manner: two pilasters or columns supporting an entablature, possibly topped by a segmental or triangular pediment. As the 1760s progressed, however, the doorway became increasingly dominated not by the doorcase entablature - which if anything tended to project less obviously into the street - but by an ever-larger fanlight. The fanlight had only first appeared over front doors during the 1720s, and as interpreted by the Palladian architects of the period was subservient to the general composition of the doorcase, in which every element was nicely, if predictably, balanced. In the hands of Robert Adam and his contemporaries, however, the fanlight was liberated from this supporting role, and was encouraged to blossom as never before. Fanlights of the Adam period were large, elaborate confections of iron and lead (some with applied brass ornamentation), which not only dominated the doorcase - often extending the whole width of the composition - but became the most striking feature of the whole façade. They appeared with increasing frequency in the fashionable squares of London, Bath, Edinburgh, Dublin and the other popular watering-holes of mid-Georgian Britain; until 1776 they were also shipped directly to America, to adorn the middle-class homes of New York, Philadelphia, Georgetown or Charleston. In many ways the Adam fanlight neatly summarizes the style and approach of the whole period in architecture and the decorative arts: breaking out from rigid, architectural confines, its exuberance and Neo-Classical delicacy brought wit and grace back into house design.

*Graceful Adam Style
fanlight tracery from
Dublin's Merrion Square,
begun in 1762. Dan
Cruickshank has called this
handsome square 'the most
imposing of Dublin's urban
spaces'.*

'Hopetoun was pleased with the chimney I sent him, which shows how much any trifle from Italy will impose, even on a sensible man'

(John Adam, 1755)

Opposite: *the first floor room from 20 St James's Square.* This page: *delicate designs for brass door furniture from the Adam brothers'* Works.

Adam's sumptuously-coloured library ceiling at Kenwood, London, of 1767-9. Such extravagant use of ceiling colour was largely limited to the newest great houses - where its initial effect must have been shocking.

By the middle of the eighteenth century the practice of simply painting panelling was becoming rather unfashionable in the wealthier homes of Britain, although it stayed in widespread use in America for the rest of the century. The trend was now to leave the wall above the dado wholly flat, and to cover this with wallpaper, with raised plasterwork or even with built-up papier mâché. Of these alternatives, the former was very much in vogue. In 1756 Ware noted sadly that 'Paper has, in a great measure, taken the place of sculpture [i.e. wood or plaster mouldings] and the hand of art is banished from a part of the house in which it used to display itself very happily.' Ware was clearly not much of a fan of the new fad of wallpapering.

Decorative plaster, if rarely employed to cover whole walls or ceilings, had long been used to embellish the surface of individual mouldings. The plaster used for this internal work was generally gypsum plaster: simple plaster of Paris, mixed with a binder of animal hair or straw, and applied in three or more coats over fir laths. In most houses pre-moulded ornaments were fixed on site; only in the grandest houses were workmen employed to execute this complex decoration in place. The modern practice of buying off-the-peg, prefabricated mouldings to install where none now exist thus has a perfectly good historical precedent. Take care, though, that the mouldings you buy are appropriate for the house's period and the room's character and function; many firms offer a disappointingly small range of 'Georgian' mouldings, which are often radically different from the historic forms they are supposed to imitate. Alternatively, papier mâché could be used in place of plaster for elaborate decorative work. Papier mâché was stronger than its name suggests; it could even be used to form whole areas of wall or ceiling. In 1759, for example, Horace Walpole fitted out the 'Holbein chamber' in his delightfully eccentric home Strawberry Hill in Middlesex; the ceiling he installed - based on a medieval interior at Windsor Castle, no less - looked initially as if it was of plaster, but was actually made entirely of papier mâché. Immediately it was finished, the poet Thomas Gray observed admiringly of the chamber that 'The ceiling is coved and fretted in star and quatrefoil compartments, all in papier-mâché.'

Virtually all mouldings were painted, creating a light and refined, low-relief effect often ruined by the modern fashion for indiscriminately stripping old woodwork. Whether it was of plaster or of papier mâché, the decorative work was generally painted the same colour as the flat ground, or perhaps painted white. Neither mouldings nor decorative relief-work, however, were ever picked out in another colour save white or gilt. Even the heavy gilding which had so characterized the rich Palladian interiors of the 1730s and 40s was, by 1760, shunned by most of the up-to-date homeowners of Britain and America.

The relation of the decoration to the wall areas, and of the walls to the rest of the room, is of central importance to anyone seeking a true understanding of the mid-Georgian room. Knowledge of proportion, and of the correct use of mouldings and motifs, was considered essential to any Georgian designer worth his salt. As Stephen Riou pointed out in his manual *The Grecian Orders of Architecture* of 1768: 'Since mouldings do, as it were, compose the alphabet of architecture', one needed 'a perfect knowledge of their several attributions and

Opposite: *typical plaster mouldings of the 1760s and 70s, from houses in London and Bath. Gone is the freedom and licence of the Rococo; in its place is architectural precision and elegant restraint.*

Far right: *a Neo-Classically-influenced ceiling design for Kedleston, Derbyshire, of c.1760, and,* below, *plasterwork details from a ceiling at 20 St James's Square.* Right: *more plasterwork details from Bristol* (top) *Wells* (centre) *and Bath* (below).

combinations, ... their uses and shapes.'

In the early years of the eighteenth century mouldings were often employed simply to cover a structural joint or an unsightly transition between different planes - allowing the parts beneath to settle and move, as well as providing a more visually cohesive display of light and shadow. The type of applied mouldings in common use during the Early Georgian era were the box cornice and 'bolection' moulding, linking two adjoining planes; both of these types were common by 1700, and by 1750 they had been joined by a variety of other, classically derived forms.

In most cases skirting, dado and cornice mouldings were carefully placed about the wall to correspond to the vertical intervals of the classical column. Thus the skirting corresponded to the base of the ancient orders, the dado to the pedestal, and the cornice to their entablature. This firm Palladian rule was reiterated by Isaac Ware in 1756: decorating the wall 'to make it correspond with the orders' was, in his opinion, 'the origin of the inside finishing of apartments; and to this it is necessary the architecture adhere.'

This architectural allegory held true throughout the Georgian era and beyond. However, as the eighteenth century progressed architects were increasingly concerned to conceal all of the real structural elements of a building; accordingly, mouldings became flatter and less pronounced, and surface decoration took the place of depth - a typical characteristic of much of the work of Adam's day.

The complexity of mouldings and their decoration corresponded directly to the dimensions and the relative social significance of the rooms in which they were used. Thus, while drawing rooms on the ground or first floors may have included elaborate cornices and rich doorcases, the rooms at the top of the house may have possessed only simple box cornices, a rudimentary dado and perhaps no skirting mouldings at all. The decoration was proportional to the pretension of the room; the humbler the function (and indeed the fewer the visitors), the more modest the mouldings. If re-introducing period mouldings of plaster or wood into a house which has lost all trace of the original pattern, it is very important to keep this context firmly in mind. Wooden mouldings and panelling bought wholesale from architectural salvage outlets, for example, are often re-used in unsuitable and incongruous settings. Over-sized and over-elaborate mouldings set in a small, modest room inevitably look cramped and ridiculous. Remember that what looks splendid in a grand country house - or a cavernous warehouse - may be highly inappropriate for your own home.

Proportion remained the key to the whole house, no matter how modest or humble the home. Many of the pattern-book authors of the time devised elaborate guides to the ideal dimensions of the walls and rooms of the average home, and laid down rules to be followed by builders and decorators. The miracle formulae proffered by some of these manuals could, though, become ludicrously over-complex. In 1766, Crunden and Milton declared that a room that was ten feet square in size should be provided with a chimneypiece that was precisely two feet five inches wide and two feet eleven-and-a-half inches high, and a cornice that was four inches high; furthermore, 'the architraves to chimneypieces should be about one sixth or one seventh of the width of the opening.' Nine years

Panel designs for the drawing room frieze at Fisherwick Park, Staffordshire, by Joseph Bonomi. Rome-born Bonomi's elegant, Neo-Classical restraint is clearly evident here. As Howard Colvin has noted, in his interiors 'Bonomi preferred a chaste simplicity to the elaborate decorative schemes of Robert Adam'.

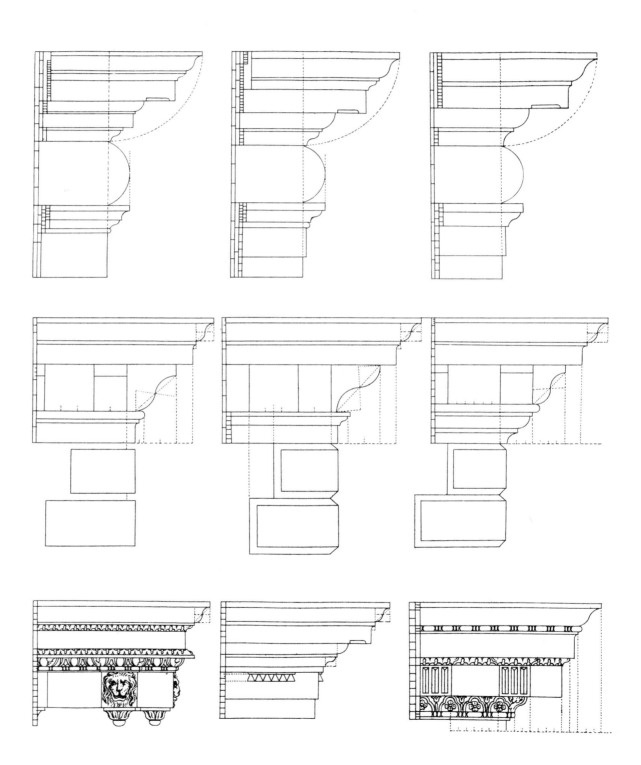

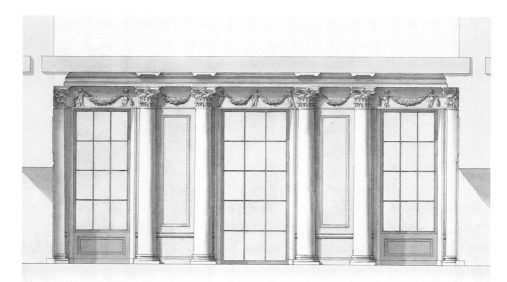

Opposite: *Typical domestic entablature mouldings for windows, doors and cornices, from Chambers's* A Treatise on Civil Architecture *of 1759.*

Sumptuous wall treatments: designs by Joseph Bonomi for the window wall of an unidentified Great Room (top) *and for the Saloon at Burley on the Hill, Leicestershire* (below).

Opposite: *multicoloured Adam ceiling design from 20 St James's Square. Note the subtle interplay of the vaulting and the reiterated ellipses and semicircles.*

Top: *detail of a ceiling at 20, St James's Square with inset painted medallion by Antonio Zucchi.* Bottom: *Zucchi's ceiling painting of Cupid and Psyche from the tapestry room at Nostell Priory, Yorkshire.*

earlier Abraham Swan suggested that if the room was ten feet high, the dado should be two feet five inches from the ground (and three-quarters of an inch higher for every foot increase in the room height), and the cornice should be one-eighteenth the height of the room. These and other manuals proffered simple solutions to amateurs (or professionals) puzzled by the basic tenets of Palladian proportion. However, the builder or houseowner who consulted more than one of these guides would have been easily confused by the contradictory advice they gave, each authority offering a magic solution which did not necessarily correspond to that of its rivals.

By 1770 the pattern-book authors were beginning to argue in print over the respective merits of the new, subtler and more archaeologically-correct Neo-Classical mouldings being introduced by Robert Adam, James Stuart and their fellow-Grecians. These were designed to supplement and even to replace the traditional Palladian forms which had been meat and drink to the architectural pattern-book writers of the 1730s, 40s and 50s. Whereas the Roman-derived mouldings of this Early Palladian era had been distinctly robust, projecting boldly into the room, the new 'Greek' forms were of lower relief and more modest profile. Thus while the Palladian ovolo moulding represented an exact quarter-circle in cross-section, the profile of its Greek equivalent was flatter and segmental, being only a part of this quarter-circle.

The battle between Greek and Roman mouldings was first joined in the pages of the Adam brothers' *Works in Architecture* of 1773. 'The mouldings in the remaining structures of ancient Rome', they declared, 'are considerably less

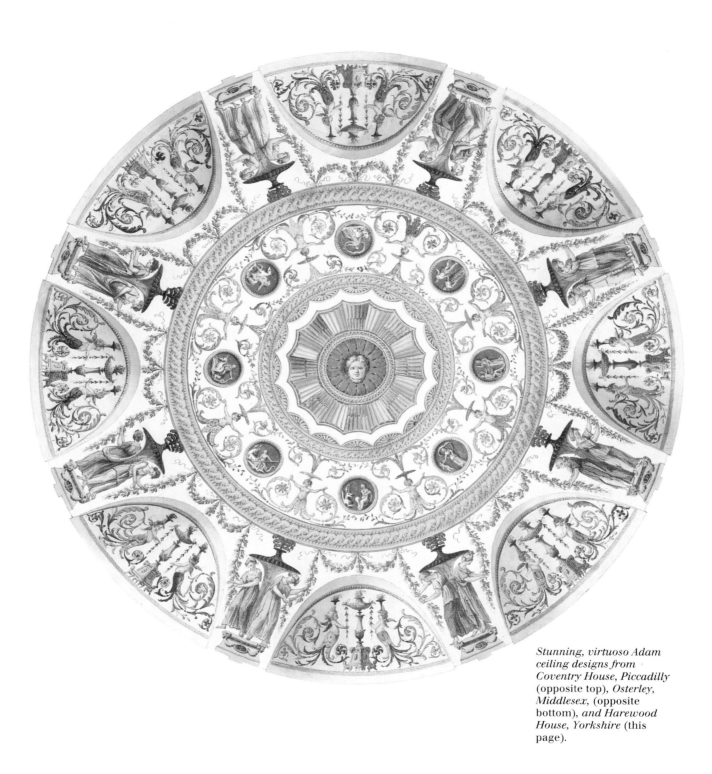

Stunning, virtuoso Adam ceiling designs from Coventry House, Piccadilly (opposite top), *Osterley, Middlesex,* (opposite bottom), *and Harewood House, Yorkshire* (this page).

Ceiling details from Syon House, Middlesex: Neo-Classical geometry at its most precise and pleasing. The house was extensively remodelled by Robert Adam for the First Duke of Northumberland in 1762-5.

curvilinear than those of the ancient monuments of Greece.' Furthermore, they announced, 'We have always given a preference for the latter, and have even thought it advisable to bend them still more in many cases, particularly in interior finishings, where the objects are near, and ought to be softened to the eye.' Clearly the Adams, while espousing the new cause of the Greek style, were also prepared to improve upon the antique forms if they deemed it necessary. Such a bold move was regarded with horror by the more traditional designers, schooled in the forms of Ancient Rome and Renaissance Italy.

The interior feature on which Adam himself effected the most dramatic change was the grand ceiling. This was an instance where Adam chose to adapt, rather than to reproduce, the ideas of the Greek masters. In his designs for the great houses of the 1760s and 70s, the ceiling became the dominant feature of each the room. Profusely patterned and richly coloured - not just with the pastel shades we so readily associate with 'Adam Style' today, but with vivid greens, blues, lilacs and pinks - the startling effect was heightened by the now famous device of weaving the carpet to a design that mirrored the format of the ceiling. The overall impression was stunning: a shocking revolution in taste for those used to the white-and-gilt ceilings of the preceding sixty years. If wished, the ceiling could be further adorned with plaster or ceramic plaques or, for the wealthier *cognoscenti,* embellished with painted panels or medallions painted by the great decorative artists of the time: Angelica Kauffmann and her one-time husband, Antonio Zucchi. Angelica Kauffmann's panel paintings were by 1770 all the rage in the country houses of Britain. And not only was Kauffmann a hugely gifted artist; she was also famously beautiful, and proceeded to charm and enrapture the great European artistic figures of the day. Goethe - one of her most ardent admirers - observed that she was not only 'very sensitive towards all that is beautiful, true and tender' but also 'incredibly modest'.

Devised as it was to enrich the rooms of a great house, Adam's ceiling decoration was not a luxury that could easily be transplanted to the average home of the period. Few could afford the talents of an Adam or a Kauffmann, let alone spend large amounts of money on paints that often proved very expensive. William Chambers himself remarked in his 1759 *Treatise* that 'Painted Ceilings, which comprise one of the great embellishments of Italian and French structures, are not at all in use among us'. Most ceilings, aside from those installed within the great mansions of the wealthy and powerful, remained much as they had been during the preceding decades: plastered flat, and painted in white distemper. (Never, incidentally, did the cornice mouldings ever intrude upon the ceiling during Adam's day. The frieze and cornice remained part of the wall both physically and in terms of decorative treatment; it was only in the 1840s that mouldings began to appear on the plane of the ceiling itself.)

Floors of the period, too, followed much the same patterns as those of the first half of the eighteenth century. Although oak was the preferred material for good, wide timber floorboards, in practice most households had to make do with deal: squared boards of pine or fir, imported from the Baltic or from North America. There were no particular rules as to the dimensions of floorboards, although any exposed boards were generally far wider than is common today. Nor were the boards always of consistent size within a single floor; machines able to plane timber uniformly were only introduced in the 1790s, and it was not until the 1830s that identical floorboards could be produced by steam-powered, mechanical saws.

Parquet floors - floors created by a decorative arrangement of tessellated wooden boards - were still being installed in grander homes. Ware attested to the continuation of this fashion in his *Complete Body of Architecture* of 1756: 'boarded floors in some rooms', he remarked, 'are inlaid with wainscot [i.e. oak], and other handsome woods in various forms.' However, parquet flooring was prohibitively expensive and, with the spread of fitted carpets, becoming both irrelevant and distinctly old-fashioned. In 1756 Ware noted of the wealthier British homes that:

'The use of carpeting at this time has set aside the ornamenting of floors in a great measure; it is the custom almost universally to cover a room entirely; so that there is no necessity of any beauty or workmanship beneath.'

Seven years earlier the architect John Wood had also attested to this fact, declaring that in recent years 'Carpets were introduced to cover the Floors though laid with the finest clean Deals, or Dutch oak boards.' Parquetry could still, though, be used for the narrow border between carpet and skirting. Any such exposed wooden floors were waxed and polished, and occasionally stained brown to imitate finer woods or, more commonly, limewashed to give an attractive, silvery sheen reminiscent of aged oak. The boards were cleaned using fresh flowers and herbs, or rubbed with dry or wet sand or fuller's earth.

Left and below: *the splendid scagliola floor in the ante-room at Syon Park. One of Adam's most powerful and lively compositions, it proved as fragile as its more humble plaster cousins; constant wear and tear meant that it had to be completely relaid by William Croggan in 1832.*

Opposite: *the strongly geometric black-and-white marble floor in the hall at Syon Park. Adam's bold Greek key pattern, running diagonally across the surface, transforms a traditional tessellated marble floor into a powerful Neo-Classical statement.*

If oak proved too expensive, a deal floor was installed. This was never left bare or varnished. In sharp contrast to the modern fervour for stripping any internal woodwork, regardless of its quality, the Georgians took care to hide the awkward and unsightly knots and blemishes inherent in common pine or fir. If carpets were too costly, then the boards might be painted, either in imitation of black-and-white marble flooring, or in a single (preferably dark) colour which was then decorated with stencilled patterns, executed in distemper or even, in more rural homes, in soot. In humbler households, floorboards were often painted dark terracotta-red to recall the old clay floors of former centuries. If even deal floorboards were too expensive, or were locally unobtainable, simple clay or composition floors had to suffice for the ground floor and basement. In 1759 Chambers recorded that:

'The common floors used in mean buildings are made of loam [a type of clay-based composition] well beaten and tempered with smith's dust, and with or without an addition of lime. Some also make them of pure clay ... and a moderate proportion of ox blood.'

An alternative to the clay floor, much used for the ground floors of rural cottages, was the tessellated brick floor. In 1756 Ware acknowledged that 'In country buildings floors are frequently made also of bricks and tiles'. Often these materials would be further reddened with a natural madder, ochre or an oxblood-based pigment, to make the floor look as bright red as when it was first laid.

For the aspiring middle classes, however, the solid marble or stone floor still represented the acme of taste, a status symbol to be treasured and displayed as publicly as possible. The tessellated

Opposite: *the superb inlaid wooden floor at The Winds, Mountstewart, Co. Down, designed by James Stuart. A wide variety of motifs vye for attention on the chimney surround behind.*

James Stuart's drawing of the Temple of the Winds at Athens, reproduced as a plate in The Antiquities of Athens. *Most of the decorative motifs found in* the Adams' floors, ceilings and walls came from the antique buildings sketched by Stuart, Revett and their fellow-Grecians.

marble floor, comprising black-and-white marble squares or, perhaps, light-coloured squares interset with small dark diamond shapes, was still the most sought-after floor treatment, much as it had been in the seventeenth century. Yet for those with even more money to spend, there was now a new and excitingly different option: the multicoloured scagliola floor. Scagliola had long been used to create columns, pilasters and panels that looked suspiciously like real marble. It was in reality a far cheaper material than marble, being made from a moulded and polished compound of basic plaster mixed with marble chips, appropriate pigments and other aggregates. However, at first or even second sight a scagliola floor looked just like the real thing - a vast (and hugely expensive) floor comprising a multitude of rare marbles.

Robert Adam fitted perhaps the most famous scagliola floor of all in the rather mis-named Ante Room at Syon House in Middlesex. This house was built in the years after 1761 for the 1st Duke of Northumberland, a crony of George III's whom Adam sycophantically termed 'a person of extensive knowledge and correct taste' (by which he presumably meant the ability to afford ambitious flights of fancy such as the new Ante Room floor). However, in the same way that Adam's espousal of the early stuccoes turned to disaster, so his brave championing of the scagliola floor proved fruitless. Just like its humble cousins of clay or composition, the delicate scagliola floor responded poorly to everyday wear and tear. By the end of the century scagliola floors were being taken up all over the country, and being replaced with more durable materials such as marble or stone. The Syon House example is thus a very rare survival; even this had to

be completely relaid by an indulgent owner in 1831-2.

A more lasting revolution was being effected in the area of staircase design. By the 1750s, turned stick balusters were out of fashion, replaced at first by the (still astonishingly modern-looking) 'Chinese' fretwork patterns popularized by Thomas Chippendale, and then by graceful iron balusters.

In 1745, W. and J. Welldon's *The Smith's Right Hand* had provided the first collection of British designs for wrought ironwork. Twenty years later, however, the elaborate Rococo scrollwork which featured so prominently in the Welldons'

The staircase from a house in Rivers Street, Bath of c.1770. The wooden balusters and tread-ends are simple and old-fashioned, but nonetheless highly elegant.

Opposite: *the double staircase at 37 Dover Street, London. The twisted wooden balusters are a traditional element in what is otherwise an Adamesque interior.*

Adam period staircases from 20 St James's Square (above), Somerset House (above right and far right) and Barton End Hall (opposite); and a detail from a balustrade by Maurice Tobin at Fairfax House, Yorkshire.

manual had given way to a more architectural, yet still very elegant, Neo-Classical style. Iron allowed for a grace and a lightness in baluster construction that was simply not structurally possible in wood. Designers could now link the thin uprights with delicately-wrought, typically Greek motifs such as the anthemion or the palmette, or indeed dispense with the vertical uprights altogether, supporting the handrail with a series of graceful balusters in the form of lyres or other popular Neo-Classical motifs. The handrail itself often remained the only element of the balustrade still made of wood. Accordingly, the wood chosen would have been an impressive one - usually oak or a West Indian mahogany. In 1774 Mrs Kenyon, examining her new London home for the first time, observed that 'The front staircase is a very good one, with a neat mahogany rail to the top of the house.'

Iron balusters were, at least in the grandest homes, painted a bright mid-blue. The intention may have been to emphasize the blueness of the iron; more probably, however, the colour was not only demonstrably bright - contrasting emphatically with many of the subdued, 'common' colours of the time - but was also recognizable by all as being vastly expensive. Ironwork, like so many other elements of the Georgian house, afforded a welcome opportunity for the blatant public display of wealth as well as taste.

Early in the eighteenth century one of the blue colourings occasionally used for internal ironwork was 'smalt', a bright, lustrous and extremely costly finish of ground blue cobalt glass dusted on top of a base coat of white lead, producing an attractive, glittering visual effect. The lead paint acted as a vital preservative for ironwork, both

inside and outside the house. By the 1750s, however, a cheaper - but nevertheless still expensive - alternative had been introduced: Prussian blue, a vibrantly powerful pigment first invented in 1704 and originating from animal blood. In 1765 an oil paint using Prussian blue was applied to the external lamps and railings at London's Mansion House. The use of Prussian blue on the graceful iron stairs at great houses such as Osterley Park and Somerset House during the 1770s made the paint doubly fashionable; by 1770 blue-painted ironwork was probably fairly common in the grander houses of Britain and America. However, since Prussian blue-derived oil paints were still three times the price of ordinary common colours, more modest homes used cheaper lead-greys - made from combining indigo with white lead - to protect and decorate their ironwork.

While the iron-balustered staircase was a major influence on the appearance and plan of the house of Adam's day, perhaps the most important element within each individual room was the fireplace. In Britain's clammy and chilly climate the fireplace quickly became the natural focus of attention in any well-used room, providing the axis about which the occupants and events of the house revolved. As Ware acknowledged in 1756: 'With us no article in a well-finished room is so essential. The eye is immediately cast upon it on entering, and the place of sitting down is naturally near it.'

The basic disposition of the Adam-period chimneypiece was still much as it had been in the mid-seventeenth century: a projecting lintel-entablature supported by columns, pilasters or consoles which carried a large overmantel. Until the early eighteenth century chimneypieces had

Adam chimneypieces. Left,
top and bottom: *decorative
details from the Adam
brothers'* Works in
Architecture *of the 1770s.*
Above and top:
*chimneypiece details from
20 St James's Square.*

Below: *Rococo chimneypiece
and grate from Thomas
Johnson's* Collection of
Designs *of 1758. This
somewhat over-the-top,
indisciplined composition
demonstrates the type of
approach to which the Neo-
Classicists of the 1760s were
reacting.* Right: *highly
architectural chimneypiece
and overmantel designs
(with the inevitably
prominent anthemia) by the
Adams, made for the first
and second drawing rooms
at Derby House.* Far right:
*strongly architectural Adam
chimneypiece designs for
Coventry House, Piccadilly,
of 1765.*

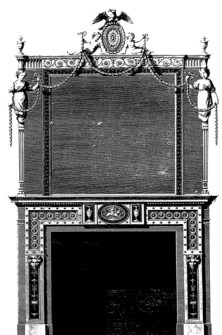

Left and far left: *delicate but sumptuous fireplace designs by the Adams for Derby House in London's Grosvenor Square (built 1773-4). Note the large area of highly expensive mirror glass above the mantelpieces. Below: section of the ante-room at Derby House, showing an anthemion frieze, semicircular niches decorated with classical medallions, three-armed sconces and a fairly restrained chimneypiece under a large, plain rectangular mirror and 'fanlight' spandrel. Compare these compositions with the Rococo fireplace, opposite.*

remained very plain and were rarely decorated; it was only with the new Palladian designers of the 1720s that profuse decoration became the norm for chimneypieces in important rooms. In the early 1760s, however, designers such as Robert Adam began to react against the ponderous swags, scrolls, shells and robust mouldings of the Palladian chimneypieces of previous years - and indeed against the lighter, more indisciplined Rococo designs which had begun to appear in fashionable, French-influenced interiors of the 1740s and 50s. Adam's chimneypieces were comparatively restrained, relying on architectural form, colour (in the form of different marbles)and a judicious use of modest Neo-Classical ornament in place of the lush decoration which so characterized the vocabulary of the Palladian and Rococo styles. Large-scale high-relief Palladian decoration was replaced by the type of low-relief, small-scale motifs popularized by Stuart and Revett and the Adam brothers. Urns, delicate swags and figures from classical mythlogy were especial favourites. After the 1760s even Adam's own chimney surrounds became increasingly plain, as he ceased to use ostentatious elements such as caryatids to support the mantelpiece.

Shortly after Robert and James Adam's return to Britain, William Chambers's *Treatise on Civil Architecture* of 1759 laid down what he considered to be the basic rules for the proportion of chimneypieces. 'The size of the chimney', he sensibly declared, 'must depend on the dimensions of the room wherein it is placed.' Similarly, while chimneypieces could be constructed from a wide variety of materials ('stone, marble, or ... a mixture of these, with wood, scagliola, or-moulu or some other unfragile substances'), Chambers insisted that in decorating them 'regard must be had to the nature of the place where they are to be employed.' Chambers's advice was both practical and aesthetic. He recommended that fireplaces should not be placed on an outside wall, since the unsupported stacks above would be more liable to collapse. More unusually, he was quick to warn his readers of the moral dilemmas presented by the licentious classical ornamentation of the day:

'All nudities and indecent representations must be avoided, both in chimneypieces; and indeed, in every other Ornament of Apartments, to which Children, Ladies, and other modest and grave persons, have constant recourse; together with all representations capable of exciting Horrour, Grief, Disgust, &c.'

As Chambers also noted, chimneypieces could be constructed from a broad range of materials. White, grey or black marble, often with an inlaid relief of exotic coloured marbles, was the most sought after - and, of course, the most expensive - material. A cheaper and lighter alternative to genuine marble was coloured scagliola. Even ceramic chimneypieces were made. Both Wedgwood and Coade made complete surrounds in addition to their ranges of mantelpiece ornaments, and by 1784 the Coade factory at Lambeth, south London, could boast a broad range of highly affordable chimneypiece designs ranging in price from 25 shillings to 14 guineas.

Companies such as those run by Coade, Wedgwood and Chippendale - who were not only the leading manufacturers of the day, but also the keenest marketing brains - remained ever alert to the changing whims of fireplace fashion. In 1781

Left: *the chimneypiece from The Princess's Dressing Room at Harewood House, Yorkshire.* Above: *two ornate bracket designs for marble slabs, from Chippendale's* Gentleman and Cabinet-Maker's Director, *originally published in 1754.*

Above: *T. Carter's designs for entablatures from* The Builder's Magazine *of 1774, and,* right: *chimneypiece panels from P. Columbani's* A New Book of Ornaments *published in 1775. Here the Neo-Classical decoration, whilst still featuring the obligatory anthemia and classical figures, is rather more free, recalling some of the Rococo licence of the 1750s. More severely classical is the marble and scagliola fireplace* (opposite) *from Syon House, designed by Adam and executed by Domenico Bartoli in the 1760s.*

Chippendale, Haig and Company charged Sir Gilbert Heathcote five shillings and sixpence for 'men's time taking off the large gilt ornaments of the 2 Chymney Pieces, and £10 18s. for Finish the pilasters - and mouldings with additional new ornaments - and making very neat carved antique ornaments to the frizes'. Heathcote obviously did not want to install a wholly new surround, but it was still out with the old, heavy gilt work and in with the new, Neo-Classical motifs. The small scale and the ease of replication of the latter allowed many householders to do the same at comparatively little expense.

By 1700 tiles for fireplace surrounds were beginning to be imported from the United Provinces. The characteristic Dutch tin-glazed 'Delft' tile - often termed 'maiolica' after the island of Majorca, a trading centre for tin-glazed pottery - was white, with painted surface decoration in blue or, occasionally, brown. By 1750 a number of English factories were producing large numbers of 'Delftware' imitations, and were becoming increasingly independent of the Dutch manufacturers. New colours were added to the traditional restricted Dutch palette of blues, browns and purples: green, yellow, red, and the typically Bristolian 'bianco sopra bianco', white-on-white. In 1756 John Sadler and Guy Green began producing copperplate-printed tiles at their Liverpool factory. Although they could print remarkably detailed patterns from the copper plates onto the Delftware blanks, the fact that the tiles were then fired at a comparatively low temperature meant that the patterns were not as durable as they might have been. Today, unfortunately, few copperplate tiles survive with their printed patterns intact.

Tiles were not the only decoration applied to

the mid-Georgian chimneypiece. Chimneyboards, used to cover the grate area during summer, were very common by 1760. They were especially prevalent in America, where they rapidly became a popular type of folk art, decorated, often by itinerant artisans, with painted or stencilled patterns or, more commonly, with ambitious landscapes and seascapes. In Britain chimneyboards were usually painted a single colour, covered in plain paper or with black-and-white prints, or painted with a realistic scene. A vase of flowers, depicted in the manner of seventeenth-century Dutch interiors, was perhaps the favourite subject for the boards. *Trompe l'oeil* scenes were also very popular; the Society of Sign Painters' public exhibition of 1762 included a chimneyboard which depicted 'a large, blazing fire painted in watercolours'. Occasionally, hand-painted

Opposite, top and bottom left: *door architrave details from Robert and James Adams'* Works *of the 1770s;* top and bottom right: *architraves from 20 St James's Square.* Above: *tin-glazed tiles printed with classical medallions of 1775-85.*

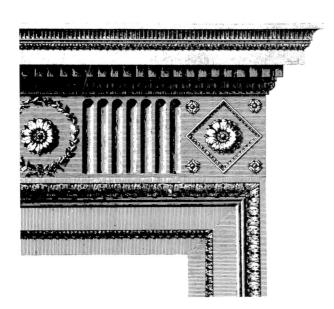

Chinese papers were imitated: as early as 1754 Dr Richard Pococke discovered that at Longford Castle in Wiltshire there were 'chimney boards throughout' which were decorated with 'Chinese pictures'. Even Robert Adam and Thomas Chippendale did not consider that the decoration of chimneyboards was beneath them. And for those who could afford it, the great decorative artists of the day would be employed to paint scenes upon these most visible of ornaments. In 1769 the renowned painter Biagio Rebecca made a particularly splendid set of chimneyboards, painted with *trompe l'oeil* antique vases and intended for the principal rooms at Audley End in Essex.

The Adam-style chimneypiece remains the most popular reproduction or salvaged Georgian item in both Britain and America. However, many modern reproductions bear little resemblance to genuine Georgian examples, being crudely decorated and with their pine surfaces left wholly unpainted. At the same time many 'salvaged' Adam chimneypieces and grates have actually been stolen from houses in Britain or Ireland. If you do use a salvaged chimneypiece, establish from the salesman exactly where it has come from. Without precise records of provenance, a salvaged item could well be stolen - and in purchasing it, you are helping to promote the theft of such splendid pieces. It is equally important to make sure that the chimneypiece is appropriate for your own home. Oversized and over-elaborate Adam-style chimneypieces can look ridiculous in a small space. Remember, too, that the position of the fireplace was governed largely by the function, not the appearance, of a room. Thus, as William Chambers was keen to point out, the less important the room, the smaller and plainer the fireplace should be. Unfortunately this basic common sense is often forgotten today.

If you do buy a reproduction, ensure that the style as well as the size is applicable to your own home. Many modern 'period' products are sad, clumsy pastiches based on genuine historical precedents. Many, too, are in bare pine - in stark contrast to Georgian (and Victorian) practice. Georgian wood or plaster chimneypieces were *always* painted; stripping historic paint layers away to reveal the basic structure exposes inferior timber that was never intended to be seen. Robert Adam would shudder to see many of the chimney surrounds and grates that are sold today using his august name.

Above left: *a Neo-Classical urn incorporated into the design for a chimneyboard, painted by Biagio Rebecca in 1769 for Audley End in Essex.*

Opposite: *the stark Neo-Classicism of the Adams' best domestic work can be seen in this view of a doorway and fireplace at 20 St James's Square.*

'I went to the duke of Kingston's private Bath, and there I was almost suffocated for want of free air; the place was so small, and the steam so stifling'

(Tobias Smollett
Humphry Clinker, *1771)*

Opposite: *the Adam fireplace in the third drawing room at Derby House, Grosvenor Square - demolished in 1862.* Left: *candelabra and tripod stand from Adam's* Works in Architecture.

In contrast to the image regularly presented in period dramas on television, Georgian interiors were generally very poorly lit, both at night-time and during the day. The Georgians, it is important to realize, were particularly sensitive to the detrimental effect of direct light on their important furnishings, and went to great lengths to minimize its effect during the day. Muslin sub-curtains helped to filter the harmful light entering via the window; shutters or blinds, too, were often pulled during the day in order to preserve the furniture and fabrics. It must also be remembered that even relatively modest, middle-class households retained servants who would be directed to turn furniture out of the sun, to apply furniture covers when necessary, and to safeguard carpets with druggets or floorcloths. The absence of such hired help in the twentieth century has inevitably caused many Georgian fittings to deteriorate rapidly.

At night interiors were even more gloomy - though hardly, this time, by choice. Few households could afford the glittering chandeliers we so readily associate with Georgian entertainments; until the 1780s most homes were lit at night solely by candles. And even this most basic form of lighting had to be used sparingly. As architectural historian Dan Cruickshank has pointed out in *Life in the Georgian City,* 'prodigality with candles was not the Georgian rule and the average room was very underlit by the standards of the nineteenth and twentieth centuries.' The light sources were usually near or on the walls: either candlesticks or candelabra, placed on side tables, or wall-mounted sconces. The latter were often fixed in front of mirrors, in order to reflect more light about the room, and generally comprised two sweeping arms projecting from a decorated

base. Grander sconce compositions were called girandoles.

The simplest form of candle was the rush light: a dried rush dipped in animal fat, held in a simple clip mounted on a stand. More expensive were tallow candles, made from rendered animal fat. Unsurprisingly, these burnt badly, and were as smelly as rush lights. Dearer still, but more effective, were beeswax candles. These cost on average three times as much as tallow candles. (At the beginning of the eighteenth century beeswax candles were taxed at 4d a pound, tallow at only ½d a pound.) They also smelt less, smoked less and had a higher melting point than tallow ones. They were, nevertheless, only available to the rich. Even in the grandest houses guests could still judge their relative social importance according to whether their hosts brought out wax or tallow candles. Good-quality beeswax was imported in Britain and America; hence candlemakers were often situated in ports.

Expensive candles required grand holders. And the silver candlestick, which perhaps best encapsulates the artistic goals and technological triumphs of the Adam era, became one of the most sought-after status symbols of the fashionable interior. The Adam brothers themselves helped to initiate the stylistic revolution in silver candlestick design. Gone were the sinuous lines and untrammelled foliage of the Rococo. In their stead were flat, unadorned surfaces, Neo-Classical motifs such as the swag and the urn (a form adapted to serve for much of the silver hollow-ware of the period), straight lines and, above all, an elegant simplicity based on the primacy of proportion.

The technology of silver production changed

More designs from Adam's
Works: *a candlestick, a two-armed candelabra and a tripod lampstand.*

Opposite: *tripod candelabra by Robert Adam, designed in the mid-1760s for Syon House.*

Elaborate girandoles designed by the Adams for Derby House's 'Etruscan room'.

as fundamentally as did the design of silverware. One of the principal effects of the industrial advances of the 1760s and 70s was that more everyday items were being made of silver than ever before. The great silversmithing centres of Sheffield and Birmingham were soon turning out all manner of silver products - not just candlesticks and candelabra, but tea-urns, teapots, sconces, and innumerable other household pieces of this sort. Sheffield continued to specialize in candlesticks - some designed by the celebrated sculptor John Flaxman - and popularized the simple composition in which clustered columns were combined with palm-leaf capitals. The newly introduced technique of die-stamping now allowed the constituent parts of the candlestick to be assembled far more simply and cheaply than before. Sheffield also pioneered the introduction in the 1770s of 'Sheffield Plate': copper fused to a silver veneer. This innovation opened up an even larger domestic market to the silversmiths: the consequent lowering of prices meant that silverware was now available to middle-class families the length and breadth of Britain and America. Soon the new fly-punch was able to punch out complex, perforated patterns onto Sheffield Plate with such precision that the copper still remained hidden below; at the same time stamped motifs such as Neo-Classical ribbons and urns were now far more easily fabricated and applied.

The impetus behind many of the technological breakthroughs in silversmithing came from the tireless industrialist Matthew Boulton, the world's first industrial entrepreneur. His manufactory at Soho, in Birmingham, was by the end of the 1760s producing a wide variety of silver goods. By 1770 Boulton was writing that he had

'seven or eight hundred persons employ'd in almost all these Arts that are applicable to the manufacturing' of silver and other precious metals. Boulton's stylistic ambitions mirrored those of the Adam brothers: 'I would', he declared in 1776, 'have Elegant simplicity the leading principle.' However, he remained content to follow the artistic lead provided by the Adams and their rivals. As he told his friend Mrs Montagu in 1772:

'since the present age distinguishes itself by adopting the most Elegant ornaments of the most refined Grecian arists, I am satisfy'd in conforming thereto, & humbly copying their style, & making new combinations ... without presuming to invent new ones.'

Elegant silver candlesticks by Henry Hallsworth (below) and Thomas Heming (centre), with candelabra (right) by John Wakelin and William Taylor.

*An unusual black basalt
Wedgwood oil lamp
supported by slave figures,
dated c. 1780, from Saltram
House in Devon.*

Below: *highly fanciful
designs for wrought-iron
lampirons from* The
Builder's Magazine, *1775.*

Silver was not appropriate for all forms of
candleholder. The natural sparkle of glass, and its
ability to reflect light, made this, not silver or brass,
the preferred material for chandeliers, although
wood and brass examples were both cheaper and
easier to maintain. For those who could afford them,
elaborate chandeliers could by 1755 be had in a
wide variety of shapes and sizes. They were,
however, generally far simpler in design than the
elaborate, cut-glass examples that dominated the
grand rooms of the Regency period. The simple
sweep of their brass, wooden or ormolu arms made
for a most elegant composition which, when not in
use, was often wrapped in fabric as a protection
against dust and summer flies.

While historic glass chandeliers are now
prohibitively expensive, good reproductions of many
Adam-period brass models can still be bought at a
fairly reasonable price. It is important to remember,
though, that whereas the rich could afford to install
chandeliers, the rest of mid-Georgian society had to
make do with flickering candlepower. It was only in
the mid-1780s that a viable alternative became
available, when colza-oil lamps began to appear. In
1783 the Swiss chemist Ami Argand patented this
new form of lamp - known in Britain as a 'colza-oil
lamp' after the thick, greenish-yellow rape-seed oil
it burned - constructed around a revolutionary new
circular cotton wick with an internal air channel.
Although initially rejected in France, Argand's
invention was enthusiastically taken up across the
Channel by Matthew Boulton, who readily agreed to
manufacture Argand's lamps. Boulton's initiative
was soon, however, overtaken by the pace of
progress (and Argand's lethargy): following the
accidental lapse of Argand's temporary patent in

A view of the fireplace from the saloon at Saltram House, attributed to Thomas Carter the younger. Notice the bright, steel-and-brass grate and the symmetrically-arranged firescreens.

Pre-Adam grates: two of 1765 (right) *and* (far right) *four Chippendale Rococo and Gothic grates of 1760-62.* Bottom right: *Neo-Classical influences are rather more to the fore in this eccentric grate design from* The Builder's Magazine.

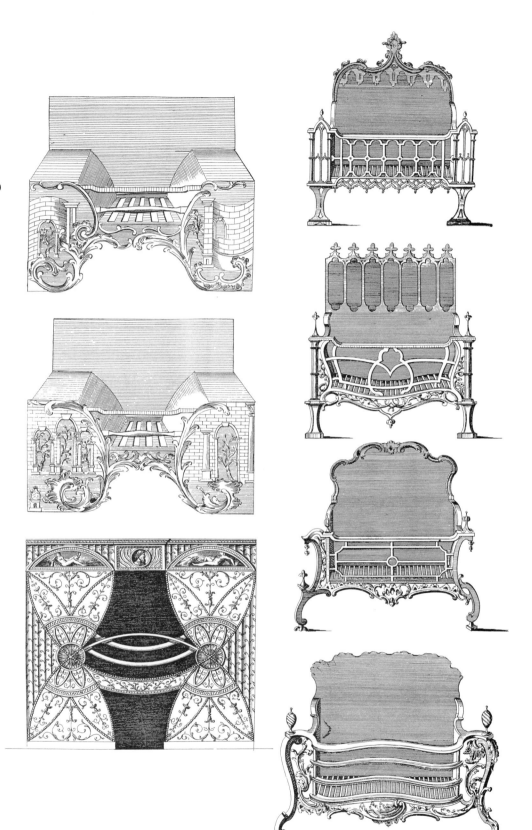

1786, imitations began to flood onto the market, and by the end of the century 'Argand' lamps could be found in large numbers of British and American homes.

As the equipment required to light the home became more refined during the years of Adam's career, so did the paraphernalia needed to heat it. By 1755 the 'stove grate' - a freestanding, rectangular basket with three fire bars placed between two andirons and a grid for falling ash at the bottom - was very common in middle-class homes, being cast not only in orthodox Palladian forms but also in more exotic Chinese and Rococo styles. As the period progressed, however, the stove grate was replaced by the hob grate. This form first appeared in the 1720s, and comprised a basket flanked by flat-topped hobs, designed to keep kettles and pots warm. By 1780 this type had become hugely popular; original or reproduction examples of these can still be widely found. The hob grate was not, like earlier versions, freestanding, but set into the fireplace. It was available in three basic patterns: 'Bath', 'Pantheon' and 'Forest', each distinguished by the form of the central plate linking the two hobs. A further improvement was the provision of movable iron plates to regulate the size of the chimney opening and thus the efficacy of the updraught - creating what became known as a 'register grate'. Isaac Ware's *Complete Body of Architecture* of 1756 found much to praise in this arrangement. 'The placing of a moveable vane at the top of the chimney is', he declared, 'often succesful; this keeps the opening of the funnel screened against the efforts of the wind.' Register grates did much to solve the problem of smoke coming into the room while heat disappeared up the chimney flue; however, a wholly efficient grate did not appear until the very end of the century.

Most of the grates of the period originated in one of two of the new foundries of the period: Carron and Company, of Falkirk in Scotland (one of whose partners was Robert Adam's brother, John), or the Coalbrookdale Company, based in the very birthplace of the Industrial Revolution in Shropshire. The products of these two manufactories have proved perenially popular. Even after the introduction of smaller, more efficient grates in the early nineteenth century, Carron and Coalbrookdale Adam-style grates continued to be sold in large quantities; today they still remain the best-selling type of reproduction grate.

To the great entrepreneur-inventors of the day, however, even the classic Adam grate could be improved upon. In 1742 that amazing polymath Benjamin Franklin had patented a double-skin metal stove fitted with an integral grate. This not only heated the immediate area around the fireplace, but also warmed the far corners of the room, carrying the air heated in the skin of the stove through a system of pipes and vents. In Britain these were called 'Philadelphia Stoves', after their city of origin; by the mid-1760s, they were actually being produced in British foundries for export back to America.

Mid-Georgian fire-grates were not intended to be purely utilitarian machines, but stylish pieces of room furniture, too. Many of them were provided with applied ornament made of brass, steel or 'paktong' - an expensive, silvery alloy of copper, zinc and nickel, first introduced from China into Britain and her colonies by Robert Adam. Paktong was easy to cast, highly lustrous, simply engraved, and did not

Left: *brightly-polished Adam firegrate in the Marble Hall at Kedleston, Derbyshire.*

tarnish. It was, at least by the early 1760s, being widely employed to decorate the fender, an innovation of the 1740s which was provided with pierced decoration designed to match the style of the accompanying surround and grate. (Prior to this the fender was generally executed in brass; in 1749 John Wood remarked that 'the Furniture for every Chimney was composed of a Brass Fender with Tongs, Poker and Shovel agreeable to it.') Other elements of the Adam fireplace were also expressly designed to harmonize with the grate in order to give the whole ensemble an overall 'look'. In Robert Adam's own unified fireplace schemes the fire irons, tongs and shovels were all made of the same material as the grate and fender, upon which they would be formally arranged.

When the fire was unused for long periods, the fender and fireplace furniture would be bodily removed and a decorated chimneyboard installed in their place. When the fire was in use, seat furniture nearby would be protected from the heat by wooden, cane or fabric fire screens. These were either freestanding, supported on a stand or pole, or were made to fit directly onto chair backs. In 1779 the family firm of Gillows submitted a bill for 'six neat fire screens to drop upon the backs of chairs' in the Dining Room at Heaton Hall, north of Manchester.

The kitchen was the one room in the house where the occupants rarely needed additional

heating. Indeed, many servants would habitually sleep overnight under the kitchen table, warming themselves from the dying hearth or stove. By 1750 cooking in most up-to-date homes was no longer conducted on the floor of an open fire in the kitchen, but over a more sophisticated wrought-iron basket - the grate. In many humble houses and cottages, on the other hand, cooking was still taking place over an open hearth as late as the middle of the twentieth century. However sophisticated the home, though, the kitchen fire always remained one of the focal points of the house. In Oliver Goldsmith's *The Vicar of Wakefield* of 1766, for example, this most cosy and welcoming of environments was where the great issues of the day were invariably debated. 'We sate beside his kitchen fire, which was the best room in the house, and chatted on politics and the news of the country.'

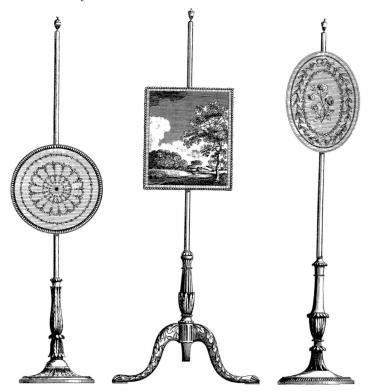

Right: *pole firescreens of the mid-1780s, by the enigmatic furniture designer George Hepplewhite.*

Left: *Adam-designed chimneyboard of 1778 from the State Bedroom at Osterley. Covered with 'Etruscan' ornamentation, it is removed by means of a brass knob situated at the top of the frame.* Top: *the Adam chimneypiece from the tapestry room at Nostell Priory, probably executed by John Devall.* Above: *Thomas Carter's glittering, ormolu-mounted chimneypiece of 1763 in the drawing room at Syon surrounds a splendid brass inset and fender. The ormolu decoration on the surround was probably made to Adam's design by Diederich Anderson, who also executed the gilding on the room's fine doorcases and window-shutters.*

As the century progressed, the workings of the kitchen grate or range became ever more complex and heat-efficient. The ancestor of the range - the 'perpetual oven' combining oven and grate - first appeared in the 1750s, and by the 1780s the iron boiler was being combined with the grate and the oven in a cast-iron, wood- or coal-fired kitchen range. In 1780 Thomas Robinson took out a patent for a range that combined an open fire with an oven and draught-operated mechanical spits, while Joseph Langmead's patent range of 1783, an improvement on the Robinson format, effectively provided the basic pattern for ranges for the next two centuries.

To complement the range were other freestanding kitchen aids such as the metal Dutch oven, made of tin to reflect the heat in as efficient a manner as possible. Dutch ovens were much in use by the end of the eighteenth-century for that staple of the British diet, the Roast Beef of Old England, whose accompanying batter pudding was cooked in a tray underneath the joint.

Although the early Georgian kitchen grate was fairly crude by modern standards, around it were installed a wide variety of surprisingly sophisticated technological aids. Spits were rested on hooks joined to the two front legs of the grate, and were turned by use of an ingenious mechanical device powered by clockwork or simply by a 'smokejack', which used the force of the updraught up the kitchen chimney. Pan supports ('trivets'), also attached to the grate, could swing out over the fire; later this arrangement metamorphosed into the kitchen hob grate. The 1710 Inventory of the Great and Little Kitchens at Dyrham Park, Gloucestershire, included a daunting array of

kitchen technology: an 'Iron Crane', iron racks, '5 Spitts', '2 Dripping panns', four brass kettles, brass pots, '2 Bell metall Skillets', and a bewildering variety of other brass, iron and pewter kitchenware. By 1760 yet more complex items, such as plate warmers and coal-filled warming pans, had been added to this impressive list.

Running water was a great rarity in most kitchens and bathrooms of the mid-eighteenth century. Houses in urban centres may have been lucky enough to have water piped to the ground floor through lead-lined wooden pipes, which were gradually replaced by cast-iron piping as the Industrial Revolution gained pace. Otherwise, lead cisterns, to hold the water needed for kitchen use, were placed immediately inside (not outside) the kitchen. Increasingly, cisterns were supplemented

Above: *traditional brass and copper kitchen implements, and,* opposite, *the re-created kitchen at Fairfax House, York (a house remodelled by John Carr in 1762), which* *includes a smoke-jack spit, chimney crane, ratchet hooks, boiling pot, kettle and an original, water-filled warming pan.*

by sinks, which were usually placed behind a partition to create a scullery area quite separate from the space in which the food was prepared. These sinks were generally made of stone or wood, and lined with lead, although, as Neil Burton has pointed out, some were actually hewn from a single piece of stone.

The lead cistern of the Adam era looked much as it had earlier in the century. It was large, rectangular and handsomely-decorated with strapwork, an odd survival of a common sixteenth-century decorative practice; it was also often inscribed with the initials of the house owner and (most helpfully for any historian) the date of its original installation. Cisterns were not always made by hammering, cutting and stamping lead sheets; some were cast in huge sand beds impressed with carved moulds. The kitchen cistern was filled from a street pump or fed by a rainwater pipe, and was connected to the rest of the kitchen and, if necessary, the other rooms on the ground floor, by a series of lead pipes. Hot water was obtained by transferring the contents of the cistern into a boiler; from the boiler servants carried it around the house in jugs.

Aside from the cistern, sink and hearth, the other principal element in the mid-Georgian kitchen was the wooden dresser. Interestingly enough, in sharp contrast to many of the other kitchen fixtures and fittings to be found at the time, the wooden dresser remains an integral feature of today's traditional kitchen, still widely available and still wholly compatible with the technology of the modern household. Unlike the range, the dresser was not a Georgian invention; yet it is certainly true that by the end of the eighteenth century it had

become far more widespread, featuring in the most modest as well as the grandest homes. Simple pine, elm or oak dressers - *always* painted if not of good, seasoned oak - took pride of place in the kitchen, and provided an invaluable storage area and an additional work surface. Their widespread provision during this period can be seen from the details of a lease of 1760 for a typical London townhouse: 36 Dover Street, in London's new Mayfair district. The laundry here possessed 'two large dressers'; the butler's pantry (which was 'wainscotted about 8 feet high') one dresser; the two larders two dressers each; and even the washhouse had one. The kitchen itself contained 'one large elm dresser and two turned feet and three drawers' and 'one deal dresser, two turned feet and potboard'. Equally illuminating is Mrs Kenyon's detailed description, contained in a lengthy letter to her mother, of her new Lincoln's Inn Fields home in 1774. The kitchen of this medium-sized townhouse was, as she depicted it, equipped with 'a butler's pantry, with a dresser that has two drawers and a cupboard under it, shelves over it for glasses etc, a lead cistern, and a pipe with water'.

Although this book is primarily concerned with the construction and decoration of the mid-Georgian house, it is certainly worth having a brief glimpse at the types of food that were prepared in the kitchens of the time. Main dishes were primarily roasted, boiled or stewed, or baked in the nearby oven or stove. For the higher echelons of Georgian society, the principal emphasis for main meals was on meat dishes and, to a lesser extent, on fish. The wealthier classes, disdaining vegetables except to garnish the meats or to make the soups - which, as today, preceded the main courses - actually ate far

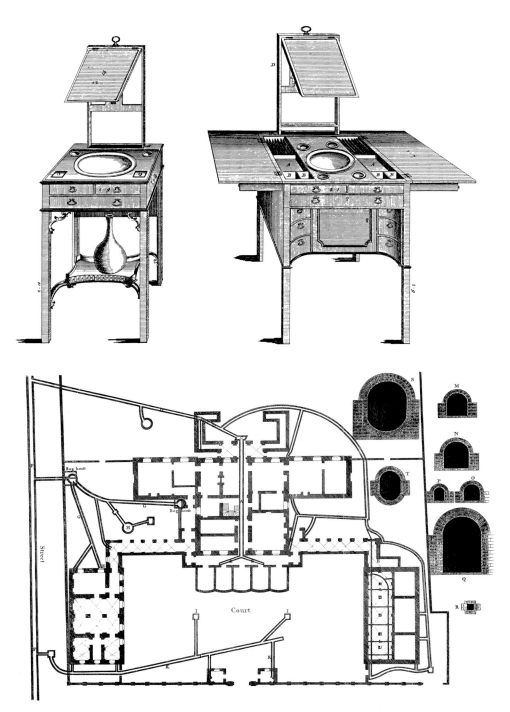

Above, from left: *a
sophisticated 'Bidet Shaving
Table' and night table of the
mid-1780s by Hepplewhite,
and a basin stand and
shaving table from the third
edition of Chippendale's*
Gentleman and Cabinet-
Maker's Director, *published
in 1762.* Left: *a fascinating
plan showing the vast
network of sewers necessary
to drain a new, modestly-
sized country house.*

less healthily than the lower classes. The latter had to make do with vegetables from the brassica (cabbage) family, pulses, beans, root vegetables, oatmeal, barley, bread and the odd piece of bacon. Many of the meats now came from farms rather than the wild, while pickles and bottled sauces, including commercial products such as Harvey's Sauce (the ancestor of many modern 'brown' sauces and ketchups), became increasingly popular as garnishes for meat. In fact, much Georgian food was remarkably unhealthy by modern standards. If vegetables were eaten in the more pretentious households, they were generally smothered in butter sauce. By the mid-eighteenth century heavy puddings, which replaced the cereal porages so common in former centuries, had become ubiquitous, most often in boiled, suet form. Sweet puddings which did not use suet were often provided with a puff pastry crust. It was only by the end of the eighteenth century that raw fruit was widely accepted as being safe enough to eat.

Breakfast was very much a Georgian invention. By 1750 it was being taken at 9 or 10 in the morning, encouraging middle-class housewives to postpone dinner from noon to 2 or even 3 o'clock. By the last years of the eighteenth century the most fashionable homes had their dinner at 4 or 5, to be followed by a supper of cold collations at about 10pm. The increasing gap between breakfast and dinner was, by the 1780s, in turn filled for the upper and middle classes by another new meal: luncheon. This was an informal meal, often designed only for women - the men being out hunting, drinking or whatever else men did during the day.

The re-created kitchen at Fairfax House in York (the decoration of which was completed

Opposite: *the dining room at Fairfax House, as set out for a fully-documented meal taken in the house on 15th April 1763. Vying for prominence are the delicate epergne and the ostentatious peacock pie.*

by John Carr in 1762) has been carefully devised around a dinner actually taken in this house at 4pm on the 15th of April 1763. The menu for that meal typifies the type of dinner prepared for comparatively wealthy middle-class Georgians of the period. The first course consisted of boiled meats, fish and soups arranged formally around an impressive table centrepiece; the second course concentrated on roasted meats, ragouts and other savoury dishes. (As Peter Brown has pointed out, 'The English as a whole disapproved of the French developments in *Nouvelle Cuisine* that had taken place in the eighteenth century.') The first course included anatomical delicacies such as boiled calf's head and florentine of rabbit - for which the rabbits were boned, and their heads served whole. Peacock Pie took pride of place on the table for the second course; this luxurious dish, however, probably did not contain actual peacock meat, which was very unappetising: the peacock was included entirely for display. A mock boar's head, executed in sponge and chocolate and decorated with a coat of arms, preceded the dessert of fruit, nuts, liquorice, calves-foot jelly, meringues and macaroons.

Many of the implements which the Georgians used for eating and drinking on such grand occasions underwent a substantial metamorphosis during this period. Most importantly, tableware which, until the mid-eighteenth century, was largely associated with the upper classes, now, through the agency of the Industrial Revolution, became available to all. At the same time the great inventors of the day devised yet more sophisticated, efficient and attractive means of dispensing food and drink. The 1760s, for example, saw the introduction of the tea-urn. This everyday

piece, generally in the form of a classical vase (and sometimes called, most confusingly, a 'kitchen'), quickly superseded the old tea-kettle; by 1770 tea-urns were very popular on both sides of the Atlantic.

Tea-drinking was now a highly fashionable, if still none too cheap, recreation in both Britain and America (although the Boston Tea Party and subsequent events in the colonies did little to encourage tea consumption there). The habit of ladies 'withdrawing' after dinner actually began as a way of allowing the mistress of the house sufficient time and space in which to brew the after-dinner tea properly. Nor was tea-drinking restricted to the grander homes (which in former times had locked their tea-caddies for fear this precious commodity would be stolen). In 1773 (ironically, the year of the notorious Tea Party) Dr Richard Price noted with patrician pessimism that 'the circumstances of the lower ranks of the people are altered in every respect for the worse, while tea, wheaten bread and other delicacies are necessaries which were formerly unknown to them'. Subsequently Dr Gilbert Blane was moved to remark, in a rather more celebratory vein, that 'Tea is an article universally grateful to the British population and has to a certain

extent supplanted intoxicating liquors in all ranks, to the great advantage of society.' ('The modern use of tea', he concluded in a somewhat more controversial fashion, 'has probably contributed to the extended longevity of the inhabitants of the country.')

To fill the growing demand for tea, silver urns and tea-sets, newly liberated from the shackles of exclusivity by the Industrial Revolution, were produced with increasing efficiency by the factories of Birmingham and Sheffield. When designed by the great silversmiths of the day such as Hester Bateman, tea-urns and their related apparatus could become objects of great artistic worth. For those who could not afford silver or even Sheffield Plate, though, a new and comparatively cheap form of everyday ware had become available by 1770: the revolutionary ceramic products produced in great quantities by Wedgwood and his rivals in the region of Stoke-on-Trent, in Staffordshire. Such wares were not only comparatively inexpensive; they were also more practical for hot liquids than silver and pewter, which conducted heat too well, and glass, which could crack.

Josiah Wedgwood is one of the most impressive figures of the eighteenth century. It was he who fused the increasing demand for ceramic drinking wares with the new fashion for Neo-Classicism. It was Wedgwood, too, who devised most

Opposite: left, *a set of delicately-decorated silver tea-caddies of 1777, with their original satinwood and yew-wood case;* and right, *Neo-Classical tea-caddies from Hepplewhite's* The Cabinet Maker and Upholsterer's Guide *of 1788.*

Far left: *a two-handed, vase-shaped tea urn of 1768. Its design looks both back to the Rococo and forward to Neo-Classicism.*

Classical lines and minimal decoration are evident in these four teapots and tea caddy, ranging in date from the 1760s to the early 1780s.

Wedgwood tea-service creamware of 1774. Wedgwood can be credited with popularizing this highly successful ware, which by this date was being sold to the Empress of Russia as well as to the middle classes of Britain and America. The modernity of Wedgwood's clean, sharp lines is particularly striking.

of the new ceramic products of the period. He was constantly experimenting with new bodies and glazes: inventing the green glaze which helped to realize the fruit and vegetable tableware so popular during the 1760s, by 1765 he had perfected a consistent creamware, and by 1776 had invented jasper, a ceramic of (in his own words) 'exquisite beauty and delicacy proper for cameos, portraits and bas-reliefs', and the product by which he is best known today. Yet Wedgwood's most profound achievement was to make what were formerly regarded as unattainable luxuries freely available to the 'Middling Class'. (In 1772 he asserted that 'The Great People have had these vases in their Palaces long enough for them to be seen and admired by the Middling Class of People', who 'would probably buy quantities of them at a reduced price'.) This goal was achieved not only by the mass-production of high-quality products, but also through a large measure of skilful marketing. After, for example, Queen Charlotte had bought some of his creamware, Wedgwood rapidly changed the range's name to 'Queensware' and began to style himself 'Potter to the Queen'. Such actions helped bring him popular success as well as critical acclaim. By 1778 Wedgwood was claiming of his creamware that it was 'no longer the choice thing it used to be, since every shop, house and cottage is full of it'.

Wedgwood's contribution in the area of form and style was also most significant, since he was the first ceramicist to harness the simplicity and purity of the Neo-Classical age to everyday 'china' wares. Much of this is directly attributable to the influence of his partner after 1769, Thomas Bentley, a Liverpool merchant and connoisseur who became responsible for the export of Wedgwood's products to America. In design historian Adrian Forty's words, Bentley was 'the first to see that pottery and Neo-Classicism, hitherto unassociated, might be suited to one another ... His espousal of neoclassicism transformed Wedgwood from an ordinary, though successful, potter into a leader of *avant-garde* taste.'

For the first time ceramics, in the form of cameos, tablets and urns, could be used as a type of interior decoration, their style and tone exactly matching the fashionable Adam-style room. Yet Wedgwood's Neo-Classicism, like Adam's, was not grounded in a slavish adherence to the precise forms of the ancients. 'I have endeavoured', wrote Wedgwood, 'to preserve the stile and spirit or if you please the elegant simplicity of the antique forms ... but not with absolute servility.' He was careful, though, not to depart too far from the Neo-Classical norm as established by Adam and his rivals. 'They certainly are not Antique', he wrote of one of his less successful range of pots, 'and that is fault enough to Damn them with most of our customers.' His jasperware was designed to be particularly appropriate for the latest Neo-Classical interiors, the translucence of its unglazed, white form closely resembling marble. (Coloured jasper, today the most enduringly popular of all Wedgwood's products, was rejected by the architects of the day for the very reason that it did *not* resemble antique marble.) Even the name of his new factory, 'Etruria', was meant to evoke the Ancient Etruscan landscape - in the extremely unlikely setting of Stoke-on-Trent.

Wedgwood broadened the horizons of the household ceramics industry immeasurably. He was the first to foster a close relationship with the great artists of the day, inviting famous painters such as

George Stubbs and Joseph Wright, and celebrated sculptors such as John Flaxman, to design his more ambitious pieces - much in the way that Eleanor Coade employed the talents of the great sculptor John Bacon. He also substantially raised the status of the trade as a whole. Not only did he make, as Adrian Forty says, 'modern methods of manufacture fashionable' - proving that technology and the antique arts were perfectly compatible; he was also the first potter to be elected a Fellow of the Royal Society.

For those of Wedgwood's time who preferred wine to tea, coffee or chocolate, a highly fashionable alternative to the humble ceramic cup or the ostentatious silver goblet was becoming widely available. By the 1750s drinking-glasses provided with an air-twist stem (often embellished with one or two 'knops' or swellings) were becoming increasingly common in fashionable homes. This delightful, delicate type of composition was achieved by drawing out tears of glass while they were still hot, and twisting them to produce an exceptionally attractive pattern of filaments just below the surface of the glass. This 'air twist' stem could be made yet more complex by interlacing two twists, or by using white or coloured glass to produce what was then called a 'cotton twist' stem. The glasses which resulted from these fascinating processes - all the rage by 1770, although old hat by 1790 - were breathtakingly delicate yet sturdily-proportioned.

While the Georgians were particularly enthusiastic about drinking and eating, they were, however, far less keen on washing. Baths were taken infrequently - but then the majority of baths were still of the cold-plunge variety, which were expensive to build, took up a considerable amount of basement floor space, and were decidedly trying on the constitution. (In 1715 a London lawyer reported that a cold bath was supposedly 'extremely good against the headache, strengthens and enlivens the body, is good against the vapours and impotence, and that the pain is little'. 'I have almost determined', he added spinelessly, 'to go in myself.') The invention of the shower-bath had to wait until the nineteenth century; however, by 1780 movable wooden or even ceramic bath-tubs, filled with jugs of water, had at least begun to replace the plunge-bath in more sophisticated homes. In *Humphry Clinker* of 1771, Smollett's middle-class lawyer Mr Micklewhimmen relates how 'he always stayed an hour in the bath, which was a tub filled with Harrigate water, heated for the purpose'.

An unusual Wedgwood teapot. Its form and decoration could easily be credited to the 1920s rather than to the 1770s.

Below right: *a jasperware teapot from the Wedgwood factory of c.1775. Jasperware is not always conceived as white decoration on a blue ground. This is a rare example of green-on-white.*

Above: *a group of Staffordshire, Yorkshire and Derbyshire creamware with delicate enamel decoration, dated 1770-80.*

Left: *a white salt-glazed pierced dish of 1760-70, with contemporary red stoneware coffee pot and punch pot with sprigged decoration.*

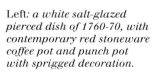

The development of the modern water closet was largely a Regency innovation - although Joseph Bramah's ball-cock WC (a superior version of Alexander Cummings's invention of 1775) was patented in 1778, and had already proved very successful by the mid-1780s. The Britons of the mid-eighteenth century were not too fastidious in their personal hygiene: generations of French and American visitors testified to this unpleasant fact. But at least they were improving.

The relatively simple technological requirements of the Georgian kitchen and bathroom are obviously not compatible with today's demands, to say nothing of health, fire and safety standards. The search for 'authenticity' in the context of servicing is bound to involve a large element of compromise. So if you are modernizing a traditional kitchen or bathroom, the best policy is always to try and ensure that most of the changes you make are to a large extent reversible. While you may not wish to retain many features of the last two centuries which have helped to create your home's history and character, later owners may wish to celebrate these elements, and will be able to indulge their enthusiasms only if sufficient original fabric or fittings are left. It is, for example, especially important not to demolish internal partitions in an effort to 'streamline' the kitchen interior. These partitions can be very useful, separating the sink area or creating a cool, walk-in larder or pantry. Subsequent owners of the house may not thank you for demolishing all traces of such sought-after features as the invaluable and spacious slate-shelved larder so often found in Georgian and Victorian homes. Instead of taking down internal divisions, it may be preferable to introduce freestanding equipment into the kitchen, rather than altering the room beyond recognition in order to accommodate fitted kitchen units.

Modern, freestanding lights are also often the best idea for illuminating a mid eighteenth-century room if you cannot obtain or afford - or simply do not want - to buy reproductions of Georgian lighting equipment. These can be removed when you wish, and do not effect any lasting visual or structural damage to the walls. When choosing light fittings for any old and characterful room, the most important factors to bear in mind are simplicity and sympathy. Bright, over-shiny brass designs of an alleged 'Victorian' or 'Edwardian' origin are liable to clash hideously with the quiet restraint of the original Georgian features which remain. Although it is now possible to find historically accurate reproduction fittings that blend harmoniously with historic interiors, if you are in any doubt, understated modern examples are often the best choice. Simplicity, restraint and elegance should be your guiding principles - as they were in Adam's own day.

A group of Staffordshire and Yorkshire creamware with underglazed oxide colours, typical of the 1750s to 80s.

'She has shewn me all her secrets, and learned me to wash gaze, and refrash rusty silks and bumbeseens, by boiling them with winegar, chamberlyne and stale beer'

(Tobias Smollett Humphry Clinker, *1771)*

Right: *Adam design for a curtain cornice.* Opposite: *Francis Wheatley's family scene of c.1770 shows fine, damask-upholstered seat furniture (with prominent nailing) and a splendid oriental carpet.*

Above right: *the famous
Reinagle picture of* Mrs
Congreve and her
daughters *of 1782 says
much about the typical
interior of the period. Note
the dark skirting, the Bath
hob grate, the Axminster
carpet, the vertically hung
curtains, and the formal,
symmetrical hang of the
paintings.* Below right:
*Hussey's painting of an
interior of twenty five years
earlier shows a stunning,
blue-grey architectural
wallpaper design, of the type
common at this time.*

During the forty years, prior to our period, which followed the Palladian revolution in taste, designers began to move away from the dark timber colours which had so characterized the seventeenth century, towards lighter and brighter tones. White became of central importance, either left plain, or relieved with gilding. This was not the brilliant, bleached white which we know today, but a colour which could be as pale as the slightly off-whites known as 'broken whites' - so-called because the white lead was 'broken' with tiny amounts of black or ochre - or as deep as the creamy 'stone colours'. Even the whitest Georgian white lead would soon turn yellow, as a result of the aging of the linseed oil used to bind the pigment. The bright whites that we use today are very much a modern innovation, and should never be used on the exteriors or interiors of Georgian buildings.

Plaster walls and ceilings in the eighteenth century were painted with cheap white distempers, made from whiting or chalk and bound with glue. But the white paint applied to internal woodwork was an oil paint: white lead. This was far more hard-wearing than distemper, which, being soluble in water, was not washable and tended to brush off with friction. (Until the twentieth century, incidentally, the term 'paint' was applied solely to oil-based colours; 'distemper' was another animal altogether.) Making white lead, which served not only as a colour in its own right but as the basis for numerous other oil paints, was a dangerous and messy business. To obtain the highly toxic pigment, vast lead sheets would be steeped in vinegar, with the result that 'the corrosive fumes of the vinegar will reduce the superficies of the lead into a white calx which ... separate by knocking upon it with a hammer', as the standard eighteenth-century guide to paintmaking described it. The pigment - obtained at the cost of countless instances of lead poisoning in the workforce - was then mixed with linseed oil to make the final paint. To this was often added a small quantity of turpentine, in order to give a flat, 'dead' matt finish that would look more like real stone. Matt wall finishes were all the fashion in Britain by 1750; in America, however, gloss finishes were applied to interiors throughout the eighteenth century.

Apart from white, a variety of other cheap, 'common' colours were widely available. These included not only the various 'stone colours' (which could be mixed to resemble any type of stone, from white Portland to golden Cotswold), but also grey (often called 'lead colour'), drab, olive, the traditional timber colours such as 'oak colour' (or simply 'wainscot') and 'walnut', and chocolate - the usual colour for skirtings and internal doors. To these 'common' colours could be added colours which were a little more expensive to make, but which were still within the reach of most middle-class households. Pea green (very commonly used by 1760), sky blue, 'dutch pink', lemon and 'straw colour' all fall within this category. Such paints could in turn be supplemented by yet more costly oil colours, whose prices varied in accordance with the difficulty and expense of obtaining the basic pigments. Robert Dossie's *Handmaid to the Arts* of 1758 listed the colours then available; among these were some of the colours most commonly associated with the Georgian era, including verdigris, the 'deep fine green' derived from corroding copper. Within the range of vivid and expensive blues were ultramarine, the 'extremely bright blue colour'

which Robert Dossie noted was made from crushed and heated lapis lazuli, and smalt, the glittering finish made of powdered blue glass. Smalt's composition would not, Dossie remarked, 'permit it to be worked with either brush or pencil; but it is used for some purposes by strewing it on any ground of oil-paint while wet; where it makes a bright warm blue shining surface.' For those who could not afford ultramarine or smalt, the invention of Prussian blue proved a blessing. This very strong pigment was derived from animal blood (or, in Dossie's words, 'the fixt sulphur of animal or vegetable coal') burnt with alum. One blue never used for walls, however, was the tone now commonly termed 'Wedgwood blue', after the Wedgwood jasperware it adorns. The colours used in the production of ceramics were, it must be emphasized, wholly different in composition and thus in appearance from those used to decorate interiors. Painting walls to match the tea service was not a practice indulged in by the Georgians.

Reds were, until the invention of chemical dyes in the nineteenth century, largely obtained from natural plant pigments such as madder, or from red-brown earth pigments. Yellows, too, were often obtained from earth ochres. Some yellows, though, could be surprisingly vivid. The highly toxic 'King's yellow', frighteningly depicted by Dossie as 'arsenic coloured with sulphur', nevertheless produced 'an extreme bright colour' when made up. Even less enticing than the directions for King's yellow was Dossie's recipe for 'deep warm yellow': gall stones dissolved in water.

Both the common colours and the more expensive paints described above remained in general use throughout the century. The rediscovery of the ancient world, however, brought with it a new and vibrant palette of colours discovered amid the ruins of Rome and Greece: lilacs, bright blues and greens, bright pinks, blacks and, most characteristically, terracotta red-browns, often used in combination with black to create an 'Etruscan' colour scheme. The designers and decorators of Adam's day did not, it must be strongly emphasized, rely on the washed-out pastel hues so often associated with 'Adam Style' today; instead they took full advantage of the rich and vivid tones now given academic sanction and, moreover, increasingly available to the general public through the development of pigment technology.

Not everyone immediately took up the new Neo-Classical colours. Traditional Palladians, more used to the blander colour schemes of previous decades, adhered to the tried and trusted old common colours. In 1771 the conservative William Chambers wrote to a client about the painting of a house in London's Berners Street, stating that 'My intention is to finish the whole in fine stone colour as usual excepting the Eating Parlour which I

Section of the Drawing Room Northumberland house London

Above: *Adam was not afraid to use colour on his walls, as seen in this intricate design for the mirror room at Northumberland House, London. Note the predominance of strong pinks and greens - colours that Adam loved to use.*

Opposite: *an Adam design for the astonishing Etruscan Room at Osterley Park. Etruscan decoration, originating from Central Italy, was vigorously promoted during the 1760s by the Adams and others as the true begetter of all antique design. At Osterley the walls are decorated in the manner of a print room, and the design is punctuated by tablets of nymphs and sporting children and by groups of maidens dancing around tripods. Most of the decoration was executed in the black and terracotta tones of Etruscan pottery.*

propose to finish pea green with white mouldings.'
The previous year he had recommended that stone
colour always be used for 'Parlours if they are for
common use'; alternatively, he permitted combinations of pea green, buff or 'Paris gray' with white.

Such humdrum colour schemes contrasted
sharply with the bright, Neo-Classical hues now
being introduced into domestic interiors by Adam
and his followers. Nowhere were these colours more
vivid and more daring than in the ceilings of Robert
Adam's own great houses. Rich lilacs, pinks and
greens vied for attention with grisaille panels,
plaster cameos or medallions painted with classical
scenes by Kauffmann or Zucchi. These flights of
decorative fancy, it is true, could only be afforded by
the very richest patrons. In practice, most ceilings of
the Adam period were painted white. Yet two
important decorative lessons learned from Adam's
ceilings did permeate down to even the most basic

townhouse and rural cottage: firstly, the application
of delicate white decoration - often in relief - onto a
richly-coloured wall, an effect exploited with
considerable commercial success by Josiah
Wedgwood in his jasperware; and secondly, the
abandonment of much of the heavy gilding which
had been such a notable feature of the formal
Palladian interior of the 1720s, 30s and 40s.

The rich ceilings of Robert Adam's own
interiors were complemented by specially-woven
carpets, specifically designed to match or mimic the
surrounding ornament. And this fashion spread
elsewhere. In 1778, for example, the firm of
Chippendale and Haig confirmed to Sir Edward
Knatchbull that he would be receiving 'a design for
an Axminster Carpet to correspond with your
Ceiling'.

Overall, the carpet was more spectacularly
and comprehensively transformed during this period
than any other decorative item. At the beginning of
the eighteenth century carpets were still rare items,
gracing only the homes of the very rich. Because of
their expense, they were more usually used to cover
tables than floors. With the expansion of Britain's
trading empire after the Treaty of Utrecht of 1713,
however, this situation improved markedly: luxury
carpets became not only more widely available, but
increasingly less expensive.

The first large-scale British carpet factory
had been erected in 1735 in Kidderminster,
Worcestershire; here both pile and flat carpets were
made. By the mid-1750s factories making Turkish-
style knotted carpets were established by Thomas
Moore at Moorfields in London, at Exeter (a brief
venture which soon folded) and, in 1755, by Thomas
Whitty at Axminster in Dorset. Between them these

Opposite: *an Adam ceiling design for a music room from* Works in Architecture, *with characteristically vibrant greens and lilacs.*

This cross-section of a town mansion by John Yenn neatly demonstrates how individual rooms of the period were treated. Here the difference between the decorative treatment afforded the principal entertainment floors (ground and first) and that applied to the more utilitarian second and attic floors is most marked. The masonry colours' colour coding refers to the different materials used: pink for brick, and yellow for timber.

three factories produced nearly all the knotted carpets for Britain and the colonies. (The principal difference between Axminster and Moorfields carpets was that the latter followed the French fashion of making every tenth warp thread a different colour, a practice which made the translation of the original painted designs to the squares of carpet far easier.) English knotted carpets were soon renowned for the quality of their designs, which relied on both Turkish and Persian influences as well as the newly-fashionable Neo-Classical motifs. In 1763 the *Universal Director* commented that Moore had 'brought his Manufactory of English Carpets to such perfection, that it far excels the Persians'.

Knotted carpets were substantially cheaper than their Levantine models; nevertheless, they were still beyond the reach of most households. Far

more affordable were the woven carpets of Wilton and Kidderminster. In 1740 a workshop was set up in Wilton, Wiltshire, at the instigation of the 'Architect Earl', the 9th Earl of Pembroke, to manufacture pile carpets in the manner of the Kidderminster factory. These carpets were woven on looms, the worsted warp being brought to the surface to form a looped pile (the so-called 'Brussels' carpet), which was often subsequently cut to give a velvet-like texture (creating the 'Wilton' carpet). Brussels and Wiltons were not only cheaper than knotted carpets; they were also more versatile. Initially woven in strips up to three feet wide, they were usually provided with small, frequently-recurring patterns which allowed them to be cut to cover all manner of room dimensions.

By the 1760s British-made fitted carpets were more than popular. As early as 1753 William Parratt, complaining that his wife had 'so disguised and altered' their house 'that I hardly knew it again', observed that, although wooden floors had been 'new laid, and in the most expensive manner', every room in the house had been 'completely covered with Wilton carpet'. By this time the new fashion for fitted carpets (carpet strips cut to accommodate the shape of the floor) had made fancy floor parquetry or surface decoration quite redundant. Fitted pile carpets could be cut to fit any shape of room, and could be easily provided with a suitable border. By the mid-1750s even King George II was using them, and business was prospering. In 1769 Lady Shelburne noted that there were an astounding 150 looms in operation at the Wilton factory, and 'to each one of these looms are only one Man & a boy.'

Carpet designs were originally committed to 'point paper' - squared paper much like modern

Anonymous carpet designs in the vein of Adam's work of the 1760s. The use of coloured ornament on a white ground was particularly popular at the time.

Opposite: top right, *Adam paint colours in the long gallery at Syon House, Middlesex. A visitor to the house of 1768 noted the recent application of 'a very faint Sea Green Stucco & also a very faint Bloom colour, which gives an elegance & delicacy I cannot describe'. More recently, architectural historian Gervase Jackson-Stops has judged that 'The present muted pinks and blue-greens, although dirty, give a wonderfully soft tone that may not be so far away from the original'. Top left* and below: *sections of plaster ceiling from the Adams' 20 St James's Square, and a detail* (bottom right) *of a ceiling at Somerset House designed by William Chambers.*

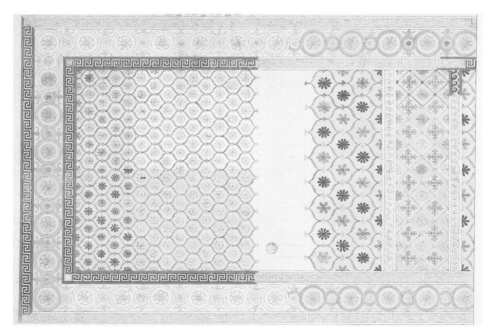

Right: *the red drawing room in Syon House, with a detail of its carpet* (above) *showing the prominent use of the Greek key pattern.*

Opposite: *an Axminster hand-knotted carpet of c.1780, based on an Adam design.*

Below right: *an Adam design for the carpet in the gallery at Syon House.*

graph paper. They were then transferred to equivalent carpet squares. The looms of the mid-eighteenth century produced carpet strips that were 27 or 36 inches wide, and almost any length. In 1758 Benjamin Franklin sent carpet strips (with 'Bordering for the same') from England to his wife in Philadelphia, advising her that they were to be 'sow'd together', with 'care taken to make the Figures meet exactly'. These early designs could rarely, though, employ more than five colours.

Laying fitted carpets was a complicated and labour-intensive process which could take a long time. When, for example, Thomas Chippendale's workmen were fitting carpets at Harewood House in Yorkshire, twelve hours were spent merely 'straining a Carpet for the Dressing Room'. And once installed, their maintenance was by no means trouble-free. Hannah Glasse's *Servant's Directory* of 1760 recommended that, to clean carpets properly, they should be turned over for two days to allow the dirt to fall onto the floor; damp sand should then be strewn over the floorboards, and the resulting mess swept away. Rather more ingenious, and less time-consuming, was the solution proposed in Susanna Whatman's *Housekeeping Book* of 1776: wet tea leaves were to be sprinkled over the carpet surface, then brushed away when dry.

By 1770 needlework carpets, traditionally embroidered by the ladies of the house, were quite out of fashion, probably because the new fad for repetitious Neo-Classical motifs made their working distinctly tedious. However, other types of flat carpet were now being professionally manufactured to take their place. The Kidderminster factory not only produced knotted and pile carpets; the name 'Kidderminster' was also (most confusingly) applied

to a quite different product: the flat, reversible and hard-wearing 'ingrain' carpet. Made by intersecting two webs of cloth - using the same basic principle as that used in the weaving of damask cloth - the back of the ingrain had exactly the same pattern as the front, but with the colours reversed. Popularly regarded as coarse and cheap, ingrains served very well as utilitarian coverings for hallways, servants' rooms and stairs. By 1770 ingrain manufacture was based at two principal centres: at Kidderminster and at Kilmarnock in Scotland, where a factory had been established ten years before. After 1769 the London-based American merchant John Norton was regularly sending 'Kilmarnock carpets' to his clients in the colonies.

Less prestigious even than the useful ingrain carpet were the painted floorcloth and the woven

drugget - a green or brown covering of serge, baize or frieze, designed to protect expensive carpets from excessive wear and tear. Given their susceptibility to the ravages of time, very few Georgian druggets or floorcloths (and indeed few ingrains) survive today. The floorcloth or oilcloth was the direct ancestor of that ubiquitous invention of the 1860s, linoleum. It was made from canvas, which was stretched tight, coated with glue, painted, smoothed with pumice, and then painted again, with up to twelve coats. Sometimes the top surface was patterned; in the 1770s Nathan Smith devised a method of block-printing finished floorcloths in a similar manner to wallpaper, using pearwood blocks. All types of grand floor coverings could be imitated in the design. The most popular was a painted pattern which resembled black-and-white marble or stone blocks. The marbled floorcloth created for the chapel of 1768-72 at Audley End in Essex (and recently re-created by English Heritage) was, according to the bill of 28 November 1772, designed specifically to look like 'Portland and Bremen stone'.

Floorcloths took a long time to dry and to harden, not surprisingly, and for obvious reasons their manufacture was usually confined to the summer months. Thus customers would rarely order one to be specially made - the waiting time would be too long - but instead chose one from those already in stock. British-made floorcloths were frequently exported to America, although there the fashion for stencilled floorboards persisted throughout the whole of the eighteenth century.

Stencilling - now undergoing an enthusiastic revival - was not only commonly used on the floors of American homes, but on the walls, too. Here it enjoyed the status of an important decorative art, a

A fine oriental carpet and traditional green walls dominate this splendidly lively Zoffany portrait of John Pento, Fourteenth Baron Willoughby and Louisa, his wife, of c.1770.

variety of complex and symbolic patterns being executed in rich distemper colours. In Britain, however, it remained a technique employed only in rural areas - at least until 1836, when wallpaper suddenly became more plebian, and stencilling correspondingly more fashionable, following the abolition of the wallpaper tax. Before this, in both countries, wallpapers were still being hand-coloured by 1780. Indeed as the duties imposed on printed wallpapers accumulated, hand-colouring, which avoided any such taxation, became increasingly attractive, especially for poorer households. In 1778 the Paper-Stainers Company was sufficiently alarmed by the spread of hand-colouring of walls that they petitioned Lord North's government to extend the wallpaper tax to wall paintings. Such a measure was, however, clearly unenforceable, and was never enacted.

In the most fashionable urban homes of Britain and America, printed wallpapers had by 1760 supplanted not only hand-painted decoration but also fabric hangings and applied stucco wall ornamentation. And only the great houses of England retained fabric wall hangings. Already in 1725 a French visitor to England noted that 'hangings are little used in London on account of the coal smoke which would ruin them', a situation which was even more true of Britain's towns and cities fifty years later. Middle-class households were tearing down watered silk or damask wall hangings and replacing them with wallpaper - which was not only cheaper, but also more easily hung in, and more appropriate for, smaller rooms.

The father of British wallpaper was John Baptist Jackson. Born in 1701, he visited Paris, Rome and Venice, where he studied the methods of the

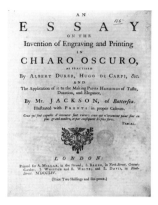

Italian chiaroscuro engravers and produced
woodblock engravings of Old Masters. Returning to
England in 1746, he adapted his new-found
knowledge to the production of wallpaper, then in
its infancy. In 1754 Jackson published the first book
in English to deal with wallpaper: *An Essay on the
Invention of Engraving and Printing in Chiaro
Oscuro*. This was, it is true, largely a thinly disguised
advertisement for the products of his own wallpaper
factory, situated at Battersea:

'It need not be mentioned to any Person of
the least Taste, how much this Way of Finishing
Paper exceeds every other hitherto known; 'tis true,
however, that the gay glaring Colours in broad
Patches of red, green, yellow, blue etc. which are to
pass for flowers and other Objects that delight the
Eye that has no true Judgement belonging to it, are
not to be found in this as in Common Paper.'

Jackson's designs were particularly well-
drawn, and had a great influence on later papers.
Less successful was his pioneering of the use of oil
colours, rather than distemper, in the printing
process. Jackson asserted that his oil colours would
'never fly off' and that 'no water or Damp can have

the least Effect'. Unfortunately, these claims proved
far too optimistic: oil colours were always
unreliable, and never caught on.

By the time of Jackson's death in 1777 most
papers were being printed in distemper colours, a
technique long thought to have been borrowed from
France in the 1760s, but which the great French
wallpaper manufacturer Papillon declared in 1766
had been invented by the English. In 1753 Edward
Dighton had devised a rolling mill to print engraved
black-and-white papers; these copperplate papers
were, however, still hand-coloured. In 1764 Thomas
Fryer, Thomas Greenhough and John Newberry
patented the first cylinder-printing machine, which
could print coloured fabrics as well as coloured
wallpapers. And in 1774 production of papers was
improved still further by the introduction by A. G.
Eckhardt of a device, based on woodblocks, to
transfer designs made on squared paper quickly and
easily to the wallpaper.

By 1760 papers could be found printed with
a wide variety of patterns. Sir William Robinson's
townhouse, fitted up in 1759 by Thomas
Chippendale, included 'sprig stripe, cathedral
gothic, green mock-flock, rose and sprig, and
crimson embossed paper'. Many papers mimicked
stonework or stucco. Particularly popular, too, were
the architectural papers which featured repeated
Neo-Classical niches or Gothic temples. At
Strawberry Hill in the 1750s Horace Walpole hung
rooms with papers imitating Gothic stonework and
Delftware tiles, and even hung one paper which
attempted to mimic the walls of Prince Arthur's
Chantry Chapel in Worcester Cathedral. 'Imagine',
Walpole asked his friend Horace Mann, 'the walls
covered with (I call it paper, but it is really paper

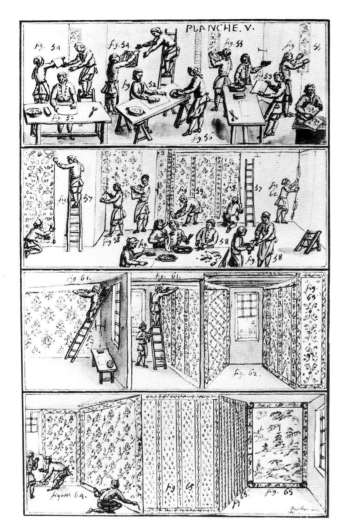

Two cartoons showing the hanging of wallpaper from Diderot and D'Alembert's Encyclopaedia *of 1751-7. This type of documentation, demonstrating exactly how trades were carried out, is extremely rare; there is, for example, nothing comparable in the English language.*

Top right: *'Royal Crescent'
wallpaper design of 1775;*
bottom right: *a flowered
paper, with delicate border;*
right: *a modern copy of the
eighteenth-century stork
design found at Temple
Newsam, Leeds.*

Opposite: *Mid-Georgian
wallpapers.* Top left and
bottom right: *papers from
Doddington Hall,
Lincolnshire;* top right, *an
architectural design of
c.1770 from a house in
Wallbridge, Gloucestershire.*
Bottom left: *an eclectic
architectural paper of 1769
from The Old Manor,
Bourton-on-the-Water,
Gloucestershire.*

Left: *a fragment of wallpaper from Norwood House, Kent, with an architectural design, printed from wood blocks, which is almost certainly based on James Gibbs' Radcliffe Camera in Oxford, completed in 1748.*

painted in perspective to represent) Gothic fretwork.'

Printed architectural forms - columns, pediments, urns and swags - were also used to border and fill the newly popular print rooms, where engraved views, arranged symmetrically on a strongly coloured ground, almost covered the wall above the dado. As early as 1753 Horace Walpole noted of his own home of Strawberry Hill that:

'The room on the ground floor nearest to you is a bedchamber, hung with yellow paper and prints, framed in a new manner by Lord Cardigan, that is with black and white borders printed.' On the floor above, Walpole continued, 'Mr Chute's bedchamber' had been 'hung with red in the same manner.'

The fashion for print rooms became more widespread than ever following the introduction of Neo-Classicism. During the 1760s Thomas Chippendale was called on to fit up large numbers of print rooms for the rich and fashionable; yet even the most modest middle-class home could now indulge in this fad, and its occupants were to be found cutting up popular engravings and pattern-book borders to cover the walls of a small closet or chamber.

Even more popular by 1760 than the creation of the print room was the hanging of flock wallpaper, an enthusiasm not widely shared today. By 1755 flock papers - plain or coloured grounds covered with glued patterns of powdered wool - were hung in the most important rooms of the house. Before the advent of flock, wallpaper had often been regarded as the poor man's wall hanging; now flock papers were often hung in place of fabric hangings. Superior, multicoloured flocks were almost as expensive as the damask silk hangings they replaced. In 1749 Lady Mary Wortley Montagu recorded that 'I have heard the fame of paper hangings and had some thoughts of sending for a suite, but was informed that they are as dear as damask, which put an end to my curiosity.'

English flock papers were exported not only to the colonies, but also (except during the period of the Seven Years War) to France. 'Papiers d'Angleterre', as they were known, were soon the height of fashion. No less an arbiter of taste than Madame de Pompadour, the notorious mistress of Louis XV, had English flocks hung on her walls in the royal palace of Versailles. By 1780, however, when France was once again at war with Britain, the fashion for flock had waned on both sides of the Channel, though not in America.

A further refinement of the flocking process produced 'lustre paper', made by sprinkling powder-paints or powdered glass, rather than wool offcuts, onto a glue pattern. Whereas only the most expensive flocks were printed in more than one colour (Thomas Bromwich of Ludgate Hill in London is known to have printed a number of double-colour flocks for Chippendale), lustre papers could be printed using a variety of colours and

Opposite: *chinoiserie paper of the mid-eighteenth century, one* (left) *from Nostell Priory, the other anonymous.*

textures, and even combined with flocking.

For those who wished for less exotic wallcoverings, papers could also be made with the standard blue, green or grey grounds, and possibly printed with the popular sprig, striped or pin-ground patterns. At Temple Newsam House in 1766 'Green Verditure Paper', 'Fine Pea Green Paper' and 'Green Mock Flock paper' were used to redecorate the rooms. The ubiquitous use of greens, greys and blues prompted derision from the French decorators, who were used to more gaudy patterns. They were not always popular at home, either: Lady Mary Coke complained of the new paper at the White Lodge in Richmond Park that the 'dark blue ground makes the room look dismal.'

Although householders with quite modest means could now take their pick of the cheaper printed papers, those who could afford an ostentatious display of wealth demanded exquisite, hand-painted Chinese papers. These wallpapers, imported in large quantities from China after c.1750 by the East India Company, were (confusingly) often called 'India Papers' after their importer. Chinese designs were non-repeating, and generally featured some exotic combination of birds, fishes, flowers or landscape. All of these elements were delicately arranged with little regard for western conventions of perspective; in 1753 William Parratt noted that 'what adds to the curiosity' of his newly-fitted Chinese paper 'is that the fishes are seen flying in the air, or perhaps perching upon trees.' Chinese papers were so highly prized that, like the tapestry hangings popular in great houses earlier in the century (or indeed like Turkish or Persian carpets today), they were often bought by house-owners rather than supplied by professional decorators.

While Chinese wallpapers were imported into England and America, and English papers exported to France, protective trade barriers ensured that few European papers entered Britain and (at least before 1783) the colonies. In 1773 the official ban on foreign 'painted' papers, originally imposed during the reign of Richard III three centuries before and still in force (although the government had long exempted the East India Company's Chinese trade), was finally repealed. However, a customs duty of eleven shillings and twopence (raised to thirteen shillings and fourpence in 1777, to help pay for the American War) was immediately applied to all foreign papers, again excepting those imported by the East India Company. The duty stamp recording the payment of this tax can help to date foreign papers; from 1778 each sheet of imported wallpaper was stamped twice, once at either end, and from 1786 a 'Duty Charged Remnant' stamp was added. America relied solely on imported English and Chinese papers until 1765, when John Rugar established a wallpaper factory in New York. By 1790 there were wallpaper factories all along the east coast, while French

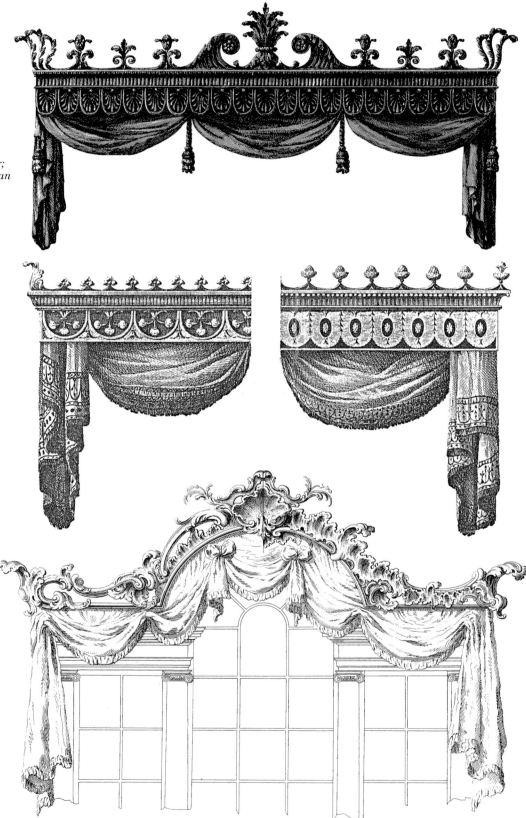

Spectacular designs for curtain cornices. Above right: *design from the Adams' Works of 1773-8;* centre: *designs for Osterley;* below: *design for a Venetian window cornice from Chippendale's* Director.

products - many of them scenic papers of the type unique to France - had supplanted many of the British-made papers in the years following the Declaration of Independence.

As the use of wallpapers increased dramatically during this period, so did the provision of elaborate curtain displays. Simple, straight-hanging curtains, little more than pieces of material tacked above the window-frame, were still in widespread use. More sophisticated versions of this type had valances hiding the tacked tops, and tie-backs to gather the curtain in during the daytime. As the eighteenth century progressed, however, households sought increasingly ostentatious ways of decorating their window frames and excluding the light. Accordingly, curtains that drew up horizontally - in one piece (what we now call a 'festoon' curtain) or in two (now often termed 'drapery curtains') - swiftly became popular, with their ruched swags and bunches impressing the visitor far more than a flat piece of cloth.

By 1760 festoon curtains, like flock wallpapers, represented the height of taste both in Britain and America. In 1765 Benjamin Franklin declared that 'The Fashion is to make one Curtain only for each window,' indicating that the festoon had eclipsed both the two-part pull-up version and draw curtains in popularity. Although festoons probably originated in France, and were accordingly termed 'French curtains' by some, across the Channel they were, confusingly, known as *'rideaux á l'italienne'*. Since festoons were devised to be drawn up vertically in swags, they were accordingly made of light fabrics which could be raised with little effort. The lines which pulled the curtains ran through two vertical rows of brass rings on the back

of the material, over boxwood pulleys hidden behind a pelmet or board, and down - via lead plumbets to help them hang properly - to be fastened near the dado rail.

The basic principle of the festoon curtain was to let the maximum amount of light into the room by gathering the curtain material into the awkward space between the window architrave and below the room's cornice. Unfortunately, this simple idea is one that is often forgotten by professional and amateur decorators today. Festoons are made not only of heavy, bulky materials, but are also allowed to obscure most of the window, even when raised. At times the entire top half of a two-frame sash window can remain unseen behind the folds of plush, frilled fabric. Such arrangements - variously described as 'Austrian blinds', 'ruched blinds' or, more appropriately, 'tart's knickers' - would have horrified the designers of Adam's day.

An alternative to the festoon was its near relation, the two-part drapery curtain. This operated on roughly the same principle as the festoon, the two pieces of material being drawn up vertically towards the outer corners of the window, resulting in heavy swags at both sides. To neaten the effect, raised drapery curtains were often fastened at dado level by large metal cloak pins, which served to prevent the material dangling down towards the floor in an unsightly fashion, while the ends of the operating cords generally culminated in decorative tassels. Textile historian and curtain authority Annabel Westman has found few references to this type of curtain before the 1750s; but in 1758, she notes, Vile and Cobb were fitting up Croome Court in Worcestershire with a 'Green Lutestrong festoone curtain, Slitt up the middle, Lin'd & fring'd

Complete', and by 1767 leading cabinet-makers Thomas Chippendale and John Linnell were both referring to this type of two-part form as 'drapery window curtains'. Johan Zoffany's portrait of Sir Lawrence Dundas, executed in the 1770s, shows a pair of drapery curtains of blue damask.

Even in mid-Georgian Britain, however, fashions came and went with alarming frequency. By 1780 enthusiasm for both the festoon and the drapery curtain was fading fast. The latest vogue was now for 'French draw' or 'French rod' window draperies. In this arrangement a pair of curtains drew not vertically but horizontally, the two pieces of material being attached to a rod above the window architrave (which could itself be hidden by a pelmet) by wooden or brass rings. This easily-operated arrangement is still, of course, very much in use today.

Behind the heavy, outer curtains many households installed a muslin 'sub-curtain'. Its primary function was to keep direct light out of the room during the daytime, and thus to help protect valuable furniture, fabrics and paintings from fading. Originally only imported from India, muslins were spun in Britain after 1779, following the invention of the spinning mule. They were made from very finely spun cotton, and could be of a variety of consistencies, from cambric to dimity; today, however, the term 'muslin' is reserved for what the Georgians would recognize as a plain, gauze-like white cambric.

Blinds - more controllable than shutters, more effective than muslin - were also employed to keep the light out. The first patent for a painted cloth blind had been granted long before, in 1692. Already by 1700 spring-loaded canvas or cloth blinds, often known as 'spring curtains' and nearly always painted green, were widely available. Thomas Chippendale, for example, supplied houses with roller blinds: in 1776 his men worked ten days repairing the blinds' tin barrels in just one house. Few, however, survive today.

Venetian blinds, made from painted deal laths held by cloth tapes, had reached Britain and America by 1760. The name may not have originated from any Venetian provenance, but from the blind's early use to mask the Venetian window, a characteristic three-light opening very popular with the Palladian designers of the first half of the century. Annabel Westman notes that in 1762 Vile and Cobb invoiced Lord Coventry 'For one Italian Blind with a Circular Head to Do for the Venetian Window in your Study, with Silk lines, and Tapes, and a Man's Time fixing'. An advertisement of *c.*1766 bravely extolled the virtues of the Venetian blind, declaring that it 'draws up as a Curtain, obstructs the troublesome Rays of the Sun in hot weather, and greatly preserves the Furniture, prevents being overlooked, & may be taken down or put up in a Minute.' Yet its reliability was often disappointing: while roller blinds were notoriously fragile, these early Venetian blinds proved to be equally faulty, the laths easily becoming dislodged from the tape that held them.

In addition to spring and Venetian blinds, designed to protect the house's furnishings, were blinds or screens which covered only half or part of the window area, and which were specifically intended to avert the gaze of passers-by rather than to filter out the sun's harmful rays. Such 'snob screens', as they were often called, were fixed at the bottom of the window, and were, it seems, also

Modern handwoven silk damasks based on mid-eighteenth century designs create an excellent contrast between the exuberant Rococo of 'Romney' (below), and the more ordered and dense Neo-Classical motifs of 'Mayville' (above).

painted a green colour. When used in combination with shutters, curtains and sub-curtains, such devices easily succeeded in preventing the prying eyes of the curious or envious from glimpsing the interiors of the fashionable. In 1777 one example was famously put to this use by Joseph Surface, in Sheridan's popular play *School for Scandal:*

'Stay, stay; draw that screen before the window - that will do. My opposite neighbour is a maiden lady of so curious a temper.'

As already noted, curtain materials in the Age of Adam tended to be light, to allow for easy operation. Tabby curtains were especially popular. Tabby was a striped silk, with alternate satin and watered stripes, which was often dyed gold. Alternatively, the new chintz cottons or more traditional moreens could be used. Most of these fabrics were lined either with a simple light cotton or with tammy, a light but strong worsted material which, like chintz, could be glazed to make it more resilient and lustrous.

Curtain materials were not the only ones to metamorphose during this period. The whole family of furnishing fabrics was being revolutionized as a direct result of Britain's rapid industrial advance. It was in 1770 that Hargreaves's spinning jenny, allowing eight spindles to be wound at the same time, was patented; nine years later Samuel Crompton's 'mule' (named after the principal power source of the early eighteenth century) combined Hargreaves's invention with Arkwright's rollers in one machine. And after 1781 James Watt's steam engines began to be harnessed to both the mule and the spinning jenny, facilitating faster and less labour-intensive production.

The saving of manual labour inevitably

caused great social unrest in those areas which suffered immediate unemployment. The home of John Kay, the inventor of the flying shuttle, was wrecked by a mob, while James Hargreaves encountered such hatred in his native Lancashire that he felt forced to move to Nottingham. Yet the industrial progress which prompted such bitter ill-feeling did effect lasting changes in the home. As textile historian Mary Schoeser has commented, 'The industrialization of textile manufacture about this time precipitated a substantial change in the furnishing of interiors.' New, lighter cottons and linens could be manufactured faster and more cheaply, than ever before. Printed patterns were now within the reach of everybody, not just the privileged few. Even previously expensive fabrics such as silks were no longer the preserve of the rich. In every type of house traditional fabrics such as velvet - a notoriously heavy dust-collector - were replaced by materials that were both lighter in weight and easily washable, the latter being an important consideration in the dirty, newly-industrialized cities of Britain and America.

The greatest revolution came in the use of cotton cloths. Since 1722 no-one had been permitted to wear printed or dyed calico cotton, or to use it for covering furniture, since its importation from India threatened to undermine the native British industry, which in turn relied increasingly heavily on exports to the American colonies. (This is not to say that Asian cottons were never used: the bed that Chippendale made for Garrick's Thames-side villa, for example, was furnished with illegally-imported Indian chintz.) In 1774, however, this restriction was removed for British cotton calicoes, although the ban on Indian imports persisted. In order to tell

British from Indian cloth, the former was now made with three blue lines running through the warp, a device which makes detection and dating a great deal easier for today's textile scholars.

The immediate result of the 1774 act was that British cottons were in widespread use by 1785 as curtains, bed-hangings, seat upholstery and loose covers. In 1778 Chippendale's firm, furnishing Sir Edward Knatchbull's house in Kent, asked the owner if he was prepared to use a new cotton fabric:

'The chairs can only at present be finished in Linnen [but] We should be glad to know what kind of Covers you would please to have for them. Serge is most commonly used but as the room is hung with India paper, perhaps you might Chuse some sort of Cotton - Suppose a green Stripe Cotton which at this time is fashionable.'

Chintzes were especially popular. Their colourful large-scale flowered patterns, often derived from Chinese silks, could withstand repeated washings without fading. Home-made calicoes, too, with their small-scale patterns, were equally bright and resilient. By 1740 English textile manufacturers had begun to print good multicoloured chintz and calico designs to rival those being imported from India. Much of this production was based in central Lancashire, an area soon to become wholly dependent on cotton goods. A French visitor of 1750 remarked of English cottons that:

'This type of fabric is made in the Manchester district, especially at a small town called Blackburn. The output is so large that scarcely a week goes by without a thousand rolls [bolts 30 yards long] being sold and sent to London unbleached.'

Rare mid- and late eighteenth-century fabric designs, striking in the elaborate use of naturalistic motifs. Top right is a plate-printed cotton with a design based on a Gainsborough painting of 1783. Below it is a copperplate fabric designed in 1766 by William Chambers, and featuring his famous Kew Gardens Pagoda of the previous decade.

A somewhat comically patriotic plate-printed cotton dating from 1785 and entitled: Apotheosis of Benjamin Franklin and George Washington.

The Frenchman relished the irony of English chintzes being subsequently and successfully sold in France as Indian chintz, 'because of the special finish they are given and also because the purchasers of this type of English goods have but slight knowledge of them'.

By 1778 block-printed cottons were prevalent on both sides of the Atlantic. In many houses they were substituted for traditional silk or worsted damasks as upholstery for seat furniture. In 1759 George Washington showed he was very much in tune with contemporary furnishing fashions by ordering from London 'a Tester Bedstead', from whose cornice was hung 'Chintz Blew Plate Cotton furniture' designed to match the wallpaper sample he had sent with the order.

At the time Washington made this order, and for the next twenty years, America remained entirely reliant on Britain for sophisticated textiles, as it was to be for nearly every element which went to furnish the fashionable house. This dependency only began to be broken after the conclusion of the War of Independence in 1783; even then, the American writer Tench Coxe noted in 1794, 'we manufactured less at that time than any other nation in the world,' and necessarily remained 'the first customer for British manufactures'. Some attempts were,

however, made to establish a native textile industry before the end of the war. Clearly the most determined of these pioneers was the textile printer John Hewson, who, as Florence Montgomery relates, packed up his Philadelphia factory in 1777 in the face of the advancing British, was captured, and, escaping in 1779, set up a new calico printing works despite the fact that 'the savage foe of Britain' had 'made such a destruction of their works and materials.'

One of the most striking and most famous of the new printed cottons of Adam's day - and one which is still extremely popular today - was the single-colour printed fabric known as 'Toiles de Jouy'. Copperplate printing of fabrics was first attempted in 1752 in Drumcondra, Ireland. An advertisement of 3rd October 1752 in *Faulkner's Journal* featured 'Drumcondra printed linens, done from metal plates (a method never before practised) with all the advantages of light and shade, in the strongest and most lasting form'; two months later the Irish diarist Mrs Delaney went to see the new cottons and thought them 'excessively pretty.'

Drumcondra closed in 1757, but by then copperplate printing had been firmly established in Britain. By 1760 factories had been started south of London at Merton, and in east London at Bromley (by Talwin and Foster) and Old Ford (by Robert Jones). In response to this, the French lifted their ban on the metal-plate printing of textiles, originally imposed in 1686. Copperplate textiles - 'toiles' - were soon being printed all over France, but it was the factory established in 1760 at Jouy en Josas, outside Paris, which became most famous. It is after this factory (run not by a Frenchman but by a Swiss, Christophe-Philippe Oberkampf) that all single-

Left: *Two designs by Ince & Mayhew dating from 1762, showing the elaborate use of drapery on a field bed (far left) and a sofa bed.*

Above: *the Blackwell-Stamper Room at the Winterthur Museum. The window curtains and slipcover, of 1770-80, are plate-printed in black. The mahogany side chair is* attributed to Benjamin Randolph of Philadelphia, and probably dates from 1760-75.

Above left: *a Massachussetts bed covered with copperplate fabric, printed by Francis Nixon, featuring a design of arborescent stems with melon and flowers.*

colour printed cottons of the type, whether English, American or French, have since been named.

Before the 1750s textile printing was done with pearwood or sycamore blocks, in the same manner as wallpapers were printed. Dots at the corners of each block pattern served as registration marks for placing the next block by hand. The new copper plates were far larger than these wood blocks, being generally about a yard square. The toiles they printed were only of one colour; it was not until the later 1780s that two- or three-colour printing became possible. The colour chosen was usually red (obtained from the dye produced by the madder plant), but could be black, blue, purple or even yellow. In 1765 Richard Baucher of New York advertised 'red, blue and purple copperplate furniture, calicoes and chintz', recently imported from London. The patterns printed in these colours were naturalistic scenes, often landscapes, much in the vein of hand-painted Chinese wallpapers. And following the introduction of printing by copper rollers by Thomas Bell in 1783, the way was open to yet more sophisticated scenes and, ultimately, to multicolour printing, a technique still much in vogue today.

Cottons were not the only fabrics to be liberated by the industrial revolution. As expensive tapestry and needlework hangings and coverings became less popular, strong and durable linens were far more widely used than they had been in previous decades - for upholstery, curtains, sheets, tablecloths and especially for loose covers.

By 1785 furnishing fabrics such as linens, cottons and silks were increasingly being coord-inated with the rest of the room, a novel doctrine which took some time to gain wide acceptance. In 1758 Benjamin Franklin, then resident in London, told his wife that he had bought '56 yards of cotton printed curiously from copper plate, a new invention, to make bed and window curtains' and also 7 yards of the same pattern for 'chair bottoms'. 'These were my fancy', he explained, 'but Mrs Stevenson tells me I did wrong not to buy both of the same colour'. A year later George Washington's copperplate bed-hangings were, in contrast, expressly designed to match the colour and pattern of the wallpaper, the festoon curtains and the bed coverlet, in order to make the bedroom 'uniformly handsome and genteel'. By 1765 Franklin had learned his lesson and was ordering, through his son, 'three curtains of Yellow Silk and Worsted Damask' to match chairs covered in yellow damask. By the mid-1770s co-ordinated interiors could be seen in many of the fashionable urban centres of Britain and America. In 1774, when Lloyd Kenyon moved into his modest London townhouse in Lincoln's Inn Fields, his wife described the planned interiors in great detail to her mother. And all was matching: the dining room was to be hung with 'blue, small-patterned flock', the back room with blue flock paper and 'blue moreen curtains', and the white-painted bedroom was to be dominated by a 'blue moreen bed'. In the same year Mrs Delaney visited the grand mansion of Luton Hoo in Bedfordshire, and observed that all the rooms were 'hung with plain paper, suited to the colour of the beds', while at the same time Thomas Chippendale was providing for Paxton House '16 pieces of fine Chintz paper for the Bedchamber and Closet, the pattern made on purpose to match the Cotton'. The modern age of harmonious interior decoration had truly begun.

A bold English design for woven silk, with sprays of flowers and leaves, dating from 1765-75.

'. . . quick, quick - fling *Peregrine Pickle* under the toilet - throw *Roderick Random* into the closet - put *The Innocent Adultery* into *The Whole Duty of Man* - thrust *Lord Aimworth* under the sofa - cram Ovid behind the bolster . . . and leave Fordyce's *Sermons* open upon the table'

(R.B. Sheridan,
The Rivals, *1775)*

Opposite: *an array of Adam Style furniture, including shield-back chair, from a drawing room in Baltimore, Maryland.* Right: *a 'Design for a China Case' from* Chippendale's Director.

By the mid-eighteenth century English and American furniture could be found in a bewildering array of exotic styles. Gone were the heavy swags and high-relief carving of the Palladians; in their stead flowered Rococo and Chinese, Gothick and Classical.

The indiscipline of the French-derived Rococo ultimately failed to win the hearts of the serious British - a race which historically had always eschewed decorative exuberance in favour of linear and more obviously architectural forms. As Christopher Gilbert has noted, in Britain (and in the colonies) the Rococo was 'little more than a passing fashion which flourished within the orderly framework of Palladian interiors'. Far more pleasing to eyes more accustomed to straight lines and evident structural relevance was the fashion for "Chinese' furniture - a fad which was ignited by the popular passion for imported Chinese ceramics, textiles and wallpapers. By the mid-1750s 'Chinese' chairs and tables with diagonal fretwork, and 'Chinese' beds with their pagoda-like testers, could be found in many fashionable homes. Few of these pieces, however, bore much resemblance to real Chinese designs. In 1757 William Chambers's *Designs of Chinese Buildings,* which included numerous plates depicting items of furniture, attempted to correct this imbalance by providing a series of 'genuine' oriental designs; however, Chambers's pieces were still little more than vague approximations of the real thing. Nevertheless, what Mary Wortley Montagu had in 1749 termed 'the barbarous *goût* of the Chinese' outlived the taste for Rococo, surviving well into the 1760s.

'Gothick' furniture also survived into the Neo-Classical era; in the mid-1770s even

Chippendale was still producing chairs with 'Gothic window' splats at the centre of their backs. As with the fashion for Chinese, though, the academic origins of 'Gothic' pieces were often spurious. Rightly did Matthew Bramble in Smollett's *Humphry Clinker* (published in 1771) exclaim that contemporary designers 'who have adopted this stile, don't seem to have considered the propriety of their adoption'. Such strictures had not, however, deterred patrons such as the tireless Horace Walpole from filling their small-scale domestic interiors with fittings derived from the nation's greatest ecclesiastical monuments.

By the mid-1760s all this had changed. Rococo and Chinese - and to a large extent Gothick - were banished from fashionable, interiors, and replaced by expressions of the new, delicate Neo-Classical taste. Out went elaborate scrolls and rich friezes, serpentine curves and over-bowed fronts; out went pagodas and fretwork. In their place came squared corners, right angles, low-relief carving, regimented hierarchies and sedate, architecturally-derived forms and motifs.

A departure from the norm. Chippendale designs for Chinese chairs, from the Director.

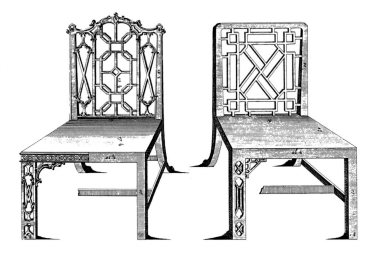

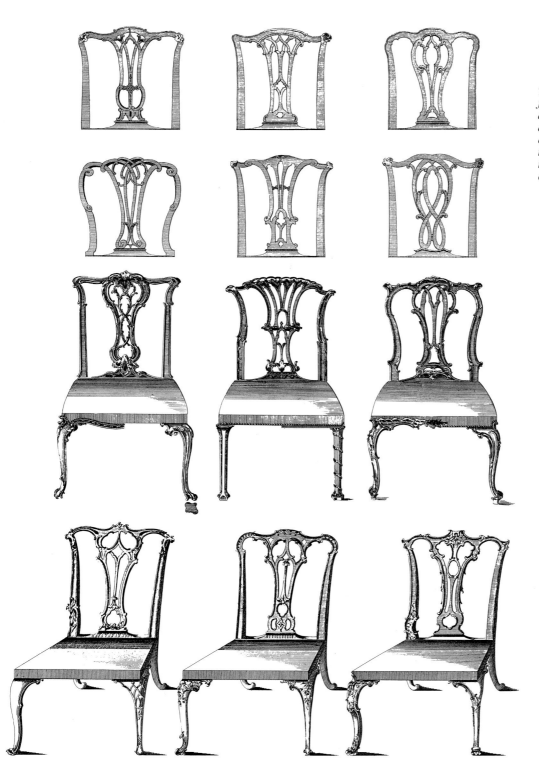

These alternative designs from Chippendale's Director *demonstrate how inventive and graceful Chippendale could be. Here he transforms the established splat-back into a variety of sinuous, organic forms.*

Opposite: *oval forms
dominate this engaging
cartoon of* 'Frederick
elegantly furnishing a new
house' *of c.1785. The oval-
backed chairs incorporate
the Prince of Wales's
monogram of three feathers.*

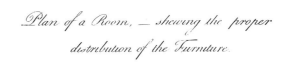

Plan of a room, from
Hepplewhite's Cabinet-
Maker and Upholsterer's
Guide *of 1788, 'showing the
proper distribution of the
Furniture'. Hepplewhite
himself had actually died in
1786, so this design
probably dates from the
early 1780s. The formal,
rigid symmetry of every wall
is a far cry from the
haphazard clutter of the
nineteenth century and the
studied informality of the
twentieth.*

Some designers were, by the fact of their youth and enthusiasm, well-placed to make the transition from the florid exotica of the 1750s to the more disciplined classicism of the 1760s. Other, more conservative figures were not. One of the older cabinet-makers who fell by the wayside was the renowned William Vile, who continued making the carved mahogany furniture with which he had made his name. Faced with the radical new Neo-Classicism of Stuart and Revett's plates and Adam's buildings, Vile decided to retire in 1764. His young partner, John Cobb, however, responded very differently. Cobb used imported woods such as tulipwood and kingwood, together with stained native fruitwoods, to create fabulous, distinctly Neo-Classical marquetry tables and cabinets. Cobb was a larger-than-life figure. Contemporaries noted his 'singularly haughty character' and called him 'one of the proudest men in England'; in 1829 J. T. Smith recollected how Cobb, 'in full dress of the most superb kind, strutted through his workshops giving orders to his men'. In 1772 Cobb was implicated in the smuggling of furniture from France in the diplomatic bags of the Venetian Resident and the Neapolitan Minister, although the charges were dropped. Yet throughout all this he remained a superb furniture designer.

The cabinet-maker who coped best with the arrival of Neo-Classicism was the incomparable Thomas Chippendale. His *Gentleman and Cabinet-Maker's Director* of 1754 was the first English-language pattern-book to deal with furniture alone, the 161 plates portraying a vast range of everyday household items. As befitted the time, the 1754 edition was permeated by the Rococo, Gothick and Chinese tastes. When the third edition was completed in 1762, however, many of the Rococo designs had been abandoned in favour of Neo-Classically-influenced pieces. The replacement plates illustrated items of furniture that were lighter, more linear and, most importantly, simpler than their predecessors. In place of the Rococo's foliate fripperies and serpentine extravagances, Chippendale substituted hard lines and graceful modulations.

Chippendale - since called 'the Shakespeare of English furniture-makers' - was born in Otley, Yorkshire in 1718. Moving first to York, then to London, in December 1753 he set up shop in the heart of London's fashionable West End, in St Martin's Lane, with his partner James Rannie. The following April disaster almost struck. A fire broke out in the workshops which, reported the *Public Advertiser,* 'in its beginning, the Wind being very high, and a great scarcity of Water, raged very furiously', especially since 'there was a great Quantity of Timber on the Premises'. These were violent times, and the fire attracted an unruly mob bent on looting the premises; however, help was at hand: 'by the timely Assistance of the Guards and the Peace Officers, the useless Part of the

Mob was beat off … and the flames were subdued.'

Following the success of the first and second editions of the *Director,* Chippendale was elected to the prestigious Society of Arts in 1760. Six years later, on Rannie's death, he entered into a partnership with the accountant Thomas Haig and later (in order to secure more reliable financial backing) with Henry Ferguson. Despite his evident success, however, Chippendale never enjoyed the social status of other masters of the visual arts such as Adam and Reynolds, and always regarded himself as a tradesman. He was, nevertheless, well aware of his genius. Gilbert relates how he called one of his own cabinets 'not only the richest and most magnificent in the whole, but perhaps all Europe' and three of his chairs 'the best I have ever seen (or perhaps have ever been made)'.

Like Adam and Wedgwood, Chippendale was greatly fêted by his contemporaries as well as by modern-day critics - a distinction enjoyed by few great artists. His significance, like that of Adam and Wedgwood, derived not only from his proficiency as a craftsman but, perhaps more importantly, from his enthusiasm and aptitude for self-promotion. To attract passers-by to his London shop, for example, he hung a chair from the shopfront. Following his move to St Martin's Lane and the publication in 1754 of the *Director* (which his biographer, furniture historian Christopher Gilbert, judged 'a provocative publicity stunt'), Chippendale actually made no furniture himself, relying on his team of up to fifty specialist craftsmen; his achievement over the next thirty years was in the fields of design and marketing. He was so successful that not long after his death the label 'Chippendale' was being used to denote any furniture copied or derived from the

Top: *The Princess Royal's Sitting Room at Harewood showing the large commode designed by Chippendale in 1773.* Above: *the intricate marquetry is clearly seen in this detail of the top of the commode, while the detail* opposite *shows delicate ivory inlay on a satinwood ground.*

Opposite: *the metamorphic library steps, designed by Adam and executed by Chippendale, from Harewood.*

Above: *a delightful gentleman's library, with a charming, glazed bookcase from an engraving of the 1780s.*

plates of the three editions of the *Director* - whether they actually originated from Chippendale's workshops or not. Many cabinet-makers bought the *Director* specifically in order to copy Chippendale's engravings. Today, the only way of demonstrating the true provenance of a supposedly 'Chippendale' piece is to produce some corroborating documentary evidence; style alone is not enough.

Chippendale's influence on his contemporaries, and on subsequent generations, was enormous. Christopher Gilbert has declared that 'It would be difficult to exaggerate the importance of Chippendale's *Director* as a formative influence on mid-eighteenth century furniture style'; certainly its appearance triggered a whole rash of rival furniture pattern-books. The *Director's* third edition, as well as gracing the libraries of the American colonies, was also translated into French, and bought by both Louis XVI and Catherine the Great. Much of the so-called 'Louis Seize' furniture popular in France in the 1770s and 80s was directly derived from Chippendale's plates.

Robert Adam - notoriously fussy and particular about his creations - trusted Chippendale to furnish some of his finest Neo-Classical interiors - the cabinet-maker using his own designs and not, as is often believed, those of Adam. Indeed the collaboration between Thomas Chippendale and Robert Adam was of particular importance in establishing what is now known as 'Adam Style'. In Christopher Gilbert's view it was Chippendale, and not Adam, who retained the original vision of robust Neo-Classicism into the 1770s. Adam, he believes, became enraptured and sidetracked by 'ever-increasing refinement expressed as exaggerated delicacy' and was by 1780 producing what were almost caricatures of his own, original style. Adam, Gilbert judges, 'was primarily a gifted decorator whose prim designs looked very effective on paper but insipid and fussy when translated on the work-bench'.

While it is a myth that all 'Chippendale' designs of the later eighteenth century were actually made in Chippendale's workshops, it is also untrue to say that those pieces which can be definitely assigned to the St Martin's Lane firm were entirely made by Chippendale's craftsmen. Chippendale contracted out many specialized processes, such as gilding, brass work and even marquetry work, to other firms - although ensuring that the contracted work was always done to his exact specifications. Today it is difficult, even impossible, to determine which parts of a particular piece were contracted out, and which elements were made in-house.

It is also a mistake to imagine that a firm such as Chippendale's was engaged only in furniture-making. As early as 1747 an upholsterer was described as a 'Tradesman's Genius' who 'must be universal in every Branch of Furniture'. Chippendale, in the words of Geoffrey Beard and Christopher Gilbert, could offer his clients not only exquisite single pieces of furniture but also:

'a complete house furnishing service, supplying everything from the most opulent beds, mirrors and cabinets to cheap domestic wares for the staff quarters. The firm regularly provided curtains, carpets, wallpapers, chimney-pieces, loose covers and bell systems; undertook repairs, removals, hired out furniture, and were even prepared to direct and furnish funerals for respected customers.'

William Reid, a craftsman of Chippendale's

employed at Harewood House during the 1770s, was required to hang wallpapers, upholster seat furniture, make up the beds, create furniture covers, and even make the floorcloths. Interestingly, Chippendale's furniture-making commissions were less profitable than his upholstering business.

When involved in furniture-making, Chippendale or his rivals could be commissioned to create a wide variety of different pieces. Beds could range from the elaborate 'state' tester beds, destined for the bedrooms of the most opulent households, to the simple, pulley-operated servants' beds which descended from the attic wall. The former could be as ostentatious as the client wished. In 1778 Horace Walpole criticised (with some justification) Robert Adam's lavish state bed at Osterley Park for being 'too theatric and too like a modern head-dress'; 'What would Vitruvius think', he added, 'of a dome decorated by a milliner?' At the other end of the social scale to the apartments at Osterley was the typical bedroom described in a survey of 1767 on cheap rented lodgings in London:

'a half-tester bedstead, with brown linsey woolsey furniture, a bed and bolster, half flocks, half feathers ... two old chairs with cane bottoms, a small looking glass six inches by four in a deal frame painted red and black, a red linsey woolsey window curtain ... [and] an iron candlestick mounted with brass'.

Half-testers, such as the example described above, could be pulled up against the wall during the day and hidden behind a curtain or a dummy bookcase. (Chippendale created a half-tester bed for Sir Edward Knatchbull which fronted as a dummy japanned bookcase, complete with wire lattice and dummy book spines.) In grander homes by the late

Adam's stunning design of 1776 for the State Bed at Osterley.

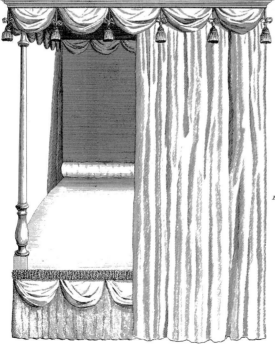

Opposite: *this elegant four-poster bed dominates the east bedroom at Harewood.* Near left: *an equally elegant and ostentatious bed of 1775 from Garrick's villa at Hampton, and designs for classical beds and bed cornices of the mid-1780s by Hepplewhite* (far left and above).

Far left and left: *general view and detail of this splendid and typical Neo-Classical cabinet of 1765. Above: even more impressive is the marvellous inlay work visible in this detail of the celebrated Chippendale library writing table of 1770, originally made for Harewood but now in the Edwardian Library at Temple Newsam, Leeds. This is marquetry at its most sophisticated and effective.*

1770s, though, 'French' canopy beds, with the canopy and draperies suspended from the ceiling rather than being supported on corner posts, were becoming more popular than the traditional four-poster or its more recent tester derivatives. Unlike the French, the British and Americans preferred bold, architectural bed cornices, eschewing the current French fashion for complex valances and elaborate bed drapery.

George Hepplewhite noted, in his *Cabinet-maker and Upholsterer's Guide,* published in 1788, that beds could be 'executed in almost every stuff which the loom produces': 'White dimity, plain and corded, is peculiarly applicable [and] produces an elegance and neatness truly agreeable.' In wealthier homes bedclothes were 'frequently made of silk or satin, figured or plain, also of velvet and gold fringe'. Blankets, cut from an original woven piece that weighed up to 100 pounds, were generally plain, but often decorated in each of the four corners. The centre for blanket-making in England, then as now, was Witney in Oxfordshire. Earlys was the leading manufacturer in Witney, and their 'rose' blankets, with corner decoration embroidered in rough, hand-spun wool, were very popular in Britain and America by the mid-eighteenth century. In 1768, for example, the American merchant John Norton was sending a valued colonial customer '3 pr best and finest double mill'd rose large Bed Blankets' from Witney via London. Beds additionally carried up to five quilts - the small bedroom fireplaces of the day being of minimal use in heating the room. Often made by the women of the house, some of these quilts would be placed over the sleeper, some underneath. On top of the quilts might be a richly decorated, hand-made counterpane; such precious

items of great sentimental value were in turn protected by a white coverlet, often made of a rough linen and wool fabric called 'darnix'.

This multitude of bedding layers was augmented by bed curtains, whose purpose was not, as is often thought, to guarantee the sleeper's privacy, but to retain heat and, more importantly, to protect valuable counterpanes from direct light from the windows.

As the period progressed bedclothes and bed hangings, in common with window curtains, became increasingly lighter, cottons and linens being preferred to the heavier traditional materials. The Indian chintzes smuggled in to adorn the bedrooms of the wealthy and fashionable were particularly prized. In 1771 Mrs Lybbe Powys noted enviously of her Shropshire neighbour that the latter had 'more chintz counterpanes than in one house I ever saw, not one bed without very fine ones'.

More important than the manufacture of beds to any self-respecting cabinet-maker was the production of chairs. Thomas Chippendale was especially renowned for his seat furniture - principally chairs, couches and the odd settee (in

Hepplewhite designs for simple, bow-fronted chests of drawers and a dressing glass of the mid-1780s. This type of basic yet elegant classical furniture remained popular throughout the nineteenth and twentieth centuries.

origin an extended, multi-seat chair). A typical Chippendale chair design, much imitated by his contemporaries and successors, was the five-piece splat-back, with straight front legs, slightly curving back legs and a Neo-Classical swag linking the central splat to the top rail. Robert Adam's own seat furniture was, predictably, even more architectural than Chippendale's later designs. Adam was the first to use the lyre motif for chair backs - a fashion which spread like wildfire - and often painted his chairs to match the painted decoration of the room. (Painted furniture was particularly common during this period; all too often today, alas, painted items are stripped to satisfy the ahistorical demand for 'honest', bare wooden furniture.) By 1780 heart-back and shield-back chairs were also much in vogue - as were more unusual hybrids such as the 'exercising chair', whose sprung leather seat, operated rather like a concertina, provided the sitter with what was alleged to be a good substitute for horse-riding.

Most seat furniture was upholstered; caned chairs had been out of fashion in both Britain and America since the 1720s. Cottons and linens were being widely used for seat upholstery as well as for hangings by 1770. As mentioned earlier, great care was taken to match them with the fabric, wallpapers and paints on the walls. In Strawberry Hill's Breakfast Room, for example, Horace Walpole installed 'plump chairs, couches and luxurious settees, covered with linen of the same pattern' as the blue-and-white striped wallpaper. Those who could afford it were by 1780 covering their chairs with the same type of French tapestry as they were using for wall hangings. These pieces were specially woven to fit the size of the chair, and were used not only for seat furniture but also to cover matching

pole firescreens. In 1771 Walpole bought a settee, four chairs and a matching firescreen, all covered with highly expensive Aubusson tapestries, for the typically extravagant outlay of £104 12s 6d.

With the advent of Neo-Classical taste, the ample, bulging upholstery of previous decades was replaced by squared stuffing, to match the new squared legs and squared backs. Chairs were generally stuffed with down, or with cheaper alternatives such as tow or horsehair, which was also increasingly used for the seat-covering fabric itself. To keep the stuffing properly squared English upholsterers stitched the corners, and secured large areas of stuffing with tufts that also pierced the cover at the front. Tufting was quickly adopted by the American colonists; surprisingly, though, the innovative French only caught on to this practice in the later 1770s. To help preserve the squared shape, and to provide additional emphasis for the seat's straight, architectural lines, British and American upholsterers also used gilt or brass nails to help fix and protect the upholstered corners, often arranging the lines of nail heads in attractive geometric patterns.

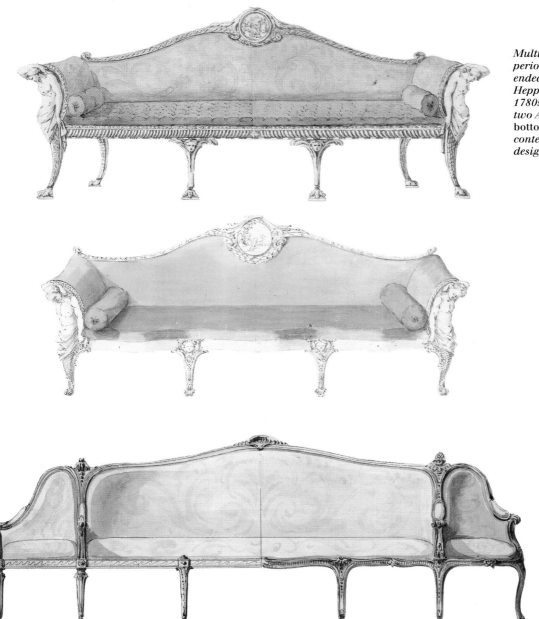

Multi-seat furniture of the period. Opposite: *a two-ended 'Duchesse' sofa by Hepplewhite, of the mid-1780s.* Top left and centre: *two Adam sofa designs;* bottom: *a roughly contemporary John Linnell design for a couch.*

Hepplewhite designs for chairs, published in his Cabinet-Maker and Upholsterer's Guide of 1788. The shield-back chair is particularly associated with Hepplewhite, and has remained exceedingly popular. Bottom left can be seen his designs for an easy chair and a 'gouty stool'.

A collection of chair designs:
Far left: *an elegant, painted
beechwood chair designed
by Chippendale for
Harewood House, Yorkshire;*
centre: *a library chair by
Chippendale from Nostell
Priory;* left: *Adam-designed
painted armchair from the
Etruscan Room at Osterley;*
below left: *a comfortable,
curved-back bergère of
beechwood and leather,
dated c.1765;* below far left:
*a lyre-splat armchair from
Osterley by John Linnell.*

The longer-established French armchair had by the 1760s become a perennial favourite across the Channel. With their curving backs and arms, and well-upholstered backs - with added squab cushions providing even greater comfort - armchairs were by now of central importance in any fashionable library or drawing room. While the new squared chairs may have reflected the up-to-date taste of the owner, the armchair offered a haven of comfort and ease in which the master or mistress of the house could forget the cares of politics, society or fashion.

An equally popular form of seat furniture - but one that needed no upholstery at all - was the Windsor chair. These chairs were entirely of wood (beech for the legs, sticks, splats and stretchers, elm for the seat), and were characterized by having their back and legs fixed independently into the seat. Windsor chairs were made principally in and around High Wycombe in Buckinghamshire, using the local labour of the itinerant 'chair bodgers' of the Chiltern woods to fashion the sticks, spindles and legs prior to assembly in the factories of Wycombe. They were probably named after the nearby royal seat of Windsor, rather than after Wycombe, either as a cunning marketing ploy, or because they were sent down the Thames to the capital via Windsor. Invented during the 1720s, these simple and highly durable utilitarian chairs could be found in a variety of forms: high, straight comb-backs; the more typical bowed backs; simple scrolled backs; or with turned spindles or a central splat, instead of the usual straight sticks, to support the back. This eminently practical piece of what is now (often erroneously) termed 'country furniture' is as popular today as it was in Adam's time. Windsor chairs have proved especially popular in America, where they were originally welcomed by the pragmatic colonists. After *c.*1750 an American variant called the 'Philadelphia Low-Back Windsor' was much in vogue in the colonies for about thirty years; this in turn provided the inspiration for the 'Smoker's Bow' Windsor chairs which dominated the smoking rooms, gentlemen's clubs and respectable bars from the middle of the nineteenth century until the Second World War - and which today are shamelessly plagiarized to create the sub-standard reproductions so often seen in refurbished pubs, bars and restaurants.

The average table of Adam's day was rarely as sophisticated as the corresponding seat furniture. In his grand room schemes Adam introduced semicircular or segmental pier tables between the large, architectural mirrors. These small tables were very much subservient to the wall decoration, their narrow profiles being reduced to little more than a subtle extension of the frieze or dado. More

Opposite: *Adam Style chair and sofa in the Yellow Drawing Room at Harewood.* Left: *Chippendale designs for brass furniture handles.*

Top: *Four Hepplewhite designs for pier table-tops;* bottom: *an excellent, Chippendale sycamore and marquetry pier table-top, orginally from Mersham-le-Hatch in Kent. Such table-tops formed an oval when reflected in an accompanying pier-glass.*

substantial than these were the marquetry-top tables which were all the rage in the homes of the wealthy and ostentatiously fashion-conscious by 1770. Their delicate but rigidly regulated, multicoloured patterns epitomized the triumph of Neo-Classical order over Rococo indiscipline. For those with more modest incomes, the comparatively plain Pembroke table, with its two side flaps, was still a popular and practical alternative, being both versatile and space-saving.

Tables of this period were always required to be returned to a position against the wall after use; it was only during the Regency era that the new trend to informality liberated both tables and seat furniture from this formal requirement. During the 1760s, however, Adam invented what was to prove a highly popular variant of the table, the sideboard, which fitted snugly against the wall while at the same time offering a wealth of functions. The sideboard swiftly became an integral part of the larger drawing or dining room, being adaptable to a wide variety of uses and providing a large surface from which to serve food or on which to display family treasures.

By 1755 the French term 'commode' was being used by English-speakers to denote a grand chest of drawers. In Britain and America this usually signified a serpentine- or bow-fronted piece, generally equipped with two doors which concealed the drawers, and which was, at least by 1770, often japanned. 'Commodes' were for the principal rooms; their humble ancestor, the chest of drawers, was still used in the bedrooms and the servants' quarters, where it was relegated to a variety of mundane purposes. Such chests were often fitted with a movable top, equipped with a mirror, or

Top right and above: *two giltwood side tables, one by Robert Adam* (top) *and, the other of c.1775, attributed to Adam's design and Chippendale's execution.* Left, top and bottom: *Adam side table designs from the* Works in Architecture *of 1773-8.*

provided with a folding easel. By 1780, too, another French invention - the cylinder-front or roll-top 'bureau' writing-desk - was becoming common in Britain. Hepplewhite's widely-read pattern-book of 1788 (actually devised in the years before before his death in 1786) included plates illustrating both forms of bureaux.

The Age of Adam was an era of great innovation in furniture design. With his *Director* of 1754 Chippendale established the fashion, persisting to this day, for octagonally- or gothic-glazed bookcases. And glass was increasingly introduced into fashionable interiors not only in glazed bookcases but also in the form of ever larger mirrors. The mirrors of Adam's day were no longer the sinuous, gilt Rococo confections of the 1750s; by 1770 they were not only of a greater size than before, but were now strictly rectangular compositions bordered by reticent, architectural frames. Mirror glass was ground from the finest quality Crown glass, and the frames gilded, decorated with ormolu, stained 'mahogany' colour or japanned.

Japanned work was vastly popular by 1780. Christopher Gilbert has determined that there was 'little evidence of a demand in England for japanned wares' prior to the mid-1750s; yet by the time Robert Adam returned to England in 1758 the technique of applying lustrous coloured lacquers to woodwork or metalwork had been comprehensively revived. In that same year Robert Dossie's pioneering decorating manual, *Handmaid to the Arts,* observed that 'The knowledge of the methods of japanning is at present more wanted than that of any other of the mysterious arts whatever.'

One crucially important aspect of the

Georgian interior that is often forgotten today is that every type of valuable furnishing was provided with its own cover, which stayed on for all but the most significant social occasions. Nowadays, of course, the army of servants which applied and maintained these loose covers no longer exists; the result has been the rapid and irreversible fading of countless historic woods and fabrics. Cottons were especially popular as loose covers, since they were light and could be easily washed. In America checked cottons - ginghams - were most often used for this purpose. And on both sides of the Atlantic linens with damasked or repeating patterns were increasingly used to cover vulnerable table-tops - the origin of the modern linen tablecloth. Chairs, couches and settees even began to be provided with 'scarves' for

An inlaid Pembroke table of c.1780. The oval top is a sliding panel fitted with a chess board on the reverse.

Far left and left:
Hepplewhite designs for two bookcases, and for glazed bookcase doors. Bottom right: *a splendid bookcase, with Gothic-glazed doors, and a painted panel in the manner of Angelica Kauffmann, dated c.1790.*

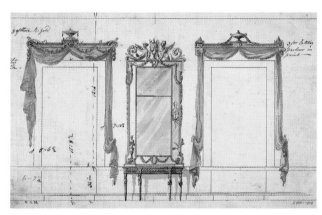

Opposite: *designs for a variety of furniture pieces, from the second edition of* Thomas Malton's A Compleat Treatise on Perspective *of 1778.*

Mirrors played an important part in Adam Style interiors. Top left: *a well-balanced design by John Linnell for two window-chests either side of* a large oval mirror and commode: top centre: *an Adam design for an oval mirror with two-branched candleholders:* top right: *a Chippendale design for an overmantel mirror of the late 1760s:* above: *a Linnell design for a tall pier-glass and side table; and* right: *an Adam design of 1778 for a mirror and commode.*

their upholstered backs. These primitive antimacassars, a form of cover that is usually associated with the Victorian era, were meant to protect the fabric from the detrimental effects not of hair oil but of hair powder, and in particular the grease used to anchor the powder to the wig. (This use of animal grease was the cause of most of the insects and vermin which infested the elaborate wigs of the day.)

Another rule followed by every interior of this period - but not, sadly, adhered to by many museum-houses today - was that all furniture, even if in regular use, was always formally arranged along the side walls. Items were only brought out when needed, and were returned to their original location (by servants, if they were available) at the end of the day. In 1759 the celebrated philosopher and economist Adam Smith testified to this practice, and provided it with a typically reasoned apologia, in his book *The Theory of Moral Sentiments*:

'When a person comes into his chamber and finds the chairs all standing in the middle of the room, he is angry with his servant, and rather than see them continue in that disorder, perhaps takes the trouble himself to set them all in their places with their backs to the wall. The whole propriety of this new situation arises from its superior conveniency in leaving the floor free and disengaged.'

This formal disposition of the room's furniture - which only began to be relaxed during the last decade of the century - was the reason why the top rail of so many chairs and tables matched the patterning of the dado, against which they would stand when not in use. It also explains why designers such as Robert Adam considered the furniture to be an integral part of the decorative scheme to be applied to the whole room.

Predictably, when the furniture designs of Adam and Chippendale were enthusiastically revived at the end of the nineteenth century, resuscitating the mid-Georgian obsession with order was considered a little too purist. Gas and later electric light had liberated the interior from the technological limitations which had previously governed the disposition of furniture; for most households, to go back and try to re-create the exact conditions of Adam's day was rightly considered both naïve and impractical.

This Adam-style torchère of c.1780 has a papier mâché tray top and is fitted with a small frieze drawer. Both top and frieze are painted with mythological motifs in the style of the popular painter Angelica Kauffmann.

Opposite: *the Du Pont Dining Room at the Winterthur Museum, of c.1785, furnished in the Adam-influenced Federal Style.*

'When a few years ago the beauty and refinement of old cabinet-work came into more general recognition, they caught up the name of Chippendale, and have been repeating it, they and their parrot-like successors - with the persistency of Poe's Raven ever since'

(H. J. Jennings, Our Homes and How to Beautify Them, *1902)*

Opposite: *an early twentieth-century 'Adam Revival' interior, taken from the portfolio of R. Goulburn Lovell. The fireplace is perhaps the only truly 'Adam' element here.* Right: *Victorian gilt-bronze torchères in the Adam Style of c.1860 - a relatively early date for revived Adam designs.*

A reaction to 'Adam Style' from those who followed in the wake of the great man was to some extent inevitable. Even before Robert Adam's death jealous rivals and less gifted successors had begun to queue up in order to denigrate his work and his approach. In 1779 the unusually spiteful young architect Robert Smirke (later to design the British Museum) wrote a scathing pamphlet with William Porden entitled *The Exhibition,* which dismissively declared that 'Most of the white walls with which Mr Adam has speckled this city, are no better than Models for the Twelfth-Night decoration of a Pastry Cook.' Similarly vehement was James Peacock's *Nutshells* of 1784, which railed against Adam's 'excess of puerile ornaments ... modern refinement and modern finery' - sounding in the process rather too much like a young fogey trying to turn back the waves of fashion.

After Adam's death in 1792 the taunts were to grow more measured. C. H. Tatham, evangelist of the new Graeco-Egyptian taste, wearily dismissed Adam's approach as constituting 'a style productive of great fatigue to the designer ... and an infinite expense to the purse of the employer'. James Elmes's stern *Metropolitan Improvements* of 1828 warned unwary designers against Robert Adam's 'confectionary' and 'impurity', while in 1842 Joseph Gwilt's celebrated *Encyclopaedia of Architecture* expressed the amazement of an early Victorian at the light-heartedness, and in particular the spurious academicism, of Adam's designs: 'It can scarcely be believed that the ornaments of Diocletian's Palace at Spalatro should have loaded our dwellings ...'

Among Regency commentators on Adam's work, Sir John Soane predictably showed more vision than the rest. 'Mr Adam', he declared,

'deserves great praise for banishing from interior decorations the heavy architectural ornaments, which prevailed in all our buildings before his time.' However, he continued, 'it will be admitted that he sometimes indulged in the extreme of fancy and lightness.' King George III himself was inclined to agree with Soane, not as a result of any keen artistic insight, but simply because the deeply conservative monarch abhorred all newfangled things and ideas - especially in the arts, a branch of learning which he continued to regard with grave suspicion. 'I am little of an architect,' the king wisely declared in 1800, 'and think that the old school is not enough attended to.' 'The Adams', he concluded, 'have introduced too much of neatness and prettiness.'

History, however, has tended to exonerate Adam (while doing little to enhance George III's own reputation). Indeed, since the mid-nineteenth century the style of Robert Adam and his contemporaries has proved perenially popular. Thomas Chippendale's *Director* designs were being

A giltwood and composition three-part overmantel mirror, very much in Adam's manner, of c.1880. The design is based on one in the Adams' Works in Architecture *for Derby House (which, ironically, had itself been demolished some twenty years earlier).*

Two Adam Revival style English interiors, both typical of the early twentieth century.

Adam Style furniture has been extremely popular from the late nineteenth century until the present day. Here are three good Victorian examples of well-made 'Adam' pieces: *a satinwood side cabinet* (above), *a dining room urn and pedestal* (below right), *and a satinwood and marquetry commode* (below).

reprinted as early as 1834, and he was lauded by his illustrious successors Thomas Sheraton and George Smith. 'Extensive and masterly', Sheraton declared of Chippendale's works in 1793, while Smith observed in 1826 that the *Director* had 'changed the whole feature of design'. In 1828 the noted critic J. T. Smith was calling Chippendale 'the most famous upholsterer and cabinet-maker of his day'. Even a commentator of 1862, writing at a time when the general reputation of both Chippendale and his Georgian contemporaries was at its nadir, acknowledged that:

'He was a designer in the best sense, however perverted the style in which he clothes his thoughts. His fantasies may now provoke laughter, but it cannot be denied that they were inspired by genius, and guided by method.'

The International Exhibition of 1862, held at London's South Kensington, was of central importance in popularizing the style of Robert Adam - and in particular the furniture of Thomas Chippendale - for a new, High Victorian generation. The forty drawings of furniture designs by Chippendale and Lock exhibited as part of the show prompted considerable public and professional comment, and stimulated widespread interest in the taste of Adam's day. By the 1870s the Chippendale revival was, as Christopher Gilbert has noted, 'well under way, and the era of romantic hero-worship had opened'. Chippendale's designs were celebrated at the expense of equally skilled rivals such as Cobb and Linnell, while 'Chippendale' reproductions were to be found in drawing rooms, dining rooms and libraries all over Britain and America. Some pieces kept rather closer to the originals in spirit and detail than others. As H. J. Jennings remarked in 1902, the

Left: *Adam Revival furniture and decoration in a room set devised by Maple & Co and advertised in an issue of* The Studio *of March 1912.*

Above: *Heal's were in the forefront of marketing the Adam and 'Colonial Adam' styles of the early twentieth century. Here is a good example of colonial Adam, advertised in* The Studio *magazine of 15th January 1910.*

*An English dining room in
Adam Revival style, from
H. P. Shapland's* Style
Schemes in Antique
Furnishing *of 1909.*

Above: *The Portman, a chastely Neo-Classical Sandersons wallpaper of 1903.* Left: *Birds and flowers dominate both the actual block-printed chintz of c.1780 and the revival machine-printed wallpaper (above left) of c.1910 based on a design of 1785.*

public were soon enthusing over 'any article, no matter how devoid of taste, that goes by his name'.

While Chippendale's designs were reaching an enthusiastic international audience, so were the decorative schemes of the Adam brothers. The famous furniture firm of Gillows exhibited 'Robert Adam' interiors in the great Paris and Manchester exhibitions of 1878 and 1882 respectively. In 1881 the publishers Batsford produced the first volume of Adam designs to be printed since the third and last part of the Adam brothers' *Works in Architecture* had appeared (posthumously) in 1822. The same year *The Cabinet Maker and Art Furnisher* noted 'how admirably the Adams' style lends itself to the chaste decoration of bedroom furniture.' It was not until 1902, however, that the first full reprint of all three parts of the Adams' *Works* (of 1773-8, 1779 and 1822) appeared. Interestingly, the publisher was French - the firm of E. Thezard Fils. Thezard was responding to the renewed interest in Adam Style across the

Channel, and was greatly helped by the fact that the canny Adams - their eyes firmly set on the potential market of rich French clients - had produced the English originals with an additional, French text.

The Adam Revival quickly spread to America, too, where genuine Adam designs were fused with more rustic, pre-revolutionary forms to create a style known popularly as 'Colonial Adam'. The stylistic compromise was typically American. As Joanna Banham, Sally McDonald and Julia Porter recently observed of Colonial Adam:

'The classical strictness of the decorations were modified with certain concessions to quaintness, a more vigorous treatment, and a less mathematically rigid attention to form'.

The aesthetic success and practical robustness of this synthesis is proved by the fact that countless middle-class American homes were still being redecorated in this refined yet comfortable style as recently as the Second World War.

The new popular enthusiasm of the late nineteenth-century for the decoration and artefacts of Adam's day was both stimulated by, and at the same time helped to create, a new fashion for buying and trading in antiques. By 1870 householders were not only becoming interested in buying contemporary Arts and Crafts or reproduction furniture, but were, for the first time, also seeking to purchase genuine Georgian pieces - which, when compared with many of the fanciful Gothic creations and the more extravagant reproductions of the later nineteenth-century, were greatly admired for their strength and simplicity. By the 1880s the fad for antiques had gripped Britain and America, and antique shops were springing up in every town. In 1904 H. Treffry Dunn, reminiscing

'Reception Room in Adam Style', designed by Edward Thorne in the early 1900s.

Opposite: 'A Drawing Room with walls panelled in Silk', illustrated in Robson & Sons' catalogue of Interior Woodwork, *c.1910. The Adam Style is deemed here to be the acme of taste.*

on Rossetti's own delight in antique Georgian furniture, recalled that the great artist would stroll through London's Leicester Square, where 'many a Chippendale chair or table could be met and bought for next to nothing.' (Alas, today Chippendale furniture cannot be had so cheaply - nor can you find any antique shops in what is now one of the capital's most dismal and tawdry squares.)

Towards the end of the century, amateur antique-hunters sprang from every type of social background, and sought out not only items from one particular era or style, but interesting pieces from all periods. Yet the most consistently popular style remained that of Robert Adam and his contemporaries - even though the Adam Style pieces they collected were then disposed in a very undisciplined and haphazard Victorian or Edwardian manner about the room. And to match the antique chairs, silverware and ceramics they had bought, fashionable householders began to demand 'Adam Style' decoration: wallpapers and fabrics either reproduced from genuine Georgian patterns or, more commonly, adapted with some licence from eighteenth-century originals. Soon every leading department store had both an antiques section and a decorative department which dealt in 'Adam' and other Georgian reproduction styles. Inevitably, many antique-hunters, with little formal training in the decorative arts, were easily deceived by some of the less scrupulous antique traders, and some type of regulation was needed to protect the unwary enthusiast. Accordingly, in 1918 the British Antique Dealers' Association was established.

Today 'Adam Style' furniture, fittings and decorative designs are still by far the most sought-after items in the reproduction catalogues.

'Adam' surrounds outsell all other reproduction chimneypieces; at the same time genuine Adam fireplaces are admired as priceless works of art - and are, as a result, at the top of the list for architectural thieves.

For many of us today, 'Adam Style' is synonymous with the term 'Georgian' - even though the thirty-odd years spanning Robert Adam's career amount to only a quarter of the whole Georgian period. However, Robert Adam would probably turn in his grave if he was able to see some of the products which now bear his name, or which are passed off as deriving from the products of his contemporaries. 'Adam' (or, gratingly, 'Adams') swags and urns are now all too frequently applied in the most clumsy manner to coarse, flat and crudely proportioned chimneypieces, pediments, mouldings, wallpaper and furniture in a desperate attempt to convey historical pedigree to a badly designed item which plainly has none. This bogus-Adam inevitably devalues both the real thing and the well-crafted reproduction. So beware: not all that is termed 'Adam' has necessarily much to do with the work of Robert Adam's own day. A stuck-on swag or a white-painted pediment is no substitute for the decorative inspiration of Adam Style.

Adam Style survives today even in the most bizarre of contexts. This example surely qualifies as the most unlikely setting in which to find an Adam-designed room: literally suspended in the midst of Richard Rogers's determinedly hi-tech Lloyd's of London building, built to great acclaim in the heart of the City during the mid-1980s. If Adam's architectural and decorative language can survive here, it can survive anywhere.

Adam, Robert (1728-92)
Born in Kirkcaldy in Fife, the son of the architect William
Adam, Robert - often in partnership with his brothers John
(1721-92) and James (1732-94) - revolutionized interior
decoration as well as the practice of architecture, introducing a
personal, delicate variation of the new Neo-Classical taste that
was to influence all aspects of design during the last forty years
of the eighteenth century. Robert Adam's furniture, often
produced in collaboration with the furniture-maker Thomas
Chippendale, provided a marked contrast with the heavy
Palladian styles which had come before. Having travelled to
Italy in the mid-1750s, on his return he established an
architectural and design practice in London in 1758. The Adam
office's immense output was achieved only through the
participation of a large number of assistants; thus it is often
difficult to ascertain exactly how much is owed to Robert
Adam's own genius, and how much should be credited to other
members of the family, to assistants, or to manufacturers such
as Chippendale. During the 1780s Robert began to be eclipsed
by younger, more fashionable architects such as James Wyatt,
and by 1785 his practice was largely resticted to Scotland.

Asher, Benjamin (1773-1845)
While Abraham Swan's *The British Architect,* issued in
Philadelphia in 1775, was the first book on architecture printed
in America, it was actually a reissue of a thirty-year-old
London publication. Credit for producing the first original
American book on architecture, therefore, must go to Asher
Benjamin, a carpenter from Greenfield, Massachusetts.
Benjamin's *The Country Builder's Assistant,* published in 1797,
was the first of several handbooks that sought to expose local
carpenters and joiners to the latest architectural developments
in the urban centres of the eastern seaboard. Beginning with
Georgian and Adamesque designs, Benjamin's books, which
ran to some forty editions, eventually embraced the Greek
Revival as well. In general, his designs cannot be called truly
innovative, but the grace and skillful composition that they
exhibit were responsible for raising the standards of a
generation of American builders.

Bateman, Hester (17?-c.1795)
Hester Bateman was one of the leading silversmiths of Adam's
day - one of many women engaged in this trade at the time.
She began work at Bunhill Row in London in 1761; by 1780 she
was known all over Britain and America for the production of
well-finished and consistent pieces of everyday silverware. Her
especial enthusiasm was for 'bright-cut' engraving: the
creation of numerous additional facets on the silver in order to
catch the light. She retired in 1790, but her children Peter and
Ann continued the family firm.

Boulton, Matthew (1728-1809)
Boulton was, in Wedgwood's expert opinion, 'the first and most
complete manufacturer in England in metal', and also probably
the world's first true industrial entrepreneur. Having inherited
his father's Birmingham toymaking business in 1759, he
expanded the Soho factory to take on the production of
precious metal objects (abandoning his early attempts to make
ormolu and silver plate after finding that they did not pay).
Soon the factory was the most advanced in the world. As Mrs

Montagu told him in 1777: 'You have rendered the Town of
Birmingham important and honourable to this kingdom. Your
manufactures are a great national object and have been of
infinite utility in rendering our Commerce flourishing during
our Contest with America.' He collaborated with great
inventors such as Ami Argand and James Watt, and found time
amid his tireless activity to marry two heiresses. Boulton's
Birmingham home, built by James Wyatt, is currently being
restored as a public museum by Birmingham City Council.

Bulfinch, Charles (1763-1844)
America's first native-born architect, Bulfinch was the product
of a long line of Bostonians with an interest in buildings.
Having completed his studies in mathematics and perspective
at Harvard, Bulfinch embarked on a tour of Europe (following
an itinerary suggested in part by Thomas Jefferson), in the
course of which he was greatly impressed by the recent work
of Adam and Chambers. His designs for the Tontine Crescent
and the Massachusetts State House, executed soon after his
return to Boston, reflect his Americanized version of this
'modern' European Neo-Classicism. During the first two
decades of the nineteenth century, Bulfinch served as
chairman of Boston's board of elected officers, designing
scores of buildings, laying out streets, and transforming the
city into the most up-to-date, efficient, and beautiful in
America. His efforts eventually attracted the notice of President
James Monroe, who engaged him to complete the US Capitol.
Bulfinch's most lasting contribution to American architecture
may be the formulaic approach to the design of capitol
buildings, which he demonstrated in Washington, Boston and
Augusta: symmetrical wings flanking a domed rotunda, the
whole composition fronted with a columned portico.

Chambers, Sir William (1723-96)
The son of a Scottish merchant, Chambers was actually born in
Gothenburg, Sweden. Having abandoned a career in the
Swedish East India Company, he began to study architecture in
1749, setting out for Italy the following year. Returning to
England in 1755, his practice rapidly became very successful.
His style, while relying much on current French and Italian
thinking, could at times be dull; his great work Somerset
House, begun in 1776 and unfinished at his death, is perhaps
the most famous example of this. He also remained a staunch
opponent of the Adam-inspired 'Grecian taste' as well as the
less academic fashion for Gothick (although he did
occasionally build in the 'Chinese' style). However, his *Treatise
on Civil Architecture* of 1759 rapidly became, in Colvin's words,
'the standard English treatise on the use of the Orders'.
Chambers was always more politically astute than the Adams:
appointed as one of the Office of Works' architects in 1761 - the
other was Robert Adam - he became the first Surveyor-General
of the reformed royal works in 1782, when Adam was in
eclipse. Made a Knight of the Polar Star by Gustav III of
Sweden in 1770, he was later allowed by an admiring George
III to assume the title of an English knight.

Chippendale the Elder, **Thomas** (1718-79)
Born in Yorkshire, Chippendale in his early career
concentrated on work for William Kent, and publication of the
first major British pattern-book solely devoted to furniture, *The*

Gentleman and Cabinet-Maker's Director of 1754. The latter proved a great success and hugely influential; however, from the mid-1760s onwards his designs turned from the Palladian and Rococo forms illustrated in his book of 1754 to the new, lighter Neo-Classicism being espoused by Robert Adam. By the time of his death Chippendale had become (in Smith's words of 1828) 'the most famous Upholsterer and Cabinet-maker of his day'. Excellent examples of his work can still be found in numerous houses in Britain and America, while copies of his designs have been found everywhere in the world since 1779.

Chippendale the Younger, **Thomas** (1749-1822)
The eldest son of the renowned Thomas (see above), Thomas junior was brought up to run his father's business, which he took over (on Thomas senior's death in 1779) in partnership with Thomas Haig. Haig died hugely in debt in 1803, as a result of which Chippendale was declared bankrupt in 1804. However, he managed to survive this setback, largely since the demand for his furniture - produced to the same high standards of design and craftsmanship as in his father's day - was even greater than when his father had been alive.

Cobb, John (c.1715-78)
Not much is known of this furniture-maker until he went into partnership with William Vile (c.1700-67) in 1751. While Vile was unable to respond to the new ideas and forms of the Adam-inspired Neo-Classical taste of the 1760s, and retired in 1764, Cobb was keen and eager to do so. In his later years Cobb was especially respected for his fine marquetry furniture. He was also widely known for the high regard he retained for his own abilities: a contemporary labelled him 'one of the proudest men in England'.

Gillow, Robert (c.1745-95) and **Richard** (1734-1811) **Gillow**
In 1729 Robert Gillow senior had founded the family furniture-making firm at Lancaster; on his death in 1772 the concern was taken over by his sons Robert in London and Richard in Lancaster. Gillows specialized in innovative furniture, and invented such pieces as the telescopic dining table and the what-not. Much of their furniture can be identified by the special stamp they started using in the 1780s, although they also began to employ specific brand names for certain pieces, derived from the names of their aristocratic patrons. The firm also branched out into upholstery services and architectural joinery, such as chimneypieces and balusters; thus by 1785 whole houses were regularly being entirely fitted and furnished by Gillows. Their business prospered throughout the nineteenth century, merging with the firm of Warings in the 1890s, and indeed still survives today.

Hepplewhite, George (17?-1786)
Hepplewhite is said to have been apprenticed to the Gillow brothers (see above), but little is known of his life aside from the publication of the influential *Cabinet-Maker and Upholsterer's Guide* by his wife two years after his death, in 1788. Although not particularly innovative, Hepplewhite's designs - very much in Adam's later style - were easily copied by furniture makers of varying proficiency, and accordingly many 'Hepplewhite' designs survive both in Britain and in America.

Holland, Henry (1745-1806)
One of the leading architects of the second half of the eighteenth century, Holland was primarily responsible for introducing French and Neo-Classical influences into the mainstream of British architecture during the 1780s, producing a synthesis of these styles that was more chaste and refined than that of the Adam brothers. His reputation was secured by the commission to rebuild Carlton House in London for the Prince of Wales, a project which was begun in 1783.

Jackson, John Baptist (1701-c.1775)
A pupil of the engraver Kirkhill, in 1726 Jackson emigrated to France and then to Italy, where he became sufficiently fascinated by the engravers of the Renaissance to produce engraved reproductions of old master paintings by artists such as Titian and Tintoretto. In 1746 he returned to England, using his experience with engraving to produce wallpapers. In 1754 he published the first book dealing with wallpaper to appear in England: *An Essay on the Invention of Engraving and Printing in Chiaro Oscuro* - partly an advertisement for his own Battersea factory. Though one of his main achievements was to pioneer the very short-lived execution of oil-colour papers, his workmanship greatly influenced subsequent distemper-colour manufacturers, and he can truly be called the Father of British Wallpaper.

Kauffmann, Angelica (1741-1807)
Of Swiss parentage, Angelica Kauffmann dazzled contemporaries not only by her skilled painting but also by her considerable charm and beauty. The cantankerous Winckelmann was the first great artist to fall in love with her; following this episode she came to London in 1766, where she took fashionable society by storm and became one of the founders of the Royal Academy. Widely regarded at the time as having revived the ancient Greek art of painting on masonry (although her reputation has suffered somewhat in the intervening two centuries), she became very wealthy as a result of her numerous commissions to paint classical scenes on the walls and ceilings of the rich and famous. In 1767 she married the bogus Swedish 'Count', Frederick de Horn; in 1781 she married again, this time to the decorative painter and close rival Antonio Zucchi. Although Kauffmann and Zucchi worked together at a number of sites (including Adam's 20 St James's Square and Syon House), the marriage was not a success, and by the late 1780s she had retired to Rome - there to be courted by Goethe.

Linnell, John (1729-96)
The son of the furniture maker William Linnell, John took over his father's business on his death in 1763, and rapidly made it one of the most skilled firms in Britain. Together with Chippendale he pioneered the production of marquetry furniture during the 1760s, and executed many of Adam's designs. (See Helena Hayward's *William and John Linnell*, 1980).

McIntire, Samuel (1757-1811)
The mansions that Samuel McIntire and his followers designed for the prosperous merchants of Salem, Massachusetts, constitute one of the richest groups of Adam-inspired houses in

the country. McIntire himself was described by a contemporary as the product of 'a family of carpenters who had no claim on public favor...[who] soon gained a superiority to all of his occupation.' Although he designed a handsome courthouse in Salem and submitted an impressive entry in the 1792 competition for the US Capitol, McIntire's reputation rests entirely on his skill as a residential architect. His houses exhibit façades of a foursquare regularity, which can seem almost stark; inside, however, his artistry finds expression in a wealth of Adamesque ornamentation of great delicacy. Little wonder that a visitor to one of these houses felt no hesitation in writing of McIntire, 'in sculpture he had no rival in New England.'

Revett, Nicholas(1720-1804)
The son of wealthy Suffolk parents, Revett left for Italy in 1742 and in 1748 visited Naples with the architects James Stuart and Matthew Brettingham and the painter Gavin Hamilton. In 1750 Stuart and Revett travelled to Venice, and thence to Dalmatia and Athens. The fruit of their studies, *The Antiquities of Athens* of 1762, helped transform the worlds of architecture and design in Britain and America, providing an invaluable source of Greek buildings and motifs for an eager new public. In contrast to Stuart, Revett's personal wealth enabled him to eschew practising formally as an architect after 1762 - the buildings he designed are very few in number - and he chose instead to visit the Greek monuments of Turkey in 1764-9, the result of which expedition was *The Antiquities of Ionia* of 1769-97.

Stuart, James (1713-88)
Revett's companion in Athens was a largely self-taught sailor's son, who began his professional life as an apprentice to a fan-painter, Lewis Goupy. His journey to Rome in 1742 was conducted largely on foot, but once there he quickly established himself as a connoisseur of paintings, in which capacity he met Hamilton, Brettingham and Revett (q.v.). After the publication of *The Antiquities of Athens*, his natural indolence and love of life led him to pay insufficient attention to his architectural practice, and commissions became rare. In 1764 he succeeded Hogarth as Sergeant Painter at the Office of Works - a post abolished as a result of the 1782 reforms.

Thornton, William (1759-1828)
Born on a Caribbean sugar plantation and educated in Europe, Thornton arrived in the United States in 1786. Three years later, while practising medicine in Philadelphia, he won a competition for the design of Library Hall. His lack of formal architectural training notwithstanding, Thornton entered the 1792 competition for the design of the US Capitol gaining the enthusiastic support of both Washington and Jefferson. Thornton was declared the winner, and he was named the first architect of the Capitol. Although much of his original design has been lost, the general concept and configuration of today's Capitol are his. During service as a member of the Board of Commissioners of the Federal District (1794-1802) and as superintendent of the Patent Office (1802-1828), Thornton continued to dabble in architecture, producing innovative residential designs for such Washington landmarks as The Octagon and Tudor Place.

Wedgwood, Josiah (1730-8)
One of the most famous figures of the period: Wedgwood was not only a craftsman and entrepreneur, but also the most famous ceramicist the world has ever known. Apprenticed to his elder brother Thomas (who had inherited their father's Burslem, Staffordshire factory) at the age of fourteen, in 1754 he entered his first successful partnership, with Thomas Whieldon. His green-glazed ware, and later his creamware, proved a huge success. Following the sale of creamware to Queen Charlotte in 1762 he began to style himself 'Potter to the Queen', and by 1770 was producing a dinner service for Empress Catherine II of Russia. In 1769 Wedgwood established his famous pottery works at Etruria, near Stoke - providing a revolutionary model village for his workers and even local transport to get them to and from work. Over the next twenty years he revolutionized the pottery industry, providing not only startlingly new products but also making what had previously been only luxury items into stylish accessories that could be afforded by all.

Wood the Younger, John (1728-81)
The son of the celebrated creator of Georgian Bath (for whom see Tim Mowl and Brian Earnshaw's splendid biography of 1988), John junior acted as his father's assistant in Bath and, after John senior's death in 1754, as his successor. On the completion of his father's Circus, in 1767 he began work on his own Royal Crescent; finished in 1775, this provided the model for countless similar developments in Britain and America. Wood's style essentially remained that of his father - traditional English Palladianism - and not of innovators such as Robert Adam; however, he continued to be fully employed in Bath until his death.

Wyatt, James (1746-1813)
Little is known of Wyatt's early life before his journey of 1762 to Venice, where he became a pupil of the architect Visentini. Following his return to England in 1768 he worked closely with his elder brother Samuel (1737-1807). Their Neo-Classical works owed much to the Adams, but were couched in a more refined and pure 'Grecian' style. Their Oxford Street Pantheon of 1772 brought James instant fame, and he was showered with official appointments. His later life proved that he could be equally at home with Roman, Gothic, or Greek; in all his commissions, however, he displayed a superficiality in design and a personal indifference which severely marred both his executed buildings and his personal reputation.

For a comprehensive guide to the architects of the period, see Howard Colvin's *Biographical Dictionary of British Architects 1600-1840* (1978). For a similarly comprehensive guide to the furniture-makers of Adam's day, see Geoffrey Beard and Christopher Gilbert (ed.), *Dictionary of English Furniture Makers 1660-1840* (1986).

Acanthus

Plant with thick leaves which is used as a decorative motif on Antique Corinthian and Composite (a hybrid mixture of Ionic and Corinthian) capitals, and which in Georgian Britain was much used on all types of classical mouldings.

Acroterion

Originally a plinth to carry an ornament placed at the summit or the corner of a pediment. In the eighteenth century acroteria were more usually quadrant-shaped 'ears' found at the corners of pediments or cabinet tops.

Anthemion

Ornamental motif based on the honeysuckle flower and leaves; much used after the mid-1770s for mouldings and ironwork.

Architrave

Moulded door or window surround. In strict classical terms, it forms the lowest part of the entablature (above the capital and below the frieze).

Ashlar

Smoothly-dressed stonework, with very narrow joints.

Astragal

Small, semicircular-profiled moulding; also section of window glazing bar. In 1756 Isaac Ware called the astragal 'A little round moulding, which in the orders surrounds the top of the shaft or body of the column', and noted that 'It is also called the *talon*, or *tondino*'.

Attic

Top storey of a building, generally above the principal external cornice.

Baize

Heavy woollen cloth, well felted and often dyed green or brown.

Bead

Small moulding dating from the Norman era, with a semicircular profile; continuous, or resembling a string of beads. Often recessed (e.g. when separating elements of the door) and flush with adjacent surfaces.

Bombazine

Heavy fabric of silk warp and worsted weft, usually made in Norwich. Generally used for dressmaking, but also as a heavy-duty furnishing fabric.

Buckram

A coarse hemp cloth, used to stiffen upholstery or valances.

Calico

Strong cotton cloth, resembling linen; its name comes from one of its original sources - 'Calicut', in Portuguese India. Made in Britain from the 1770s.

Cambric

Fine white linen cloth, often used for bedclothes.

Canvas

Very coarse hemp or flax (linen) cloth; also known as BOLTING.

Capital

Head of a column or pilaster; often decorated, according to the type of order used (see below).

Cartouche

'An ornament representing a scroll of paper or parchment' (Ware, 1756).

Caryatid

Column or pilaster in the shape of a female figure. The male equivalents (which usually wore a more solemn if not tragic expression) were called ATLANTES or TELAMONES.

Casement

Traditional medieval window type; side- or top-hung, and opening inwards or outwards. Largely replaced by the sash window during the Georgian period.

Cassimere

Medium-weight, soft twilled woollen cloth; a cheaper version of cashmere.

Chiffonier

Commode or sideboard with open shelves (although some were provided with doors).

Chintz

Printed or possibly even painted cotton, sometimes glazed to be more washable and hard-wearing. Originally from India, where 'chitta ' meant 'spotted cloth'.

Cima recta

A very commonly found moulding which, in Ware's

words, 'is hollow at the top, and swelling at the bottom, so that its out-line has a waved appearance'.

Coade Stone

Durable ceramic, made in Lambeth by Eleanor Coade after 1769, which could mimic stone or plaster.

Corduroy

Durable cotton, with the weft raised in ribs.

Cornice

The upper part of the entablature, or the uppermost part of a wall. Also applies to any projecting moulding at the top of internal or external walls.

Damask

Reversible patterned fabric, usually in one single colour; the pattern is produced by the contrast between the warp and weft faces, the former producing the satin ground.

Darnix

A rough fabric of linen warp and wool weft, often used for bed furnishings.

Deal

Planks of fir or pine; from the Low German 'dele', meaning plank. Generally imported from the Baltic or from North America.

Dentil

Plain projecting moulding with a square profile. Repeated dentils often featured in simple cornices.

Die

'A term to express a squared naked piece' (Ware), such as the body of a classical pedestal.

Dimity

Any type of plain or patterned fabric. White dimity was often used as a furnishing fabric in humbler dwellings and cottages - particularly for curtains and bed-hangings.

Drugget

Thin cloth, often used to cover floors or carpets, or occasionally as a loose cover for furniture; it was usually twilled, and half wool and half linen.

Egg and anchor

Extremely common, often very heavily-projecting moulding used widely by the Palladian designers before Adam. Called EGG AND ANCHOR by Ware.

Entablature

Upper part of the classical orders, above the capital; consists of architrave, frieze and cornice.

Festoon

'An ornament of carved work, representing a wreath, or garland of flowers, or leaves... naturally thickest in the middle, small at each end, and tied up there, whence a part commonly hangs down beyond the knot' (Ware, 1756). More recently this term has largely come to signify the style of single, vertically-hung curtain typical of Adam's day.

Frieze

Middle section of the entablature, below the cornice, which was often decorated with motifs or representational carvings. Can also be used for the equivalent section of a wall, i.e. the wide band below the cornice of a room. In textile terms, the term 'frieze' signifies a stout, coarse woollen cloth.

Gauze

Thin, transparent fabric with a crossed-warp weave.

Gimp

A decorative, openwork band of stiff thread, often used as a border or edging for furnishing fabrics.

Gingham

Striped or checked cotton, used for cheap bedroom hangings or loose furniture covers. Particularly popular in eighteenth-century America.

Guilioche

Decorative moulding comprising interlaced S's.

Japanning

Term originally used for coloured lacquering (usually black or red) on imported Japanese cabinets. Oriental lacquer was derived from plants, whereas English black lacquer was manufactured synthetically from asphaltum or candle soot. By 1780 the term was used for any effect obtained by built-up layers of lacquering - whether on wood, papier mâché or metals.

Mastic

Any oil-based render or plaster.

Mathematical tile

Clay tile with a large nib, laid on a vertical wall in interlocking courses in order to give the appearance of brickwork.

Metope

The square spaces between the characteristic triglyphs (three vertical projections) on the Doric frieze.

Modillion

Scroll-shaped bracket appearing in the cornice or supporting a structural or projecting member.

Moire

Ribbed or grained silk.

Moreen

Worsted cloth with a waved or stamped finish. This 'watered' look, much used for curtains and wall-hangings by 1760, gradually fell out of favour as more easily washable fabrics became available.

Moulding

Contour or pattern given to projecting surfaces in architecture or furniture; generally executed in plaster, papier mâché or wood.

Muslin

Fine cotton textile originating in India. Used to make transparent sub-curtains which would filter the direct light entering a room.

Ormolu

Alloy of copper, zinc and tin, gilded; much used for mounts, frames and furniture decoration. 'English ormolu' referred to the simple lacquering of brass or similar alloy to get the same lustrous effect.

Order

Classical architectural formula of column and entablature which formed the basis for all Greek and Roman architecture. The five Graeco-Roman orders comprised the Doric (the plainest), Tuscan, Ionic, Corinthian and Composite (the most elaborately decorated).

Ovolo

'A moulding called a quarter round' (Ware, 1756). Also called an ECHINUS.

Paktong

Lustrous, durable and easily-polished alloy of copper, zinc and nickel, imported from China. The term comes from the Chinese 'pai-tung', meaning white copper.

Palmette

Fan-shaped leaf ornament resembling a palm leaf; often used in conjunction with the anthemion (see above).

Patera

Flat circular or oval ornament, often decorated with a flower-pattern.

Pediment

Classical architectural termination, either triangular or segmental (i.e. with a curved upper surface).

Pilaster

Flat-faced column projecting from a masonry or panelled surface. Not to be confused with an ENGAGED COLUMN, which refers to the effect by which a normal, cylindrical column appears to have half of (or part of) its shaft buried in the wall behind.

Pulvinated frieze

A 'swelling or rounding of the frieze' (Ware), commonly used both by Adam and his rivals as well as by Adam's Rococo predecessors. From the Latin 'pulvinatus', meaning cushioned.

Quirk

Sharp incision or undercutting between mouldings or adjacent surfaces, designed to throw a shadow.

Quoin

Stone or brick at the right-angled corner of a building; generally projecting from the wall surface to emphasize the termination.

Rail

Horizontal member of a door or window, or of a piece of furniture. The MEETING RAILS of a sash window are those two rails which interlock when the sash is shut, and which carry the sash fasteners.

Reeding

Combination moulding formed from groups of beads or similar simple, convex mouldings.

Render

Plaster covering of a wall. A general term which includes stucco and even interior (gypsum) plaster; now used generally to indicate an exterior covering.

Satin

A twilled weave with a very smooth texture which caught the light. Could be made of silk, cotton or worsted.

Scotia

A hollow moulding, also called a CASEMENT, which produces 'an effect, just opposite to the quarter round' (Ware).

Serge

A twilled fabric with a worsted warp and woollen weft.

Settee

Multi-seated chair. Distinct from a sofa in being derived directly from the form, height and pattern of adjacent chairs.

Shag

Cheap worsted fabric with a heavy pile. Used in Adam's day for bed coverings and the upholstery of simple seat furniture.

Stile
Vertical structural members of a door, window or piece of furniture.

Stock

Originally the board on which a brick was hand-shaped; by the late eighteenth century this term, short for 'stock brick', indicated an average-strength brick of reasonable quality and finish. 'London stocks', grey or yellow facing bricks (their colour deriving from the local clays) were much used in the speculative building of the period.

String Course

Projecting masonry course (i.e. horizontal band) on the exterior of a wall.

Stuff

General term referring to worsted cloths.

Tabby

A heavy, plain silk, often watered or waved, which was much used for curtains.

Taffeta

Plain woven silk, with thicker weft threads. Popular for window or bed hangings.

Tammy

A strong but light worsted fabric, often glazed. Frequently used to line curtains.

Term

A pedestal topped with a human or animal figure, tapering towards the bottom. Stone, plaster or Coade terms were often used as garden ornaments.

Ticking

Strong linen twill woven in a herringbone pattern and often striped. Much in vogue for mattresses and pillows, since their feathers could not force their way through its dense texture.

Torus

A thick, projecting moulding which looks rather like a cable. From the Greek meaning 'thick rope'.

Tuck pointing

The process by which inferior or badly-cut bricks are set in a mortar of the same colour as the brick itself; in order to give the impression of expensive, thin-jointed brickwork, a straight line of white 'tucking' mortar is then set into this original mortar.

Twill

A type of weave in which each weft row starts one thread further on than the last row, producing a diagonal line.

Velvet

A cut-pile fabric, made from cotton, wool or silk.

Vitruvian scroll
Wave ornament, often used to decorate friezes. Also called RUNNING DOG. The name was originally derived from the celebrated Roman architect Marcus Vitruvius Pollio.

Warp

Strong threads arranged lengthwise in the loom to form the basis of any fabric. WEFT are the threads interlaced at right angles to these.

If you are seeking to renovate or redecorate your Adam-period home, or simply wish to find out more about the houses of the time, there are many sources of information. These can help with methods of repair, types of materials, with advising on suitable local suppliers and craftsmen, and suggesting other expert sources.

Remember, many directories of suppliers and services which pose as authoritative and critical guides to the best experts in the subject are actually nothing of the sort. Neither are salesmen the best sources of balanced information about their own products. It is always important to get the advice of a disinterested expert before you begin any type of repair or redecoration.

Contacts and sources of information in the United Kingdom

1   Conservation Officers
The Conservation Officer of your local District or Borough Council (usually associated with the council's Planning Department) is there specifically to help house-owners on all aspects of period house renovation. He or she can advise on local joiners, plasterers, ironworkers and other good, reliable craftsmen in the area. They can also let you know about possible local authority grant aid for your repairs or alterations. Some county councils have expert conservation groups who can be of similar help.

Architectural salvage outlets can be very useful. They can also be horribly mis-used, encouraging over-enthusiastic house-owners to install over-sized or over-elaborate elements in inappropriate settings. While some salvage companies are exemplary in their dealings with suppliers and public alike, others are not so scrupulous - at worst effectively acting as fences for the hugely expanding trade in art and architectural theft. As with local craftsmen, do not just rely on consulting the Yellow Pages or a magazine directory to get the names of random architectural salvage companies; talk to your local Conservation Officer before choosing one.

If your building is listed, your Conservation Officer should also be able to provide you with details of the listing, which should tell you more about the history of your home.

2   English Heritage
As the principal body regulating the conservation and maintenance of historic buildings in England, English Heritage (officially known as the Historic Buildings and Monuments Commission), and its equivalents in Wales (Cadw) and Scotland (Historic Scotland), are well equipped to help in a variety of ways.

The Conservation Service of English Heritage in London (Keysign House, 429 Oxford St, London W1R 2HD, tel 071 973 3000) can advise on all matters of repair or redecoration. John and Nicola Ashurst produced a five volume-series on Practical Building Conservation for the section in 1988; this series - available from English Heritage, or from good bookshops - is

easily the best guide to problems and solutions in the area of repair and maintenance. Subjects covered are stone masonry (vol.1), terracotta, brick and earth (vol.2), mortars, plasters and renders (vol.3), metals (vol.4), and wood, glass and resins (vol.5).

English Heritage's Architectural Study Collection, also run from Keysign House, is an excellent source of decorative treatments and artefacts, from roller blinds to original wallpaper. The experts who administer the Collection have a wide knowledge of structural and decorative solutions for all types of building. Contact Treve Rosoman on 071 973 3637.

Local English Heritage historic buildings inspectors should be able to help with methods of repair and types of decoration as well as with reliable local suppliers. He or she may even be able to visit your home to give on-the-spot advice. To find out who your local inspector is, ring the general English Heritage number (071 973 3000).

3   National Amenity Societies
The National Amenity Societies not only serve as legal consultees on alterations to listed buildings involving demolition, but also offer advisory services on all aspects of period homes, whether listed or not.

The Georgian Group (37 Spital Square, London E1 6DY, tel 071 377 1722) produce a series of introductory guides on key aspects of the Georgian house. The series currently comprises No.1 *Windows*, No.2 *Brickwork*, No.3 *Doors*, No.4 *Paint Colour*, No. 5 *Render, Plaster and Stucco*, No.6 *Wallpaper*, No.7 *Mouldings*, No.8 *Ironwork*, No.9, *Fireplaces*, No.10, *Roofs*, No.11, *Floors and Floor Coverings*, No.12 *Stonework*, No.13 *Lighting* and No.14 *Curtains and Blinds*. The Group can also provide general booklists for those beginning or contemplating repair or redecoration.

The Society for the Protection of Ancient Buildings (37 Spital Square, London E1 6D Y, tel 071 377 1644) publishes a series of Technical Pamphlets and Information Sheets on maintenance and repair and advises on suitable surveyors and craftsmen. It also produces a quarterly Period Property Register of historic houses for sale, available to members.

4   Specialist Societies
The British Brick Society
Woodside House
Winkfield
Windsor
Berks SL4 2DX

The Furniture History Society
Flat 1
78 Redcliffe Square
London SW10 9BN

The Garden History Society
35 Picton Street, Montpelier
Bristol BS6

The Glass and Glazing Federation
44 Borough High St, London SE1 1XB

The Men of the Stones
The Rutlands
Tinwell, Stamford
Lincs PE9 3UD

The Stone Federation
82 New Cavendish St
London W1M 8AD

The Tiles & Architectural Ceramics Society
Reabrook Lodge
8 Sutton Rd, Shrewsbury
Shropshire SY2 6DD

The Wallpaper History Society
The Victoria and Albert Museum
South Kensington, London SW7 2RL

5   Museums
Local and national museums often serve as a source of expert
knowledge on internal and external decoration.
Here are some of the leading authorities:-

Birmingham Museum and Art Gallery
Chamberlain Square, Birmingham B3 3DHA
021 235 2834

The Bowes Museum
Barnard Castle
Co Durham DL12 8NP
0833 37139
(Houses a superb collection of historic textiles)

Bristol Museum and Art Gallery
Queens Road, Bristol BS8 1RL
0272 299711
(Includes an excellent collection of furnishing fabrics)

The Brooking Collection
Thames Polytechnic, Dartford, Kent
(A vast collection of architectural artefacts, including doors,
windows, glazing bars, sash mechanisms, fanlights and
ironwork, due to open in 1992. View by appointment:
tel 0483 504555)

Heaton Hall, Heaton Park
Prestwich
Manchester M25 5SW
061 998 2331
(Manchester City Art Galleries also run the excellent Queen's
Park Conservation Studios in Harpurhey, tel 061 205 2645.)

High Wycombe Chair Museum
Priory Avenue
High Wycombe
Buckinghamshire
0494 421895

The Museum of English Rural Life
Whiteknights Park, Reading
Berkshire RG6 2AG
0734 875123

Pilkington Glass Museum
Prescot Road, St Helens
Merseyside WA10 3TT
0744 28882

Temple Newsam House
Temple Newsam Park
Leeds LS15 0AE
0532 647321
(As well as splendidly restored rooms and an unrivalled
archive, Temple Newsam has an expert staff available for
advice, and produces invaluable guides on key aspects of the
Georgian interior)

The Department of Furniture and Interiors
The Victoria and Albert Museum
South Kensington
London SW7 2RL
071 938 8500
(An excellent source of expert knowledge, of artefacts, of
pictures - and of original Georgian room sets)

6   Houses Open to the Public
It is always useful to have a look at extant houses of the Adam
period which are open to the public and which have interiors
in a reasonably original state. While these may be very useful
sources of reference, though, remember that the scale,
complexity and pretension of their interiors may be
inappropriate for the more modest dimensions and differing
character of your own home. Useful, domestically-scaled
interiors include:
No.1 Royal Crescent, Bath, Avon
The Georgian House, Charlotte Street, Bristol
Pickford's House, 41 Friar Gate, Derby
The Georgian House, 7 Charlotte Square, Edinburgh (run by
the National Trust for Scotland) and Soho House, Birmingham
- Matthew Boulton's own home, altered after 1787 and now
being splendidly restored by Birmingham City Council.

Large country houses are not always the most appropriate
models for modest domestic redecoration, nor do they
represent a typical reflection of what life was like for most
people in the mid-Georgian era. However, houses such as
those listed below still serve as splendid examples of what
Adam and his contemporaries could achieve:
Claydon House, Buckinghamshire (National Trust)
Culzean Castle, Ayrshire (National Trust)
Harewood House, North Yorkshire
Kedleston Hall, Derbyshire (National Trust)
Kenwood, Hampstead, London (English Heritage)
Newby Hall, Yorkshire (National Trust)
Nostell Priory, Yorkshire (National Trust)
Osterley Park, Middlesex (National Trust)
Saltram, Devon (National Trust)
Syon Park, Middlesex.

Contacts and sources of information in the United States

1   State Historic Preservation Offices

Each state has a designated state historic preservation officer (SHPO) whose responsibilities include carrying out statewide inventories of cultural resources, nominating properties to the National Register of Historic Places, administering grant and loan programmes, operating historic properties, and providing public education and information, on preservation techniques, the National Register nomination procedure, federal tax credits for rehabilitation, and a number of other subjects. A list of SHPOs can be found in *Landmark Yellow Pages* (see 'Further Reading' section).

2   Statewide and Local Preservation Organizations

Local preservation organizations exist in hundreds of communities, conducting tours of historic homes and neighbourhoods, offering advice on preservation techniques and sources of assistance, and issuing newsletters and other publications as well as linking local groups with one another, lobbying for state and local legislation supportive of preservation interests, administering funding programmes, and serving as information clearing-houses. Your National Trust regional office (see below) may be able to provide the names of statewide and local organizations in your area.

3   Local Historic District Commissions

If your house has been designated a local landmark or is situated in a locally designated historic district, you may be required to obtain the approval of a review board before making certain alterations to the property. Titles of these boards vary widely as do the provisions of the ordinances which they administer. Check with the city hall (the planning and zoning commission is a good place to start) for information on whether your house or neighbourhood is governed by local preservation regulations.

4   Historic American Buildings Survey

Founded in the 1930s, the Historic American Buildings Survey (HABS) is a valuable collection of photographs, measured drawings and documentary research on hundreds of historic structures. To find out whether a particular property may have been documented by HABS, or to obtain copies of photos and drawings of documented structures, contact:

Historic American Buildings Survey
Division of Prints and Photographs
Library of Congress
Washington, DC 20540
(202) 707-6394

5   National Trust for Historic Preservation

Chartered by Congress in 1949, the National Trust is a nationwide nonprofit organization with more than 250,000 members, which aims to foster an appreciation of the diverse character and meaning of the American cultural heritage and to preserve and revitalize the nation's historic environments. The Trust publishes a monthly newspaper, *Historic Preservation News*, a bimonthly magazine, *Historic Preservation*, and a wide variety of books and other materials; conducts conferences, workshops and seminars on a range of preservation-related topics; supports the work of local and statewide preservation organizations; administers a nationwide collection of historic museum properties; and, through its network of regional offices, offers advice and information to preservationists. For general membership information, contact:

National Trust for Historic Preservation
1785 Massachusetts Avenue, N.W.
Washington, DC 20036
(202) 673-4000

For information on a particular subject, contact the appropriate regional office:

Mid-Atlantic Regional Office
6401 Germantown Avenue
Philadelphia, PA 19144
(215) 438-2886
(DE, DC, MD, NJ, PA, VA, WV, Puerto Rico, Virgin Islands)

Midwest Regional Office
53 West Jackson Boulevard, Suite 1135
Chicago, IL 60604
(312) 939-5547
(IL, IN, IA, MI, MN, MO, OH, WI)

Northeast Regional Office
7 Faneuil Hall Marketplace, 5th Floor
Boston, MA 02109
(617) 523-0885
(CT, ME, MA, NH, NY, RI, VT)

Southern Regional Office
456 King Street, Charleston, SC 29403
(803) 722-8552
(AL, AR, FL, GA, KY, LA, MS, NC, SC, TN)

Mountains/Plains Regional Office
511 16th Street, Suite 700
Denver, CO 80202
(303) 623-1504
(CO, KS, MT, NE, ND, OK, SD, WY)
Texas/New Mexico Field Office
500 Main Street, Suite 606
Fort Worth, TX 76102
(817) 332-4398
(NM, TX)

Western Regional Office
One Sutter Street, Suite 707
San Francisco, CA 94104
(415) 956-0610
(AK, AZ, CA, HI, ID, NV, OR, UT, WA, Guam, Micronesia)

6   Old-House Journal

Published bimonthly, the *Old-House Journal* is an excellent source of 'how-to' advice for the handyman, as well as information of interest to the old-house *aficionado*. In addition to the magazine itself, the magazine's staff also publishes an annual catalogue which lists sources of traditional products. For subscription information, contact:

Old-House Journal
PO Box 50214
Boulder, CO 80521
(800) 888-9070

7   Other Organizations
American Association for State and Local History
172 2nd Avenue, North Suite 202
Nashville, TN 37201

Decorative Arts Society
c/o Brooklyn Museum
200 Eastern Parkway
Brooklyn, NY 11238

Society of Architectural Historians
1232 Pine Street
Philadelphia, PA 19107

8   Museums
Cooper-Hewitt National Museum of Design
2 East 91st Street
New York, NY 10128

Diplomatic Reception Rooms
US Department of State
2201 C Street, NW
Washington, DC 20520

Essex Institute
132 Essex Street
Salem, MA 01970

Henry Francis du Pont Winterthur Museum
Route 52
Winterthur, DE 19735

Metropolitan Museum of Art
5th Avenue at 82nd Street
New York, NY 10028

Museum of Art
Rhode Island School of Design
224 Benefit Street
Providence, RI 02903

Museum of Fine Arts
465 Huntington Avenue
Boston, MA 02115

Philadelphia Museum of Art
26th Street and Benjamin Franklin Parkway.
Philadelphia, PA 19130

9   Houses Open to the Public
Boscobel
Route 9D

Garrison-on-Hudson, NY 10524

Gardner-Pingree House
128 Essex Street
Salem, MA 01970

Homewood
3400 North,Charles Street
Baltimore, MD 21218

Joseph Manigault House
350 Meeting Street
Charleston, SC 29403

The Octagon
1741 New York Avenue, N.W.
Washington, DC 20006

Harrison Gray Otis House
141 Cambridge Street
Boston, MA 02114

Peirce-Nichols House
80 Federal Street
Salem, MA 01970

George Read II House
42 The Strand
New Castle, DE 19720

Nathaniel Russell House
51 Meeting Street
Charleston, SC 29401

Tudor Place
1644 31st Street, NW
Washington, DC 20007

Woodlawn Plantation
9000 Richmond Highway.
Mount Vernon, VA 22121

Introducton **The Age of Adam**

(a) Contemporary sources

Boswell, James, *The Life of Dr Johnson* (1799 etc)
Goldsmith, Oliver, *The Vicar of Wakefield* (1766)
    Betsy Sheridan's Journal (ed. W. LeFanu, OUP, 1986)
Smollett, Tobias, *Humphry Clinker* (1771)
Sterne, Laurence, *Tristram Shandy* (1759-67)
Woodforde, James, *The Diary of a Country Parson*
    (OUP, 1924-31)

(b) Modern sources

Ed. Black, Jeremy, *British Politics and Society from Walpole to*
    Pitt 1742-89 (Macmillan, 1991)
Borsay, Peter, *The English Urban Renaissance - Culture and*
    Society in the Provincial Town 1660-1770 (OUP, 1989)
Brooke, John, *George III* (Panther, 1972)
Bryant, Julius, *Robert Adam (1728-92) Architect of Genius*
    (English Heritage, 1992)
Butler, Marilyn, *Romantics, Rebels and Reactionaries - English*
    Literature and its Background 1760-1830 (OUP, 1981)
Denvir, Bernard, *Art, Design and Society 1689-1789*
    (Longman, 1988)
George, M. Dorothy, *London Life in the 18th Century* (1925;
    reprinted Peregrine 1966)
Hay, Douglas, etc, *Albion's Fatal Tree - Crime and Society in*
    Eighteenth Century England (Allen Lane, 1975)
Mitchel, Leslie, *Charles James Fox* (Oxford University Press,
    1992)
Porter, Roy, *English Society in the Eighteenth Century*
    (Penguin, 1982)

Chapter One **Adam Style**

Adam, Robert and James, *The Works in Architecture of Robert*
    and James Adam (1773, Academy Editions 1975)
Banham, Joanna, McDonald, Sally, and Porter, Julia, *Victorian*
    Interior Design (Cassell, 1991)
Binney, Marcus, *Sir Robert Taylor* (George Allen and Unwin,
    1984)
Colvin, Howard, *A Biographical Dictionary of British Architects*
    1600-1840 (John Murray, 1978)
Cruickshank, Dan, and Burton, Neil, *Life in the Georgian City*
    (Viking Penguin, 1990)
Fleming, John, *Robert Adam and his Circle* (John Murray, 1962)
Harris, John, *Sir William Chambers* (Thames & Hudson, 1970)
Harvey, John, *Restoring Period Gardens* (Shire, 1988)

Hussey, Christopher, *English Country Houses: Mid-Georgian*
    (Country Life, 1955)
Irwin, David, *English Neoclassical Art* (Faber, 1966)
Lees-Milne, James, *The Age of Adam* (Batsford, 1947)
Longstaffe-Gowan, Todd, *The London Town Garden* (Yale, 1992)
Mordaunt Crook, J., *The Greek Revival* (John Murray, 1972)
Rowan, Alastair, *Robert Adam* (V&A catalogue of drawings,
    1988)
Stillman, Damie, *The Decorative Work of Robert Adam* (Alec
    Tiranti, 1966)
Stroud, Dorothy, *Henry Holland, His Life and Architecture*
    (Country Life, 1966)
Summerson, John, *Georgian London* (Barrie & Jenkins, 1989)

Chapter Two **The Architectural Shell**
and
Chapter Three **Fixtures and Fittings**

(a) Contemporary sources

Chambers, William, *A Treatise on Civil Architecture* (1759)
Crunden, John, and Milton, Thomas, *The Chimney Piece*
    Maker's Daily Assistant (1766)
Crunden, John, and Milton, Thomas, *The Carpenter's*
    Companion (1770)
Darly, Matthew, *The Ornamental Architect* (1771)
Pain, William, *The Practical Builder* (1774)
Pain, William, *The Carpenter's and Joiner's Repository* (1778)
Swan, Abraham, *A Collection of Designs in Architecture* (1757)
Swan, Abraham, *Designs for Chimnies* (1765)
Ware, Isaac, *A Complete Body of Architecture* (1756)
Welldon, W. & J., *The Smith's Right Hand* (1765 ed.)
See also Harris, Eileen, *British Architectural Books and Writers*
    1556-1785 (Cambridge , 1990).

(b) Modern sources

Amery, Colin, *Period Houses and their Details* (Butterworths,
    1978)
Brunskill, R.W., *Brick Building in Britain* (Gollancz, 1990)
Byrne, Andrew, *Bedford Square* (Athlone, 1990)
Cruickshank, Dan, and Burton, Neil, *Life in the Georgian City*
    (Viking Penguin, 1975)
Davey, Heath, etc, *The Care and Conservation of Georgian*
    Houses (Edinburgh New Town Conservation Committee
    /Butterworths, 1986)
Gilbert, Christopher, and Wells-Cole, Anthony, *The*
    Fashionable Fireplace (Leeds City Art Galleries, 1985)
Gilbert, Christopher, Lomax, James, and Wells-Cole, Anthony,
    Country House Floors (Leeds City Art Galleries, 1987)

Graham, Clare, *Dummy Boards and Chimney-Boards* (Shire, 1988)

Harris, John, *The British Iron Industry 1700-1850* (Macmillan, 1988)

Kelly, Alison, *Mrs Coade's Stone* (Self-Publishing Assoc, 1990)

Kelsall, Frank, 'Stucco' in ed. Hobhouse and Sanders, *Good and Proper Materials* (London Topographical Society, 1989) and 'Liardet versus Adam' in *Architectural History*, vol.27 (Society of Architectural Historians, 1984)

Kitchen, Judith L., *Caring For Your Old House* (The Preservation Press, 1991)

Lloyd, Nathaniel, *A History of English Brickwork* (1925; reprinted Butterworths, 1983)

Sambrook, John, *Fanlights* (Chatto & Windus, 1989)

Shivers, Natalie, *Walls and Molding* (The Preservation Press, 1990)

Chapter Four **Services**

Bickerton, L.M., *English Drinking Glasses 1625-1825* (Shire, 1984)

Brears, Peter, *The Kitchen Catalogue* (York Castle Museum, 1979)

Brown, Peter, *Pyramids of Pleasure* (York Civic Trust, 1990)

Butler, Joseph T., *Candleholders in America 1650-1900* (Crown, New York, 1967)

Ed. Cooke, Lawrence S., *Lighting in America* (Main Street Press, 1984)

Cruickshank, Dan, and Burton, Neil, *Life in the Georgian City* (Viking Penguin, 1990)

Dickinson, H.W., *Matthew Boulton* (Cambridge, 1937)

Elville, E.M., *A Collector's Dictionary of Glass* (Country Life, 1961)

Eveleigh, David, *Firegrates and Kitchen Ranges* (Shire, 1983)

Forty, Adrian, *Objects of Desire - Design and Society 1750-1980* (Thames & Hudson, 1986)

Gilbert, Christopher, and Wells-Cole, Anthony, T*he Fashionable Fire-Place* (Leeds City Art Galleries, 1985)

Gilbert, Christopher, etc, *Lighting the Historic House* (Leeds City Art Galleries, 1992)

Glossop, William, *The Stove-Grate Maker's Assistant* (1771)

Goodison, Nicholas, *Ormolu: The Work of Matthew Boulton* (Phaidon, 1974)

Hayward, Arthur H., *Colonial Lighting* (1927, reprinted Dover, 1962)

Laing, Alastair, *Lighting* (V&A exhibition catalogue, 1982)

Mankowitz, Wolf, *Wedgwood* (Batsford, 1953)

Moss, Roger, *Lighting for Historic Buildings* (NTHP, Washington DC, 1988)

Moss, Roger W., *Lighting for Historic Buildings* (The Preservation Press, 1988)

Rowe, Robert, *Adam Silver* (Faber, 1965)

Shure, David, *Hester Bateman* (W.H. Allen, 1959)

Chapter Five **Colours and Coverings**

Ayres, James, 'Oilcloths' in *Traditional Homes*, July 1985

Bredif, Josette, *Toiles de Jouy* (Thames & Hudson, 1989)

Bristow, Ian, 'Floorcloths' in *SPAB News*, vol.11 no.2 (Society for the Protection of Ancient Buildings, 1990)

Dossie, Robert, *The Handmaid of the Arts* (1758)

Entwisle, E.A., *The Book of Wallpaper* (Kingsmead Reprints, 1970)

Fowler, John, and Cornforth, John, *English Decoration in the 18th Century* (Barrie & Jenkins, 1978)

Jackson-Stops, Gervase 'Syon Park, Middlesex' in *Country Life*, 16 April 1992

Ed. Jameson, Clare, *A Pictorial Treasury of Curtain and Drapery Designs 1750-1950* (1987)

Lynn, Catherine, *Wallpapers in America* (Kingsmead Reprints, 1980)

Montgomery, Florence, *Printed Textiles: English and American Cottons and Linens 1700-1850* (Thames & Hudson, 1970)

Montgomery, Florence, *Textiles in America* (W. W. Norton, New York, 1984)

Nylander, Jane C., *Fabrics for Historic Buildings* (The Preservation Press, 1990)

Nylander, Richard C., *Wallpapers for Historic Buildings* (NTHP, Washington DC, 1992)

Nylander, Richard C., *Wallpapers for Historic Buildings* (The Preservation Press, 1983)

Oman, Charles, and Hamilton, Jean, *Wallpapers* (Sothebys, 1982)

Rosenstiel, Helene Von, and Casey Winkler, Gail, *Floor Coverings for Historic Buildings* (NTHP, Washington DC, 1988)

Rosoman, Treve, 'Portraits of the Past' in *Traditional Homes*, February 1990; 'Swags and Festoons' in *Traditional Interior Decoration*, Autumn 1986; and 'In the Shade' (Blinds) in *Traditional Homes*, July 1985

Rothstein, Natalie, *Silk Designs of the 18th Century* (Thames & Hudson, 1990)

Thornton, Peter, *Authentic Decor: The Domestic Interior 1620- 1920* (Weidenfeld & Nicolson, 1984)

Wells-Cole, Anthony, *Historic Paper Hangings* (Leeds City Art Galleries, 1983)

Westman, Annabel, 'English Window Curtains in the Eighteenth Century' in *Antiques*, June 1990

Chapter Six **Furniture**

(a) Contemporary sources

Chambers, William, *Designs of Chinese Buildings* (1757)
Chippendale, Thomas, *The Gentleman and Cabinet Maker's Director* (1st ed. 1754, 3rd ed. 1760-2; reprinted 1957 etc)
Columbani, Placido, *A New Book of Ornaments* (1775)
Crunden, John, *The Joyner and Cabinet-Maker's Darling* (1765)
Ince, William, and Mayhew, John, *The Universal System of Household Furniture* (1762)
Manwaring, Robert, *The Cabinet and Chair-Maker's Real Friend and Companion* (1765)
Pryke, Sebastian, 'Revolution in Taste' in *Country Life*, 16 April 1992

(b) Modern sources

Ed. Beard, Geoffrey, and Gilbert, Christopher, *Dictionary of English Furniture Makers 1660-1840* (Furniture History Society, 1986)
Clabburn, Pamela, *The National Trust Book of Furnishing Textiles* (Viking Penguin, 1985)
Gilbert, Christopher, *The Life and Work of Thomas Chippendale* (Artline Editions, 1978)
Hayward, Helena, and Kirkham, Peter, *William and John Linnell* (Christies, 1980)
Walton, Karin, *The Golden Age of English Furniture Upholstery* (Leeds City Art Galleries, 1973)
Ed. White, Elizabeth, *Pictorial Dictionary of British 18th Century Furniture Design* (Antique Collectors' Club, 1990)

Further Reading of particular importance for the United States

Andrews, Wayne, *Architecture, Ambition and Americans* (New York: Free Press, 1979)
Aronson, Joseph, *The Encyclopedia of Furniture* (New York: Crown Publishers, 1965)
Belden, Louise Conway, *The Festive Tradition: Table Decoration and Desserts in America 1650-1900* (New York: W. W. Norton & Co., 1983)
Bjerkoe, Ethel Hall, *The Cabinetmakers of America* (Rev. ed., Exton, Pa.: Schiffer Publishing Ltd., 1978)
Butler, Jeanne F., *Competition 1792: Designing a Nation's Capitol* (Washington, D.C.: United States Capitol Historical Society, 1976)
Fairbanks, Jonathan L., and Bates, Elizabeth Bidwell, *American Furniture: 1620 to the Present* (New York: Richard Marek, 1981)
Favretti, Rudy J., Favretti, Joy Putnam, *Landscapes and Gardens for Historic Buildings: A Handbook for Reproducing and Recreating Authentic Landscape Settings* (Nashville, Tenn.: American Association for State and Local History, 1978.)
Gowans, Alan, *Images of American Living: Four Centuries of Architecture and Furniture as Cultural Expression* (Reprint, New York: Harper and Row, 1976)
Harris, Eileen, *The Furniture of Robert Adam* (New York: St Martin's Press, 1973)
Hayward, Arthur H., *Colonial and Early American Lighting* (Reprint, New York: Dover Publications, 1962)
Hiesinger, Kathryn Bloom, and others, *Bulletin, Volume 82, Numbers 551-52 (Summer 1986): Drawing Room from Lansdowne House* (Philadelphia: Philadelphia Museum of Art, 1986)
Kimball, Fiske, *Domestic Architecture of the American Colonies and of the Early Republic* (Repr. New York: Dover, 1966.)
Kitchen, Judith L., *Caring for Your Old House: A Guide for Owners and Residents* (Washington, D.C.: The Preservation Press, 1991)
Lyle, Charles T., *The George Read II House: Notes on Its History and Restoration* (Wilmington: Historical Society of Delaware, 1986)
Lynn, Catherine, *Wallpaper in America*, (New York: W. W. Norton and Co., 1980)
McAlester, Virginia, and McAlester, Lee, *A Field Guide to American Houses* (New York: Alfred Knopf, 1984)
McCue, George, *The Octagon* (Washington, D.C.: The American Institute of Architects Foundation, 1976)
Miller, Edgar G., Jr., *American Antique Furniture* (Reprint, New York: Dover Publications, 1966)
Metropolitan Museum of Art, *Nineteenth-Century America: Furniture and Other Decorative Arts* (New York: New York Graphic Society, 1971)
Montgomery, Florence N., *Textiles in America, 1650-1920* (New York: W. W. Norton and Co., 1984)
Moss, Roger W., *Lighting for Historic Buildings* (Washington, D.C.: The Preservation Press, 1988)
National Trust for Historic Preservation, *Landmark Yellow Pages: Where to Find All the Names, Addresses, Facts and Figures You Need* (Washington, D.C.: The Preservation Press, 1992)
Nylander, Jane C., *Fabrics for Historic Buildings* (Rev. ed., Washington, D.C.: The Preservation Press, 1990)
Nylander, Richard C., *Wallpapers for Historic Buildings* (Rev. ed., Washington, D.C.: The Preservation Press, 1992)
Peterson, Charles E., ed., *Building Early America* (Radnor, Pa.: Chilton Book Co., 1976)

Peterson, Harold L., *Americans at Home* (New York: Charles Scribner's Sons, 1971)

Pierson, William H., Jr., *American Buildings and Their Architects: The Colonial and Neo-Classical Styles* (Garden City, N.Y.: Doubleday and Co., 1970)

Stillinger, Elizabeth, *The Antiques Guide to Decorative Arts in America 1600-1875* (New York: E. P. Dutton & Co., 1972)

Thornton, Peter, *Authentic Decor: The Domestic Interior 1620-1920* (New York: Viking, 1984)

Von Rosenstiel, Helene, *American Rugs and Carpets* (New York: William Morrow and Co., 1978)

Von Rosenstiel, Helene and Winkler, Gail Caskey, *Floor Coverings for Historic Buildings* (Washington, D.C.: The Preservation Press, 1988)

Photographic Acknowledgements

Angelo Hornak, Photographer: 31, 38, 45, 62, 63, 112, 160 (bottom right), 188 (bottom), 189

Arthur Sanderson & Sons Ltd: 219

Athlone Press, London. Illustrations taken, by kind permission, from *Bedford Square*, Andrew Byrne (Athlone Press, 1990): 66 (drawing by Rupert Bound), 67 (drawing by James Whitehead)

Barrie & Jenkins, London. Illustrations taken, by kind permission, from *Georgian London*, John Summerson (Barrie & Jenkins): 64 (drawing by Alison Shepherd, A.R.I.B.A.)

Bridgeman Art Library, London: 12, 18 (British Museum), 19 (Trinity College, Cambridge), 36, 47 (Townely Hall Art Gallery and Museum, Burnley), 92, 121, 153 (Christie's London), 162 (top, photo: John Bethell), 164, 199 (top and centre: Sir John Soane's Museum)

Chris Salmon, The London Crown Glass Company: 83 (right)

Christie's Colour Library, London: 204, 205, 214; Christie's London: 216

Country Life (photo: Jonathan Gibson): 109

Courtesy of the Trustees of Sir John Soane's Museum, London (photos: Geremy Butler): 61, 102 (top), 103, 116 (top and centre right), 129, 156, 157, 162 (bottom), 193

Dorothy Bosomworth, Warner Fabrics Archives, Milton Keynes: 175

Edifice, London: 65 (right, top and bottom), 66 (bottom left and centre), 69, 76, 78, 79 (bottom left and right), 84 (top left), 86, 87 (top left and right, bottom left), 89

English Heritage, London: 57, 124

Fairfax House, York Civic Trust: 14, 112 (bottom, right), 139, 143

Garry Atkins, 107 Kensington Church St, London W8, photos: Alfie Barnes: 149 (top, bottom left), 150

Hamilton Weston Wallpapers Ltd, Richmond, Surrey: 168 (top right)

Harewood House, Leeds, by Permission of the Earl of Harewood: 119, 188 (top), 190, 194, 201 (top left), 202

Ian Parry, Photographer: 39, 40, 41, 50, 72, 74, 75, 79, 81 (right), 84 (bottom left), 87, 95, 104, 106, 107, 110, 137 (bottom right), 160 (top right), 162 (top left)

Jonathan Horne Antiques, 66c Kensington Church St, London W8: 122, 148

Martin Charles, Photographer: 1, 2, 4, 59, 84, 90, 94 (bottom right), 95 (centre right), 100, 101 (top left), 112 (top left), 115, 123, 125, 160 (top left, bottom left)

National Gallery of Ireland, Dublin: 154

National Maritime Museum, Greenwich: 68

National Portrait Gallery, London: 8

National Trust for Historic Preservation, Washington DC/Society for the Preservation of New England Antiquities (photos: David Bohl): 49, 54, 55

Public Affairs Department, Lloyd's of London: 223

Royal Commission on Historical Monuments, England: 111

Royal Academy of Arts, London: 159

Royal Institute of British Architects, Drawings Collection, London (photos: Geremy Butler): 34, 97, 99

The Stapleton Collection: 52, 53, 94 (top right), 102 (bottom), 116 (far left), 127, 130, 158, 161, 168 (bottom right), 171 (bottom), 172, 177, 179 (top), 181, 183, 191, 199 (bottom), 208, 209, 213, 215, 218, 220

Tate Gallery: 81

Temple Newsam (Leeds City Art Galleries): 168 (left)

The Mansell Collection, London: 11, 13, 16, 18, (below), 21, 23, 24, 33

The National Trust Photographic Library, London: 15 (photo: Geoffrey Shakerley), 37 (photo: Sheila Orme), 80, 95 (top right, photo: J. Whittaker), 101 (bottom left, photo: John Gibbons), 132 (photo: Angelo Hornak), 133 (photo: Rob Matheson), 136 (photo: Jenny Hunt), 137 (left, photo: John Bethell; top right, photo: John Gibbons), 138 (photo: Rob Matheson), 171 (photo: J. Whittaker), 201 (top centre, photo: John Gibbons; top right and bottom left, photos: John Bethell)

The Historic Charleston Foundation, Charleston, South Carolina: 60 (photo: Louis Schwartz)

Tim Mowl: 94, 113

Victoria & Albert Museum, London: 169, 170, 181.

Walker Art Gallery, Liverpool/Lady Lever Gallery, Wirral: 149, 163

Winterthur Museum, Delaware: 178, 179 (bottom), 182, 211

Photography of Syon House by kind permission of the Duke of Northumberland

Page numbers in *italics* refer to
illustration captions.
Adam, James 41
   Architect of the King's Works 41
   Italy 41
   Piranesi, meeting with 41
   quoted 44
   Spalatro 41
   Works in Architecture (with
      Robert Adam) *9*, 44, 49, 51,
      55, *91*, 101, 104, *115*, *122*, *127*,
      129, *159*, *172*, *205*, *214*, *220*
Adam, John 41, 91
   Carron and Company 80, 135
Adam, Robert 188
   Architect of the King's Works 41
   birth and family 37, 41
   ceiling designs *103*, 104-5, *104*
   Chambers compared 51
   chimneyboard designs 124
   Chippendale, collaboration
      with 191, *191*, *205*
   death 77, 214
   decorative style 44, 49
   elected Member of
      Parliament 41
   funeral 41
   influence 51, 56
   integrated interior design 49, 51
   Italy 41
   manipulation of public taste 25
   marketing 41
   metamorphic library steps *191*
   moulding designs 101
   movement, concept of 44
   Piranesi, meeting with 41
   popularity 51
   portrait by Willison *9*
   quoted 49
   reaction against 214
   retirement to Scotland 77
   seat furniture designs 198
   side table designs *205*
   sideboard, invention of 204
   Spalatro 36, 41
   state bed, Osterley Park 192, *193*
   Stuart's Spencer House
      interiors criticised by 37
   stucco patent rights 75, 77
   Works in Architecture (with
      James Adam) *9*, 44, 49, 51, *55*,
      91, 101, 104, *115*, *122*, *127*,
      129, *159*, *172*, *205*, *214*, *220*
Adam, William 37, 41
Adam Revival 210, *213*, *215*, 216,
   216, *217*, *218*, *219*, 220, *221*, *222*
agricultural production 28
Anderson, Diederich *137*
anthemion motif 79, 80, 114, *116*,
   117, *120*
Archenholtz, von 25, 27
architraves *122*
Argand, Ami
   colza-oil lamp 132, 135
Arkwright, Sir Richard
   water-frame 28
Arne, Thomas 14
Asgill House, Richmond 60
Asgill, Sir Charles 60
Ashton, T.S. 28
attic storey 68
Audley End, Essex *24*, 124
Axminster carpet 158, 160, *162*

Bacon, John
   Coade Stone designs 80, 148
balusters *80*, 110, *110*, 114
Barlaston, Staffordshire 60
Bartoli, Domenico *120*
Barton End Hall *112*
basement storey 64, 67
Bateman, Hester 14, 144
Bath *50*, 87, 88, *94*
   Camden Crescent *39*
   Circus *41*, 61, *74*
   ironwork *79*
   limestone *72*, 75
   Paragon *72*
   Queen Square 61

Bath *continued*
   Rivers Street *110*
   Royal Crescent *39*, 61, *62*
Bath Stove *134*
bathrooms 138, 148, 151
baths 148
Baucher, Richard 180
Beard, Geoffrey 192
bedrooms 68
beds *179*, 180, 192, *193*, *195*, 197
   textiles and bedding *179*, 180,
      192, 197
Bell, Thomas 180
Bentley, Thomas 147
bianco sopra bianco tiles 122
Blane, Dr Gilbert 144
blinds 128, 174
   roller 174
   Venetian 174
bog-house 68
bolection moulding 96
Bonomi, Joseph *97*, *99*
bookcases *207*
   dummy 192
   glazed 206, *207*
Boston, Massachusetts *87*
Boston Massacre *19*
Boston Tea Party 17, 144
Boulton, Matthew 14, 28, 131
   colza-oil lamp manufacture 132
Bourton-on-the-Water *168*
bow window 85
box cornice 96
Boydell, John
   print of Coalbrookdale bridge *10*
Bramah, Joseph
   ball-cock WC 151
breakfast 142
bricks 68, *69*, 71
   brick arches *70*
   brick tax 73
   chequered pattern 71
   colour 68, 71
   cutting bricks 71
   facing bricks 73
   floors 108
   gauged bricks 71
   kilns 68, *70*
   place bricks 71
   rubbed bricks 71
   stock bricks 71
   tuck-pointing 71, 73
   vitrified 71
Bridgwater, Duke of 28
Brindley, James 28
Bristol *94*
Bristol, Third Earl 22
British Museum
   Hamilton collection 56
Bromwich, Thomas 170
Brown, Mather
   portrait of George III *15*
Brown, Peter 142
Brussels carpet 160
Building Act (1774) 64, *64*, 85
building materials
   Bath stone *72*
   brick *see* bricks
   cast lead 80
   ceramics 118
   Coade Stone *76*, 77, 80, 118
   Hartley's fire-plates 80, 82
   ironwork *79*, 80, *80*, 82, 110, 114
   marble 118, *119*
   mathematical tiles 73
   parian marble 77
   Parker's Cement 77
   roofing slates 82
   scagliola 118, *120*
   stone 75
   stucco 73, 75, 77, *79*
   tiles 82, 122, *122*
building practices 73, 75
building standards 64
Buffinch, Charles
   Harrison Gray Otis House *54*, 56
Bunker Hill, Battle of *18*
bureaux 206
Burley on the Hill, Rutland *99*
Burton, Neil *68*

Bute, John Stuart, Third Earl
   10, 14, *15*, 17, *21*
   engraving by W.T. Mote *15*
   Lansdowne House *9*
   patronage of Adam *9*, 41
Byng, Admiral 20

canals, construction of 28
candelabra *127*, *129*, *131*
candles 128, *208*
   beeswax 128
   tallow 128
candlesticks 128, *129*, 131, *131*
Cardigan, Lord 170
Caroline, Queen 80
carpets *46*, 105, 108, *153*, *154*,
   158, 160, *161*, *162*, 164, *165*
   cleaning 164
   fitted 160, 164
   ingrain 164, 165
   needlework 164
   protection 128
   Turkey *26*
Carr, John
   Fairfax House kitchen *138*, 142
Carron and Company 80, 135
Carter, Thomas.
   Builders Magazine 70, *120*,
      132, *134*
Carter, Thomas
   chimneypiece, Syon House *137*
Carter, Thomas, the Younger
   fireplace, Saltram House *133*
Cawthorn, James 37
ceilings *101*, *103*, 104-5, *104*, *159*
   colour *92*, 104, 155, *159*, *161*
   moulded decoration 105
   painted decoration *101*, 104
   papier mch decoration 93
   plasterwork 93, *94*, 96
ceramics
   bianco sopra bianco 122
   Chinese *184*
   creamware *146*, 147, *149*, *151*
   Delft and Delftware 122
   jasperware 147, *149*, 158
   red stoneware *149*
   salt-glaze *149*
   sprigged decoration *149*
   tablewares 144, *146*, 147-8,
      148, *149*
   tiles 122, *122*
chairs and seat furniture *26*,
   197-8, *199*, *200*, *201*, *203*, *203*
   Chippendale *184*, *185*
   exercising chair 198
   French armchair *201*, *203*
   loose covers 206
   shield-back *183*
   Windsor chair *203*
Chambers, William 51, 108,
   124, 156, 158
   chimneypieces 118
   Designs of Chinese Buildings *184*
   Italy 51
   Osterley Park Eating Room
      ceiling *44*
   Somerset House *48*, *161*
   Surveyor-General of Office
      of Works 51
   textile design *177*
   Treatise on Civil Architecture
      51, 85, *99*, 105, 118
chandeliers 128, 132
Charlotte, Queen 147
Chatham Dockyard, Kent
   officer's gardens 68
Chatham, William Pitt, First Earl
   of *see* Pitt, William, the Elder
chimneyboards 122, 124, *124*, *137*
chimneypieces *48*, 114, *115*, *116*,
   117, 118, *119*, *120*, 122, 124,
   124, *137*
chinoiserie 170, *184*, *184*, 187
   architectural designs *170*
   "Chinese" fretwork 110
Chippendale, Haig and
   Company 122, 158, 188
Chippendale and Lock 216

Chippendale, Thomas 14, 24,
   118, 164, 166, 170, 174, 176,
   180, 187-8, 191
   Adam, collaboration with
      191, *205*
   basin stand *141*
   chimneyboards 124
   china case *183*
   Chinese Chippendale 110, *184*
   commode *188*
   complete house furnishing
      service 192
   *Gentleman and Cabinet-Maker's
      Director* 56, 119, *141*, *172*,
      183, *184*, *185*, 187, 188, *191*,
      206, 214, 216
   grate designs *134*
   library writing table *196*
   Neo-Classicism 187
   nineteenth century popularity
      216, 220
   overmantel mirror *208*
   pier table *204*
   seat furniture *184*, *185*, 197-8, *201*
   upholstering business 192
   window cornice design *172*
cisterns 138, *140*
Claude Lorrain 28, 57
Coade, Eleanor 14, 80
Coade Stone *76*, 77, 80
   chimneypieces 118
Coalbrookdale bridge 10, *10*
Coalbrookdale Company 80,135
Cobb, John 187, 216
cobbles, replacement of 27
Coke, Lady Mary 56, 171
colour 44, 155, *157*, *161*
   blue 155-6, 171
   bricks 68, 71
   ceilings *92*, *101*, 104, 158,
      159, *161*
   chimneypieces 118
   coordinated textiles and
      wall-coverings 180, 198
   doors 88
   Federal style *54*
   fireplace tiles 122, *122*
   floors 105, *107*, 108, 110
   green 155, 158, *165*, 171
   grey 171
   lead colour 155
   mouldings and decorative
      relief work 93
   Prussian blue 114, 156
   red 156
   scagliola *107*, 110
   smalt 114, 156
   staircases 114
   stone colours 155, 156, 158
   white 155, 158
   windows *81*, 85, 88
   yellow 156
Columbani, P.
   New Book of Ornaments *120*
Colvin, Howard 49, 51, *97*
colza-oil lamp 132, 135
commodes *188*, *204*, *208*
coordinated textiles and wallcoverings 180, 198
Coptfold, Essex 60
cornices 96, *99*, 101, 105, *153*, *172*
Cornwallis, Charles, First
   Marquess 25
Cotes, Francis
   Paul Sandby *81*
countryside, changes in 28
Coventry, Lord 174
Coventry, Maria Gunning,
   Countess of 22
Coxe, Tench 178
Craig, James
   Edinburgh New Town 61
creamware *146*, 147, *149*, *151*
crescents *39*
Croggan, William *107*
Crompton, Samual
   spinning mule 175

Crook, Professor 32
Croome Court,
   Worcestershire 173-4
Crown glass 82, *83*, 206
Cruickshank, Dan *89*
   Life in the Georgian City 128
Crunden and Milton 96
Cumming, Alexander
   ball-cock WC 151
curtains *154*, 173-5, *179*
   cornice designs *153*, *172*
   drapery 173-4
   festoon (French) 173-4
   French draw (French rod) *26*,
      174
   muslin 128, 174
   spring 174
   Tabby 175
   textiles used 174, 175

dadoes *26*, 96
Dance, George
   Building Act (1774) 64
Danson, Kent 60
Darby, Abraham 10, *10*
Delaney, Mrs 178, 180
Delft and Delftware tiles 122
Devall, John *137*
Devonshire, Georgina, Duchess
   of 14
Diderot and D'Alembert
   Encyclopaedia *83*, *167*
die-stamping 131
diet and meals 140, 142, 144
Dighton, Edward 166
dining rooms 68, 204
dinner 142
distemper 155
Doddington Hall, Lincolnshire *168*
   doors *87*
   architraves *122*
   Circus, Bath *74*
   Coade Stone keystones *76*
   doorcase 88
   entablature mouldings *99*
   fanlights *59*, 88, *89*
   furniture 88, *91*
   numbering front doors 88
   paintwork 88
Dossie, Robert
   Handmaid to the Arts 155-6, 206
drawing rooms 67, 68, 96, 204
dressers 140
druggets 128, 165
Drumcondra printed textiles 178
Dublin *87*, 88
   design standardization 64
   Merrion Square *89*
Dundas, Sir Lawrence
   portrait by Zoffany *26*, 174
Dunn, Treffry 220, *222*
Dutch oven 138
Dyrham Park, Gloucestershire 138

Earlys 197
Eau de Cologne 24
Eckhardt, A.G. 166
Edinburgh 88
   Charlotte Square *31*
   George Street 61
   New Town 61, 75
Elmes, James
   Metropolitan Improvements 214
enclosures 28
entablature mouldings *99*
Etruscan style 36, *36*, 156, *157*
Eveleigh, John
   Camden Crescent, Bath *39*

Fairfax House, York *112*, *138*,
   142, *142*
   sugar temple *14*
false teeth 22
fanlights *59*, 88, *89*
Fanny, Mrs *21*
Farina brothers 24
Farington, Joseph
   Diary 51
fashion and clothing 22, 24

Federal style *54*, 56, *210*
fenders 136
fenestration *see* windows
Ferguson, Henry 188
Fergusson, Adam *50*, *72*
Ferrers, Lord 20-1, *21*
fireplaces *24*, 114, *117*, 118, 122, 124, *124*, 127, *133*, 222
 ceramic 118
 chimneyboards 122, 124, *124*, *137*
 chimneypieces *48*, 114, *115*, *116*, *117*, 118, *119*, *120*, 122, 124, *124*, *137*
 colour 118
 fenders 136
 grates *133*, *134*, 135-6, *136*, 138, *154*
 marble 118, *119*
 mirrors *117*
 perpetual oven 138
 proportion 124
 ranges 138
 scagliola *120*
 tiles 122, *122*
firescreens *133*, *136*, *136*
first floor 67, 68, *159*
Fisher, Kitty *22*
Fisherwick Park, Staffordshire *97*
Flaxman, John
 candlestick designs 131
 designs for Wedgwood 148
floors 105, 108, 110
 brick 108
 carpets *see* carpets
 clay 108
 colour 105, 108
 composition 108
 druggets 128, 165
 floorcloths 128, 164, 165
 marble *107*, 108, 110
 oilcloth 165
 parquet 105
 scagliola *107*, 110
 stencilling 165
 stone 108-9
 timber 105, 108, *108*
fly-punch 131
flying shuttle 28, 176
Fort Niagara 20
Forty, Adrian 147, 148
Fox, Charles James 14, 17
Franklin, Benjamin 14, 20, 164, 173, 180
 Philadelphia stove 135
furniture *26*
 Adam Revival *213*, *215*, 216, *216*, 217, *218*, *221*
 bedroom *197*, 204, 206
 beds *179*, 180, 192, *193*, *195*, 197
 bookcases 192, 206, *207*
 bureaux 206
 cabinets *183*, *196*
 chairs and seat furniture *183*, *184*, *185*, 197-8, *199*, *200*, *201*, 203, *203*, 206
 chinoiserie 184, *184*
 commodes *188*, 204, *208*
 exercising chairs 198
 formal arrangement *186*, 210
 Gothick Revival 184
 jappaned 204, 206
 loose covers 206
 Louis Seize 191
 marquetry and inlay *188*, *196*, 204, *204*, *206*
 metamorphic library steps *191*
 mirrors 206, *208*
 Neo-Classicism 184, 187, 198
 painted 198, *201*
 protection 128, 206, 210
 sideboards 204
 tables *196*, 203-4, *204*, *205*, 206
 upholstered *153*, 198

Gainsborough, Thomas 14
gardens 67-8, *68*
Garrick, David 14, 44, 73, 176, *195*
George, Dorothy 17

George II 160
George III 10, 14, 17, 24, 41, 80, 214
 portrait by Mather Brown *15*
George IV 24, 80
Gilbert, Christopher 184, 188, 191-2, 206, 216
gilding *81*, 93
Gillows 156, 220
girandoles 128, *130*
glass
 air-twist stems 148
 chandeliers 132
 cotton twist stems 148
 Crown 82, *83*, 206
 cylinder (broad; Muff) 82
 glazed bookcases 206, *207*
Glasse, Hannah
 Servant's Directory 164
glazing bars 82, 85
Goethe, Johann Wolfgang von 105
Goldsmith, Oliver
 The Vicar of Wakefield 59, 136
Gordon, Lord George 17
Gordon Riots 16, 17, 20
Gothick Revival 184, 187
grates *154*
Gray, Thomas 93
Greek key pattern *107*, *162*
Greek Revival 37, 104
Grosley, Pierre-Jean 62, 64, 73
ground floor 67, *159*
Guadeloupe 20
Gwilt, Joseph
 Encyclopaedia of Architecture 214
Gwynn, John
 London and Westminster Improv'd 64

Hagley Park, Worcestershire 36-7
Haig, Thomas 188
Hallsworth, Henry
 candlesticks *131*
Hamilton, Sir William
 Collection of Etruscan, Greek and Roman Antiques 36
Hamilton, William
 Woodlands, Philadelphia 56
Harcourt, Earl 31
Hardwick, Thomas 60
Harewood House, Yorkshire *103*, *119*, 164, *188*, *191*, 192, *195*, *196*, 201
Hargreaves, James spinning jenny 28, 175, 176
Harleyford Manor, Buckinghamshire 60
Harrison Gray Otis House, Boston *54*, 56
Hartley's fire-plates 80, 82
Hay, Douglas 17
Heal's *217*
Heart and Honeysuckle design 80
Heathcote, Sir Gilbert 122
heating 136
 Bath Stove *134*
 fireplaces *see* fireplaces
 grates 138
 Philadelphia stove 135
 register grate 135
 stove-grate 135
Heaton Hall, Manchester 136
Heming, Thomas
 candlesticks *131*
Hepplewhite, George
 bed designs *195*
 bedroom furniture designs *197*
 bookcase designs *207*
 bureaux designs 206
 Cabinet-Maker and Upholsterer's Guide *145*, *186*, 197, *200*
 firescreen designs *136*
 seat furniture *199*, *200*
 table designs *141*, *204*
 tea-caddy designs *145*
Hewson, John 178
Higgins, Bryan
 water-based stucco 77

Hogarth, William
 Five Orders of Perriwigs 32, *33*
 frontispiece for Kirby's *Perspective of Architecture* 35
 The Times 15, *21*
Holland, Henry
 Brooks's Club 71
Howe, General *18*
Hume, David 44
Hussey, Philip
 Interior 154

Ince & Mayhew *179*
Industrial Revolution 10, 68, 142, 175-6
 and design aesthetic 28
 road and canal building 28
 steam-engine 28,175
 textile production 28, 175-6
International Exhibition (1862) 216
ironwork 79, 80, *80*, 82
 balusters *80*, 110, 114
 colour 114
 fanlights *59*
 lampirons *132*

Jackson, John Baptist 165-6
 Essay on the Invention of Engraving and Printing in Chiaro Oscuro 166, *166*
Jackson-Stops, Gervase *161*
jappaning 204, 206
jasperware 147, *149*, 158
Jennings, H.J. 216, 220
 Our Homes and How to Beautify Them 213
Johnson, Dr Samuel 24, 28
Johnson, John 77
Johnson, Thomas
 Collection of Designs 116
Jones, John Paul 14
Jones, Robert 178
Jordan, Mrs 14
Jouy en Josas 178, 180
Kauffmann, Angelica 14, 104-5, 158, *207*, *210*
Kay, John
 flying shuttle 28, 176
Kedleston, Derbyshire *94*, *136*
Kelsall, Frank 77
Kennedy, Paul 25
Kenyon, Lloyd 180
Kenyon, Mrs 140
Kidderminster carpet 158, 160, 164
Kilmarnock carpet 164
Kingston, Duke of 127
Kinross
 Robert Adam elected as MP 41
Kirby, Joshua
 Perspective of Architecture 35
kitchens 136, 138, *138*, 140, 151
 dressers 140
 Dutch oven 138
 ranges 138
 sinks 140
 water supply 138, 140
Knatchbull, Sir Edward 158, 176, 192

La Rochfoucauld 68
Lagos 20
Langmead, Joseph 138
Le Roy
 Ruines des Plus Beaux Monuments de la Grce 36
Lees-Milne, James 10, 51
Liardet stucco *66*, 75, 77
Liberty riots 17
libraries *191*, *196*
lighting 128, 131-2, 135, 151, *210*
 candelabra *127*, *129*, *131*
 candles 128, *129*, 131, *131*, *208*
 chandeliers 128, 132
 colza-oil lamp 132, 135
 girandoles 128, *130*
 lampirons *132*

Lighting *continued*
 lampstands *129*
 rush lights 128
 street 27
 torchres *210*
 wall-mounted
 sconces 128
Linnell, John 174, *199*, *201*, *208*, 216
Liverpool
 population 27
Lloyd, Robert 9
London 56, 77, 88, *94*
 7 Adam Street 79, 80, *87*
 Adelphi 41, *42*, 44, *48*, *60*, 61, 79, 80, *87*
 19 Arlington Street *26*
 Bedford Square 61, *65*, 66, *67*, 71, 76, 80, 85, *87*
 brick terraces 69
 Brooks's Club 71
 Chandos House 76
 Coade Stone 76
 Coventry House *103*, *116*
 Derby House *116*, *117*, *127*, *130*, *214*
 design standardization 64
 development 25, 27
 37 Dover Street *110*
 Home House 36
 ironwork 79
 Kenwood House 56, 77, *92*
 Lansdowne House *9*
 New Road 25, 27
 Northumberland House *157*
 Oxford Road (Street) 27
 Pantheon 51, 56
 Portland Place 76
 14 Queen Anne's Gate *46*
 Somerset House *48*, *112*, 114, *161*
 speculator-builders 25, 27
 Spencer House 37
 squares *65*, *67*
 11 St James's Square 77
 20 St James's Square *24*, *59*, *80*, *91*, *94*, 101, *112*, *115*, 122, *161*
 street lighting 27
 Syon House *81*
 Westminster Paving Act (1762) 27
 White Lodge, Richmond Park 171
Longford Castle, Wiltshire 124
Louis Seize furniture 191
Louis XV 24
Louis XVI 24
Lovell, R. Goulburn *213*
luncheon 142
Luton Hoo, Bedfordshire 180
lyre motif 114, 198

macaronis 22, *23*
Macaulay, Catherine 14
Madras 20
Malcolm, James 88
Malton, Thomas
 aquatint of *Adelphi Terrace* 60
 Compleat Treatise on Perspective 208
 perspective drawing *46*
Manchester
 canal 28
 Cleaning and Lighting Act (1765) 27
 Manchester Exhibition (1882) 220
 population 27
Mann, Horace 20, 166
Mansfield, First Earl 56, 77
Maple & Co *217*
marble
 fireplaces 118, *119*
 flooring *107*, 108, 110
mathematical tiles 73
medical care 21-2
Mersham-le-Hatch, Kent *204*
middle classes 25, 60, 61, 71, 142, 147
Mills, Thomas 60

Minden, Battle of 14
mirrors 206, *208*
 candle sconces 128, *208*
 chimneypieces *117*
 glazed bookcases 206
Moffatt Ladd House, New Hampshire *48*
Montagu, Elizabeth 56
Montagu, George 20
Montagu, Lady Mary Wortley 170, 184
Montagu, Mrs 131
Montgomery, Florence 56, 178
Moore, Thomas 158, 160
Moorfields carpet 158, 160
Mote, W.T.
 portrait engraving of Third Earl of Bute *15*
mouldings and decorative relief work 93, *94*, 96
 bolection mouldings 96
 cornices 96, *99*, 101, 105, *153*, *172*
 entablature mouldings *99*
 Neo-Classicism 101, 104
 ovolo mouldings 101
Mount Vernon, Virginia 56
movement, Adam's concept of 44
Muthesius, Stefan 39

Nathaniel Russell House, Charleston, South Carolina 60
Neo-Classicism 184, 187, 198
 influences on 28
 Antiquities of Athens (Stuart and Revett) *31*, 32, *33*, 35, 36, 56, *108*
 Baalbec, volume on (Wood) 36
 Collection of Etruscan, Greek and Roman Antiques (Hamilton) 36
 Grecian Orders of Architecture (Riou) 32, 36, 93, 96
 Reflections on the Imitation of Greek Works in Painting and Sculpture (Winckelmann) 36
 Ruines des Plus Beaux Monuments de la Grce (Le Roy) 36
 Ruins of Athens (Sayer) 36
 Ruins of Palmyra (Wood) 36
 Spalatro (Adam) 36
 moulded decorations 101, 104
Nixon, Francis *179*
North, Lord 17
Northumberland, First Duke *104*, 110
Norton, John 164
Norwood House, Kent 170
Nostell Priory, Yorkshire 101, *137*, 170, *201*
Nuneham Park, Oxfordshire 31

Oberkampf, Christophe-Philippe 178
oilcloth 165
ormolu 118, *137*
Osterley Park, Middlesex 36, *103*, 114, *137*, *172*
 Eating Room *81*
 Etruscan Room *157*, *201*
 state bed 192, *193*
oval forms *186*, 204, 206, 208
ovolo moulding 101

Pain, William
 Practical Builder 62, 64
Paine, James 60
paintwork 155
 doors 88
 furniture 198, *201*
 ironwork 114
 windows *81*, 85, 88
 see also colour
paktong 135-6
Palladian style 60, 61, 67, 88, 96, 118, 156
palmette motif 114

pantiles 82
papier mch wall and ceiling
decorations 93
Papillon 166
parian marble 77
Paris Exhibition (1878) 220
Paris, Treaty of (1765) 61
Parker, Reverend David
Parker's Cement 77
parlours 67
parquet 105
Parratt, William 160, 171
pattern books 101
fireplaces and chimneypieces
116, *119*, *120*
ironwork 110
proportion, guides to 96
pavements 27
paving commissioners 27
Paxton House, Berwickshire 180
Peacock, James
Nutshells 214
Pembroke, Ninth Earl 160
Penrhyn, Lord 82
Penzel
Setting a Limb 21
perpetual oven 138
Philadelphia stove 135
picture hangs *26*, *154*
Piranesi
meeting with Adam brothers 41
Piranesi, Giambattista *35*
Pitt, William *21*
Pitt, William, the Elder 10, 14,
15, *23*
portrayed by J.S. Copley *24*
Pitt, William, the Younger 10
plasterwork *94*, 96
gypsum 93
premoulded 93
walls 93
plate warmers 138
Pococke, Dr Richard 124
point paper 160, 164
Pompadour, Madame de 170
population growth 27, 28
Poussin, Nicolas 37
Powys, Mrs Lybbe 197
Price, Dr Richard 25, 144
print rooms 170
Pritchard 10
proportion and interior design
46, 96, 101, 124

Quebec 14, 20

Ralph, James
Critical Review 61
Randolph, Benjamin *179*
ranges 138
Rannie, James 187, 188
Rates 64, *64*
Rebecca, Biagio *24*, 124
red stoneware *149*
register grate 135
Reid, William 192
Reinagle, Philip
*Mrs Congreve and her
Daughters 154*
Revett, Nicholas 32, 49, 118
Antiquities of Athens (with
James Stuart) 31, 32, *33*, *35*,
36, 56, *108*
Island Temple, West
Wycombe Park 37, *37*
Reynolds, Joseph 14
Riou, Stephen
Grecian Orders of Architecture
52, 36, 93, 96
road building 28
Robertson, Charles *62*
Robinson, Thomas 138
Robinson, Sir William 166
Robson & Sons *221*
Rococo style 49, 184, 187
reaction against *116*, 118
Rodney, Admiral 14
roofing materials 82

room shapes 60
Rossetti, Dante Gabriel 222
Rugar, John 171

Sackville (Germain), Lord
George 14, 17
Sadler, John and Green, Guy 122
salt-glazed ware *149*
Saltram House, Devon *132*, *133*
salvaged items 124
Sandersons *219*
Sandwich, Earl of 17
Saratoga 25
sash window 82, *84*, 85
Sayer, Robert
Ruins of Athens 36
scagliola *107*, 110, 118, *120*
Schoeser, Mary 176
second floor 68
servants 128
rooms used by 68
Seven Years War 10, *15*, *21*, 24,
61, 170
sewers *141*
Shapland, H.P.
*Style Schemes in Antique
Furnishing 218*
Sheffield Plate 131
Shelburne, Lady 160
Sheraton, Thomas 216
Sheridan, Betsy 22
Sheridan, Richard Brinsley 14
The Critic 75
The Rivals 22, 183
The School for Scandal 175
Shugborough *14*
shutter boxes *81*
shutters 128
Siddons, Sarah 14
silver
candlesticks 128, 131, *131*
die-stamped 131
fly-punched 131
Sheffield Plate 131
tea-ware 144, *145*
sinks 140
skirting 96, *154*
skylights *46*
slate 82
Smirke, Robert and Porden, William
The Exhibition 214
Smith, Adam 41, 44
Theory of Moral Sentiments 210
Smith, George 216
Smith, J.T. 187, 216
smokejack 138, *138*
Smollett, Tobias 75
Humphry Clinker 127, 148,
153, 184
snob screens 174-5
Soane, Sir John 214
Spalatro 41
speculator-builders 25, 27, 62,
64, 73
spinning jenny 28, 175
spinning mule 174, 175
spits 138, *138*
Split 41
squares *65*
staircases *112*
"Chinese" fretwork 110
colour 114
handrails 114
ironwork balusters *80*, 110, 114
wooden balusters 110, *110*
steam engine 28, 175
stencilling 165
Stevenson, Mrs 180
stove grate 135
Strawberry Hill, Middlesex 93,
166, 170, 198
streets
cobbles, replacement of 27
gutters 27
lighting 27
repaving 27
rubbish removal 27
Westminster Paving Act
(1762) 27

Stuart, James 32, 49, 118
Antiquities of Athens (with
Nicholas Revett) 31, 32, *33*,
35, 36, 56, *108*
Greek arch, Nuneham Park 31
Greek temple, Hagley Park 36-7
moulding designs 101
Spencer House interiors 37
Tower of the Winds,
Shugborough *14*
The Winds, Mountstewart *108*
Stubbs, George 148
stucco *66*, 73, 75, 77, *79*
Kenwood 56
Parker's Cement 77
patent rights 75, 77
Summerson, Sir John 49, 62
supper 142
Swan, Abraham 101
Syon House, Middlesex *104*, *107*,
110, *120*, *129*, *137*, *161*, *162*

tables 26, *196*, 203-4, *204*, *205*, *206*
marquetry and inlay 204
Pembroke 204, *206*
tablewares 142, 144, *145*, *146*,
147-8, *148*, *149*
Talwin and Foster 178
Tatham, C.H. 214
Taylor, Sir Robert 49, 60
Asgill House 60
Barlaston 60
Building Act (1774) 64
Coptfold 60
Danson 60
Harleyford Manor 60
Taylor, William
candelabra *131*
tea-caddies *145*
tea-drinking 144, *145*
tea-urns 142, 144, *145*
Temple, Earl *15*
Temple Newsam House, Leeds
168, 171, *196*
terraced housing *42*, 61-2, *69*, *72*
textiles
Adam Revival *219*, 222
beds *179*, 180, 192, 197
Chinese 184
cotton 176, *177*, 178, 180, 197,
206
curtains *see* curtains
industrialization of
manufacture 28, 175-6
linen 180, 197, 206
loose covers 206
printed 176, *177*, 178, *179*, 180
Toiles de Jouy 178, 180
United States 56
upholstery 198
woven silk *180*
Thorne, Edward *221*
Ticonderoga 20
tiles
fireplace surrounds 122, *122*
mathematical 73
roofing 82
Tobin, Maurice *112*
Towneley, Charles
portrait by Zoffany *46*
transportation 28
tripod stands *127*, *129*
trivets 138
tuck-pointing 71, 73
Tucker, Josiah 28
Turkey carpets *26*
Turner, Thomas 20
turnpike trusts 28

United States of America
Adam Revival 220, 222
Adam's influence 56
Boston Massacre *19*
Boston Tea Party 17, 144
fanlights 88
Federal style *54*, 56, *210*
Harrison Gray Otis House,
Boston *54*, 56

United States of America *continued*
Moffatt Ladd House, New
Hampshire *48*
Mount Vernon, Virginia 56
Nathaniel Russell House,
Charleston 60
panelling 93
Revolution 10, 14, 17, *18*, *19*
textiles 56, 178, 180
wallpaper 171
War of Independence 25, 56,
61, 73
Winterthur Museum *179*, *210*
Woodlands, Philadelphia 56
Universal Director 160
upholstery *153*, 198
urns *24*, *44*, 118
Utrecht, Treaty of (1715) 158

Vile and Cobb 173, 174
Vile, William 187
violence in Georgian society 20-1
Voltaire, Franois Marie Arouet de
10, 20

Wakelin, John
candelabra *131*
Wallbridge *168*
wallpaper *26*, *48*, 93, 165-6, *167*,
168, 170-1, *170*, 173, 180
Adam Revival *219*, 222
architectural designs *154*, 166,
168, *170*
Chinese 171, 184
chinoiserie *170*
flock 170
hand-coloured 166
lustre 170
printed 166
tax 165
walls 99
cornices 96, 101, 105
dadoes *26*, 96
panelling 93
papier mch decoration 93
picture hangs *26*, *154*
plasterwork 93, *94*, 96
print rooms 170
skirting mouldings 96
stencilling 165
wallpaper *see* wallpaper
Walpole, Horace 10, 20-1, 25, 36,
192, Strawberry Hill 93, 166,
170, 184, 198 on Wyatt's
Portman Square house 56
Ware, Isaac 64, 67, 68, 96
Complete Body of Architecture
67, *70*, 82, 105, 108, 114, 135
Wark, Reverend David
stucco 75
warming pans 138, *138*
Washington, George 178, 180
Mount Vernon 56
water closet 151
water supply 138, 140
water-frame 28
Watt, James
steam engine 28, 175
Wedgwood, Josiah 14, 80, 188
black basalt oil lamp *132*
chimneypieces 118
creamware *146*, 147
designers used by 148
Etruria 147
false teeth manufactured by 22
jasperware 147, *149*, 158
manipulation of public taste 25
showroom in the Adelphi 44
tablewares 144, *146*, 147-8, *148*,
149
Welldon, W. and J.
The Smith's Right Hand 110
Wells *94*
West Wycombe Park,
Buckinghamshire 37, *37*
Westman, Annabel 173, 174
Westminster Paving Act (1762) 27
Whatman, Susanna

Whatman, Susanna *continued*
Housekeeping Book 164
Wheatley, Francis
Family Group 153
Whigs 14
Wilkes, John 17, *21*
Williams Wynn, Sir Watkin *59*
Willison, George
portrait of Robert Adam *9*
Willoughby, Fourteenth Baron
portrait by Zoffany *165*
Wilson, Richard 37
Wilton carpet 160
Winchester School 20
Winckelmann 49
*Reflections on the Imitation of
Greek Works in Painting and
Sculpture* 36
windows 60, 62, *81*
blinds 128, 174
bow 85
Building Act (1774) 85
Crown glass 82, *83*
curtains *see* curtains
cylinder (broad; Muff) glass 82
entablature mouldings 99
fanlights *59*, 88, *89*
furniture *81*, 85
glazing bars 82, 85
paintwork *81*, 85, 88
sash 82, *84*, 85
shutter boxes *81*
shutters 128
skylights *46*
snob screens 174-5
window size 85
window tax 85
The Winds, Mountstewart *108*
Winterthur Museum
Blackwell-Stamper Room *179*
Du Pont Dining Room *210*
Witney blankets 197
Wolfe, General James 10, 14, 20
Wood, John 105, 136
Wood, John, the Elder
Circus, Bath *41*, 61, *74*
Queen Square, Bath 61
Wood, John, the Younger
Circus, Bath 61
Royal Crescent, Bath *39*, 61, *62*
Wood, Robert
Ruins of Palmyra 36
volume on Baalbec 36
Woodforde, James 17, 24
Woodlands, Philadelphia 56
Woollet, William *35*
Wright, Joseph 148
Wyatt, James 51, 56
Pantheon 51, 56
Portman Square house 56

Yenn, John
cross-section of town mansion
159
Yorktown 25

Zoffany, Johan
Charles Towneley 46
*John Pento, Fourteenth Baron
Willoughby and Louisa, his
wife 165*
*Sir Lawrence Dundas and his
Grandson 26*, 174
Zucchi, Antonio *44*, *101*, 104-5,
158